SMOKE & MIRRORS, INC.

SMOKE & MIRRORS, INC.

MIRRORS, INC.

ACCOUNTING FOR CAPITALISM

Nicolas Véron,
Matthieu Autret,
& Alfred Galichon

Translated by George Holoch

CORNELL UNIVERSITY PRESS
ITHACA AND LONDON

This Work is published with the assistance of the French Ministry of Culture—Centre National du Livre.

Ouvrage publié avec le concours du Ministère français chargé de la culture—Centre national du livre.

Cornell Studies in Money
edited by Eric Helleiner and Jonathan Kirshner

Original French edition, *L'Information financière en crise: Comptabilité et capitalisme,*
copyright © Editions Odile Jacob, 2004
English translation copyright © 2006 by Cornell University

First published 2006 by Cornell University Press

Printed in the United States of America

Library of Congress Cataloging-in Publication Data

Véron, Nicolas.
  [Information financière en crise. English]
  Smoke & Mirrors, Inc. : accounting for capitalism / Nicolas Véron,
Matthieu Autret, and Alfred Galichon ; translated by George Holoch.
    p. cm — (Cornell studies in money)
  Includes bibliographical references and index.
  ISBN-13: 978-0-8014-4416-6 (cloth : alk. paper)
  ISBN-10: 0-8014-4416-0 (cloth : alk. paper)
    1. Disclosure in accounting.   2. Corporations—Accounting—Corrupt practices.
3. International   finance.   4. Capitalism.   I. Autret,   Matthieu.   II. Galichon,
Alfred.   III. Title.   IV. Series.
HF5658.V4713 2006
657—dc22

2006001750

Smoke & Mirrors, Inc., is a fictional company used for illustrative purposes only. Any similarity to actual companies is coincidental and unintentional.

CONTENTS

ACKNOWLEDGMENTS

We are extremely grateful to Joseph Traynor and Richard Coxon, who reviewed the entire manuscript and gave us illuminating comments. We also thank our friends and colleagues who provided invaluable help and encouragement to this book and its underlying research: Suzanne Berger, Xavier Gabaix, Frédéric Gielen, Peter Gourevitch, Augustin Landier, Jonah Levy, Sophie Meunier, Jacques Mistral, Thomas Philippon, and John Zysman.

L'Information financière en crise: Comptabilité et capitalisme, published by Odile Jacob in 2004, provided the initial basis for this text, even though it now includes significant changes and updates. *L'Information financière en crise* owes enormously to Georges Barthès de Ruyter, Michel Berry, Pierre Bollon, Étienne Boris, Bernard Colasse, Philippe Crouzet, François Engel, Gilbert Gélard, Christian Germa, Bruno Husson, Zaki Laïdi, Frédéric Martel, Thierry Pech, Jean Pisani-Ferry, Claude Riveline, Hervé Stolowy, and Philippe Trainar, and we thank them warmly again for their help. We also thank Professors Asis Martinez-Jerez, Edward Riedl, Stephen Ryan, and Philip Wolitzer for their precious comments on the differences between European and U.S. accounting practices.

Finally, we express our special gratitude to our editors, Roger Haydon and Candace Akins, without whose continuous support and patient attention this book would never have come to light.

N.V., M.A. & A.G.

PROLOGUE

It was a few years ago, in a country not so far, far away. Joseph Smith, the CEO of Smoke & Mirrors, Inc., a publicly listed manufacturer of fireworks, sat in a corner office facing the sea. He was feeling increasing pressure. The economic climate was bad. Foreign competitors were a growing threat. As the year came to a close, the total loss was expected to be as high as $40 million, meaning a negative 8 percent return on equity. Smith knew that when he announced this, it would mean trouble. Investors had long expected a positive return of 15 percent. The market was getting jittery. And as if worries about profitability were not enough, some analysts were starting to point at Smoke & Mirrors' high level of debt as an additional emerging problem.

Facing Smith was a visitor. John Wills was a partner at the advisory firm Wills & Wills, which specialized in restructuring ailing companies. A friend had told Smith about Wills' reportedly amazing skills; Smith was skeptical but had contacted Wills nevertheless. Two weeks earlier, they had had a first meeting, where Wills, a short, bald, dark-eyed man, had asked only about Smoke & Mirrors' accounting policies. Now, Smith expressed puzzlement.

"Frankly, Wills, I don't understand what we're doing. I thought we would discuss strategy. Production plans. The many changes we're experiencing right now in the fireworks market. But all you talk about is financial engineering and accounting standards. How on earth can that help?"

"It will help quite a bit, you'll see. There are assets on your balance sheet that burden it and have no strategic importance for your business. Analysts don't like that. What they love to see is less debt and more return on equity. So, make it simple, get rid of all the cumbersome assets! If you ask me, you should start with selling your head office building. It could be done quickly, and everybody will be happier."

"Are you crazy? I can't part with this headquarters building. It's so beautiful, and my grandfather had his office here. Anyway, suppose the new owner throws me out?"

"Don't worry, Mr. Smith—may I call you Joe? No one will throw you out of here. The new owner will be a shell company owned by a friendly bank. The contract we prepare for it will meet some special conditions and give you an option to buy the building back, at the end of the lease. It will feel exactly as if you still owned the building. The rationale is that, under this country's accounting standards, if you don't formally own the property then you don't book it as an asset. So, while the bank nominally owns the place, you can stay in it without recording it on your balance sheet. In effect, the outcome of the transaction is to hide part of your debt: this "sale" will lower your debt-to-equity ratio from 130 percent to 82 percent. And here's another piece of good news. The old building has been almost entirely depreciated over the years, so by selling it you can record a capital gain, and you erase all the loss you had for the year."

Smith was impressed.

"Well, I thought there was no way I could show any profit this year. I gave up hope of reducing my debt level below 100 percent years ago. This is really interesting. Please go on."

"I'm delighted you like it, Joe. Let's now turn to something else. You have a lot of receivables in your assets, and I understand that several customers may never pay you. Sure, you could write down the bad debts, but that would add losses, so I propose that you sell them instead. Here, too, your bank can help. The bank would finance a special-purpose entity that does not appear on your balance sheet, and that buys the receivables from you at face value. Of course, you may ask, who would buy such bad assets? Well, the fix here is a clause that will commit you to remaining liable for all receivables not collected by the special-purpose entity in the future. Thus, the risk remains yours but does not appear on your balance sheet, only in small print in the footnotes. Nothing too visible, but enough to keep your auditor happy."

"This is eye-opening. Does it really work?"

"Sure, and you'll not be the first nor the last one to do so. Now, to go on. I spoke with your technical staff and discovered that you use an outdated method for valuing inventories. Let me explain. The price at which you purchase raw materials varies with time. For example, you bought explosive powder for your fireworks at $15,000 per ton a year ago, but this year the price fell so that you can now buy the same powder at $10,000 per ton. The so-called first in, first out method, which you have used thus far, means assuming that the powder used first was the oldest, that is, the material bought at $15,000 per ton, while that bought at $10,000 per ton remains in inventory at the end of the year. You can change this by assuming instead that you've used some of the powder bought this year and some bought last year. That's what is called the weighted average cost method. Your unit cost of inventory at year end will be $12,500 instead of $15,000 per ton, which will increase your net profit by $35 million."

Joe Smith's mind was busy calculating the implications. "That sounds great, too. Any other suggestions?"

"For sure; I have derivatives."

"Oh, that must be complicated. If you don't mind, I'll call in my chief financial officer. He knows more about these things than I do."

"That's not necessary, Joe, because in fact it's very simple. In the past, your company issued bonds when interest rates were 8 percent. Now, the payment of interest weighs heavily, and in the meantime market rates have gone down to 4 percent. I suggest you do a swap, which will allow you to exchange payments at 8 percent for payments at 4 percent, in line with today's market conditions."

"Now, John, you're going too far. I have been convinced by your stratagems up to now, but you're asking me to believe we can turn lead into gold and that there is such a thing as a free lunch."

"You're right; no free lunch, as you say. But I haven't finished. The bank will provide that after the first four years at 4 percent, you will have to pay them over the following six years at a rate determined by a rather complicated formula. That may increase the size of your interest payments overall but not until four years down the line."

The idea of such a long delay seemed to make Smith joyful.

"In four years' time, I'll be happily retired. Let each generation have its own problems. But are you sure this commitment would not appear anywhere in this or next year's accounts?"

"You know, it's pretty much the same thing I mentioned a few minutes ago. The arrangements are described in the footnotes as 'off-balance-sheet items.' Not many people read them, because it requires too much time and work to understand, and most analysts are not that interested. Under current accounting standards, there is no negative impact from the derivatives on the balance sheet or the income statement. And your return on equity will get even better."

"I see. This off-balance-sheet stuff is just fantastic. It reminds me of stock options; they don't show up in the figures anywhere either."

"You learn quickly, Joe, and you've just guessed my next and final suggestion, which is made possible by the excellent labor relations I understand you enjoy at Smoke & Mirrors. I suggest that you call a meeting of all your employees and explain to them the serious dangers facing the company. To save their jobs, you propose that they accept the following bargain: their salary would decrease, but this would be offset by other kinds of benefits. All employees would receive extra pension entitlements, and managers would be granted additional stock options. The beauty of this is that the cost savings on salaries are recorded immediately, while the future pension payments only appear off balance sheet, and the stock options are not expensed at all, that is, they will never appear as a cost on your income statement. Therefore, nothing shows up in the financial statements but as small print items in the notes. Only your successors and your stockholders will share the burden: payment of the pensions will cost money, and the stock options will reduce the profits available to shareholders. But for now, your costs are lowered and you get a further increase in Smoke & Mirrors' return on equity, which now rises to an appealing 12 percent."

Smith was on the point of agreeing but suddenly felt a qualm.

"But isn't there a risk of being accused of accounting fraud? I don't want to end up in jail."

"Not the slightest risk. All these arrangements comply with the accounting standards applicable in this country. You risk nothing, except an increase in your share price," Wills grinned. "No one has ever been blamed for innocent accounting optimization. Besides, if you're hesitant, we can call your auditor. I guarantee that he will confirm the feasibility of all the arrangements I've proposed."

"Very well, it's a deal then."

Two years later, Smoke & Mirrors, Inc., has pulled through. Its high profits have enabled it to finalize a large bond issue and to invest in new industrial equipment. As for Smith, he has sold his shares in the company at a good price and is now planning a peaceful retirement.[1]

SMOKE & MIRRORS, INC.

INTRODUCTION

Enron's bankruptcy, in December 2001, was no small event. The Houston-based energy-trading firm had been hailed throughout the late 1990s as a model corporation, and it ranked among the best-connected U.S. companies. Its collapse caused thousands of job losses; led to the disappearance of Arthur Andersen, until then one of the world's most prestigious professional services firms; and accelerated a slump in stock prices which, by some measures, was unprecedented since the early 1930s.

But perhaps the most lasting change brought by Enron, and by the many other scandals that followed, was the realization that accounting really mattered. Enron's apparent accounting manipulations were only slightly more subtle than the ones described in our prologue (most of which are not allowed under current U.S. accounting standards but have been allowed in the past in the United States and until very recently in many other developed countries). Since the beginning of 2002, accounting issues have featured more prominently than ever before in financial media, and even in the mass media. What Enron brought to light was not that some managers were unscrupulous (which had always been the case) but that the controls on their financial disclosures were weaker than most people thought and, perhaps even more important, that the weaknesses were heightened rather than reduced by powerful trends shaping the current business environment, such as the acceleration of corporate restructuring, disruptive technology changes, and constant financial innovation.

Another trend, which also increases the importance of understanding what is at stake in accounting, is globalization. Globalization increases the opportunities for companies to hide risks or losses, as Enron and others did by creating "shell" companies in the Cayman Islands and other tax havens, or as Italian dairy-products producer Parmalat did in Latin America. But more important, globalization increases cross-border interdependence and the need for a shared language, which accounting is meant to provide for all business transactions. This has been the basis for the astounding success of International Financial Reporting Standards (IFRS), which within the past few years have been endorsed by the European Union, Canada, Australia, Russia, and many other countries, and are in a process of mutual convergence with accounting standards used in the United States. It also explains the dominance of only four major accounting firms, whose global footprint creates formidable barriers to entry. Global business requires global reporting and accounting, which leads to the gradual elimination of specific national approaches—even U.S. ones, as has been illustrated by the debate about expensing stock options. Accounting is critical to the globalization of business, because it has always been a common language of capitalism and because it is much easier to share than management styles, working habits, corporate governance patterns, or cultural references. In this book, we concentrate on the two main centers of capital-markets activity, the United States and the European Union, with France, our home country, often taken as an illustration of the broader continental European situation.[1]

Corporate financial reporting had long appeared as a dull, reliable, rational technique, a requirement for doing business but with no economic consequences of its own. Discussion about accounting was the sole preserve of a closed circle of specialists. This is no longer the case. Accounting manipulations played a central role in almost all recent corporate scandals, sometimes along with corruption and tax evasion. This has broadly called into question the reliability of the financial data on which capital markets critically rely. And issues of accounting standard-setting, such as the expensing of stock options in the United States, or the recording of bank deposits in Europe, have been seized on by politicians as key policy choices. The issue of financial reporting has surged out of the narrow remit of the accounting profession to become a matter of public interest.

The authors have come to place accounting at the center of their analysis of business transformations on the basis of the empirical observation of these broad trends rather than because of professional prejudice (the three of us originally trained as engineers, not as accountants). Nor is there any partisan or doctrinal intent in this book—even though it was initially published in France, a country prone to heated ideological rhetoric even among observers of business life. Rather, we aim to provide the layman with a better understanding of current developments in relations between companies, investors, and other economic agents, by focusing on what can be revealed by accounting. The interaction of all these parties produces a "financial ecosystem," where the "food chain" of capital circulation parallels natural ecosystems and determines the development of companies, thus playing a central role in growth and employment. Accounting is an ideal lens through which to look at this fast-changing world.

We are aware that our subject has the reputation of being unglamorous, and that it may frighten some readers. Accounting matters (as well as accountants) are commonly known for being austere, if not outright boring. But readers should not be put off by this prejudice. In fact, this subject is immensely varied, and intimately linked with the most significant developments in the economic world. To bring this out more clearly, we provide many examples and analyses of actual events and situations that have arisen in the recent or remote past. Accounting can certainly lend itself to abstract arguments, but its major concerns are deeply rooted in the day-to-day reality of business, which we have carefully tried to always keep in view. Our approach is based on historical analysis, reference to well-established facts, and insistence on the role of the different agents and their respective interests.

The structure of the book stems from the foregoing concerns. The first part, Accounting and Its Controversies, presents the key ideas and intellectual bases of financial statements, accounting standards, and their use. Chapter 1 describes the origins and historical development of accounting and the range of users it has been intended to serve; the rudiments of accounting concepts are presented in a short section that readers already familiar with these matters can easily skip. Chapter 2 starts with a description of the various possibilities for accounting manipulation, richly illustrated by the Enron case, and then broadens the discussion to question the very notion of the accuracy and fairness of accounts. To the extent that accounts include an opinion about the future, they cannot claim to be an expression of objective truth but only to a degree of neutrality and compliance with certain rules. Hence, the central importance of accounting standards, the various characteristics and consequences of which are examined in chapter 3.

The second part, The Changing World of Financial Reporting, explores the political economy of accounting and the various players in the financial ecosystem. Chapter 4 highlights the main current business trends that affect the preparation of accounts by corporations. Chapter 5 concentrates on auditors and on the recent changes in their business model and competitive position. Chapter 6 focuses on investors, asset managers, and on the many financial intermediaries on which they rely. Finally, chapter 7 examines the role of public authorities in the regulation of securities markets, which is specifically affected by two key drivers: the impact of technological change and the globalization of market activity.

Modern, double-entry accounting was born at the same time as the capitalist enterprise, among the merchants of late medieval Italy. Now, understanding the stakes of financial reporting is an integral, though often underrated, part of any effort to fully grasp the transformation of our market economy. This book's goal, and our hope, is to stimulate a taste for this field of study—the relationship between financial reporting practices and underlying economic trends—which we think will have increasing resonance in the coming years.

PART I

ACCOUNTING AND ITS CONTROVERSIES

CHAPTER 1

THE COMMON LANGUAGE OF CAPITALISM

F inancial accounting, which was created at about the same time as the earliest joint-stock companies, is an unmatched tool: a common language that makes it possible (theoretically) to describe all economic activities in the same terms and to compare all businesses with one another. For this reason, it can be counted among the few vital underpinnings of any market economy. Conversely, once the accuracy of financial information can no longer be taken for granted, the entire economic and financial system runs the risk of paralysis.

Looking at the origins of accounting is a useful introduction to the roles of the various users of corporate financial information. This historical overview serves two purposes. First, it makes it easier to understand the influence exerted on accounting by each of the economic agents that make up the financial system as a whole. Second, it helps explain the current organization of institutions and the specific practices of financial-information professionals in the light of the circumstances in which they came into being.

The Origins

Accounting techniques developed hand in hand with economic activity from the very beginning. The first written texts in human history, inscribed on Sumerian clay tablets more than five thousand years ago, are accounting documents. Later, with the invention of currency around the seventh century BC, accounting made it possible to record all exchanges in the same units.

In every Western language, the vocabulary related to writing and the faculty of reasoning is permeated with notions derived from accounting. In Latin, *ratio* (reason) originally meant "count" or "calculation," a meaning retained in the Italian word for accounting, *ragioneria*. An *écrivain*, in old French, meant an accountant or a clerk long before it meant, as today, a writer. In many European languages, "book keeping" is synonymous with accounting.[1]

The next stage, which marked the true birth of modern accounting, started in late medieval Italy, then the center of economic and financial innovation in Europe. The rise of foreign trade, with naval expeditions requiring the commitment of significant amounts of capital, led the merchants of Genoa, Venice, and Tuscany to form "companies" to share risks and profits—which could be very high for a successful expedition. In this process, the company gradually acquired a practical, legal, and financial identity different from that of its owners. On a day-by-day basis it was run by a professional manager, typically a ship's captain, who himself was generally not one of the partners or shareholders. With this separation between ownership and management, the joint-stock company had come into being, probably one of the most revolutionary inventions in history.

Thus separated from the enterprise in a joint-stock arrangement, the owners soon felt the need for a more elaborate mechanism than previously available, one that would allow them to oversee, from a distance, the development of the business. They also needed to be able to compute, and control, the profitability of their investment. This soon gave rise to the need for a proper framework of corporate governance. As Thomas Hobbes pointed out a little later in time in chapter 22 of *Leviathan*:

> The end of these Bodies of Merchants [joint-stock companies], being not a Common benefit to the whole Body . . . but the particular gaine of every adventurer [partner], it is reason that every one be acquainted with the employment of his own; that is, that every one be of the Assembly, that shall have the power to order the same; and be acquainted with their accounts. And

therefore the Representative of such a Body must be an Assembly, where every member of the Body may be present at the consultations, if he will.[2]

A new method gradually emerged, whose intent was to express the business in figures following precise rules that reduced the risk of fraud or mistake. This method involved entering each new transaction in two separate registers, debit and credit, permitting verification by comparison of the two at any time. First known as the "Venetian method," and then as "double-entry bookkeeping," it was used as early as the fourteenth century and given its first consistent expression in 1494 by one of the key humanists of the Italian Renaissance, Luca Pacioli, who had been Leonardo da Vinci's mathematics teacher in Milan.[3]

Modern double-entry bookkeeping was thus shaped by its two Italian Renaissance parents: nascent capitalism and the rediscovery of the mathematical rationality of Antiquity. Max Weber observed in *The Protestant Ethic and the Spirit of Capitalism*:

> Rational industrial organization, attuned to a regular market, and neither to political nor irrationally speculative opportunities for profit, is not . . . the only peculiarity of Western capitalism. The modern rational organization of the capitalistic enterprise would not have been possible without two other important factors in its development: the separation of business from the household, which completely dominates modern economic life, and closely connected with it, rational bookkeeping.[4]

The separation of owners and shareholders from the company—and thus from its managers—meant that shareholders had to exercise rigorous control over managers from a distance. At the same time, since the wealthiest merchants now could be involved simultaneously in several "companies," they looked for ways of choosing, with increasingly sophisticated methods, investments that would provide the best return on their capital. Accounting thus had to provide *relevant* and *reliable* information to ensure shareholder control over the managers; the information also had to be *comparable* from one enterprise to the next, and consistent over time to permit optimal capital allocation—even though this last function was still quite embryonic in the period to which we are referring.

The fundamental requirements for relevance, reliability, and comparability have not changed since then. The reader will come across them again on many occasions in the rest of this book.

From Venice To Houston

The basic principles of modern accounting were thus in place by the early Renaissance, when the "Venetian" double-entry method was codified by Luca Pacioli in his *Summa*. Since then, accounting has constantly mirrored the changes in capitalism and the recurring crises caused by the ingenuity of financiers. Following every crisis, accounting rules and their underlying principles have been adapted.

Developments were relatively slow until the second half of the nineteenth century. As the economic historian Fernand Braudel pointed out in *Civilization and Capitalism* (first published in French in 1979), the respective paths of double-entry bookkeeping and of capitalism would still be far from converging for two centuries after Pacioli. Use of the double-entry technique was patchy and spread unevenly in different countries. For example, France crossed a significant milestone in 1673, when Louis XIV's minister Jean-Baptiste Colbert adopted an "edict for trade among wholesale and retail merchants." This founding document of French accounting tradition required that merchants, wholesalers, and clothing manufacturers keep accounts that could be used as evidence in commercial disputes. It also required that the keeping of "double-entry books and registers" be part of the basic knowledge of any merchant. But the dynamic relationship between shareholders and managers that is at the origin of accounting did not turn up everywhere. It was often absent from major industrial enterprises, many of which were established on government initiative, such as military arsenals or the *Manufactures* created by Louis XIV in the 1660s. These were large and prestigious factories, which produced luxury items such as tapestries (manufacture des Gobelins, est. 1662) or mirrors and glass (manufacture de Saint-Gobain, est. 1665, the ancestor of today's Saint-Gobain Group).

As properties of a state obsessed with *grandeur*, they were subject to less stringent profitability requirements than privately owned businesses and, hardly coincidentally, often applied only rudimentary accounting. Financial markets, also, were gradually established. Shares in the Dutch East India Company, founded in 1602, were being traded on the Amsterdam exchange as early as the seventeenth century. In France the Bourse de Paris was set up in 1724, after John Law's bankruptcy demonstrated the need for some organization of the financial market; and the London Stock Exchange began operations in 1773. Most securities listed on these markets were debt instruments, however, and the link between the public listing of securities and stringent accounting rules was slow to emerge. For example, the Dutch East India Company never actually used double-entry bookkeeping in its almost two centuries of existence (it was dissolved by Napoleon in 1800).

After 1850, the development of capitalism accelerated. This was partly because of a groundbreaking innovation, the introduction of limited liability, which was adopted by law in 1862 in Great Britain and 1867 in France and opened a period of unprecedented growth for joint-stock companies. In a way, the right to limited liability effectively constituted massive government interference in the economy (and was denounced as such by opponents at the time), as losses in case of bankruptcy were assumed by the community. But, unlike other types of state aid, this interference was practically invisible as it gave the government no discretionary authority, and it eventually stimulated rather than reined in the willingness to take risks.[5]

Limitation of liability also led to a spectacular growth in share trading on capital markets, which took on an increasingly prominent role in the second half of the nineteenth century. This also spurred accounting scandals, where the manipulation techniques used by unscrupulous businessmen were strikingly similar to those observed in our times. In *L'Argent* (published in 1891), a vivid account of the rise and fall of the fictional bank-cum-transportation conglomerate Banque Universelle, the French novelist Émile Zola depicted accounting falsifications that eerily remind us of Enron or WorldCom.

The nineteenth century was also the period when the first firms of independent accounting professionals appeared, the origin of today's major global accounting giants. Namely:

- William Deloitte established his firm in London in 1845 and conducted the first independent audit when he examined the accounts of the Great Western Railway. In 1989, Deloitte Haskins & Sells merged with Touche Ross, a partnership set up in London in 1899, and with the firm created in Tokyo in 1968 by Admiral Nobuzo Tohmatsu and others, thus forming Deloitte Touche Tohmatsu (now renamed Deloitte).

- Samuel Price founded his London firm in 1849, and when he retired in 1874, the reins were taken up by his partner Edwin Waterhouse. In 1998, the firm Price Waterhouse merged with Coopers & Lybrand, itself the product of the 1957 merger of firms established in London in 1854 by William Cooper and in Philadelphia in 1898 by William Lybrand. The entity resulting from the 1998 merger was renamed PricewaterhouseCoopers (PwC).

- The accountants whose initials provide the first three letters of today's KPMG, Piet Klynveld, William Peat, and James Marwick, established their firms respectively in Amsterdam in 1917, London in 1867, and Glasgow in 1887. Peat and Marwick merged in 1911; the final "G" came from Reinhard Goerdeler, who headed Germany's oldest audit firm Deutsche Treuhandgesellschaft (founded 1890) when it merged with Klynveld in 1979. The merger of Peat Marwick with Klynveld Main Goerdeler, which resulted in KPMG, took place in 1986–87.

- The brothers Alvin and Theodore Ernst formed a partnership in Cleveland in 1903. Their firm merged in 1989 with one set up in Chicago in 1894 by a Scottish immigrant, Arthur Young, thereby creating Ernst & Young.

- Finally, Arthur Andersen, an immigrant from Norway, established his own firm in Chicago in 1913, in partnership with Clarence Delaney; both of them had previously worked for Price Waterhouse. Arthur Andersen, who was also a pioneer in consulting services, was probably the most well-known name in accounting before it disappeared in 2002 in the wake of Enron's collapse.

The details of this chronology also illustrate the shift of the center of accounting and financial innovation from London in the mid-nineteenth century to the United Sates in the early twentieth. The major financial rating agencies were also created in the United States: as early as 1860, Henry Varnum Poor began publishing the financial analyses that led to the establishment of Standard & Poor's. John Moody published his first *Manual of Industrial and Miscellaneous Securities* in New York in 1900, and started giving credit ratings in 1909. John Fitch established his financial data publishing company, also in New York, in 1913.

By the 1920s, the New York Stock Exchange (NYSE) dominated world capital markets. At the time, companies listed in New York and on other U.S. exchanges still enjoyed almost complete autonomy in their choice of accounting policies, even though the 1887 law establishing the Interstate Commerce Commission had created an embryonic common accounting system for railroad companies. Until the First World War, companies rarely published an income statement, and even when they did, the statements were open to all kinds of manipulation in the absence of mandatory accounting standards. An attempt in 1914 to impose a single format for the presentation of accounts was rejected by Congress. The use of external auditors was spreading, but they usually worked on the management's internal control needs, not for the shareholders.

The October 1929 market crash was a defining moment in the history of modern accounting. The collapse of share prices, ruin of investors, and chains of bankruptcies, together with the revelation of high-profile cases of misleading disclosures, brought about sudden awareness that the capital markets needed reliable financial information in order to function properly. This reliability, which had not been spontaneously provided by companies or professionals, would now be guaranteed by the government. The Securities Acts of 1933 and 1934 were among the most important and enduring legislation of Franklin Delano Roosevelt's New Deal. The legislation established the Securities and Exchange Commission (SEC), a federal agency for the supervision and regulation of the securities markets, and gave it the task of producing and enforcing accounting standards for all listed companies. Listed companies were also required to have their financial statements audited by an independent accounting firm and to publish consolidated accounts. A committee of private experts began the work of standardization of accounting rules under the supervision of the SEC: the expression "Generally Accepted Accounting Principles" (GAAP) appeared in 1936, and the first complete codification of the standards, from then on designated as US GAAP, was published in 1953. This institutional setting has remained relatively stable to the end of the twentieth century. The last significant change occurred in 1973, with the establishment of the Financial Accounting Standards Board (FASB), a private body responsible for most of the production and interpretation of US GAAP accounting standards, by delegation from the SEC in replacement of previously existing committees. Public accounting standards are thus a direct consequence of the 1929 crash, as is the legal requirement to use the services of an independent external auditor.

The initiatives taken by the United States were generally copied by other industrialized countries. For example, France adopted the requirement for external audit by a government decree on August 8, 1935, rendering it obligatory that at least one of the pre-existing corporate officers known as *commissaires aux comptes* (statutory auditors) be a professional accountant. Three decades later, auditing profession regulation was established by the law of July 24, 1966, still today the principal basis of corporate law in France. Accounting standards also appeared in France, for the first time in 1947 in the *Plan Comptable Général* (general chart of accounts), based on preparatory work begun by the Vichy regime, and the 1966 law required that all companies issuing shares, even non-listed ones, publish individual accounts. Compared with the United States, however, these moves were less inspired by the need for investor protection and more by the drive to reform the economic infrastructure that lingered from the postwar reconstruction years. Therefore, they responded at least as much to the state's needs as to those of investors, a fact to which we will come back later. For example, publication of consolidated accounts remained for a long time a rare practice in France, until a European directive in the 1980s made it obligatory above certain thresholds.

The U.S. model of supervision of the capital markets by a specialized government agency also spread gradually through Europe. France was among the first countries to adopt it, establishing in 1967 the Commission des Opérations de Bourse (replaced in 2003 by the Autorité des Marchés Financiers or AMF). This agency oversees the quality of financial information disclosed by listed companies and, consequently, controls the implementation of accounting standards, although, unlike the SEC, it has no direct authority over the preparation of the standards themselves.

The gradual appearance, first in the United States and then in the rest of the industrialized world, of national institutions for accounting standard-setting itself turned out to be a source of difficulties. Because capital markets have gradually become more integrated across national borders, investors in those markets have felt increasingly hampered by the diversity of national accounting rules, and often of the underlying philosophies as well. Recognizing this, some accounting professionals took the initiative in 1973 to establish a private body with a global purpose, which has been known since 2001 as the International Accounting Standards Board (IASB). The IASB developed International Accounting Standards (IAS), followed by International Financial Reporting Standards (IFRS) since 2001,[6] and promotes their adoption by the largest possible number of countries. For a long time, however, IFRS had little direct impact on developed economies, and they were mainly used as fallback standards in developing countries that had no capacity for developing accounting standards of their own.

Finally, the beginning of the twenty-first century was marked by several watersheds. The collapse of Enron in late 2001 was the first of a series of accounting scandals of unprecedented proportions, in the United States and later in Europe. As a consequence of these, the United States adopted the Sarbanes-Oxley Act of July 2002, which placed the auditors of public companies under government oversight and tightened the rules by which corporate executives are held accountable for public financial statements. In a largely unrelated but simultaneous move, since 2000 the European Union and other countries (such as Canada in 2005) have decided to require the application of IFRS by companies listed on their markets. This decision was initially greeted with indifference, but its wide-ranging effects, as we shall see later, are now unfolding and triggering profound changes in the way financial information is prepared and used in Europe.

Accounts for Whom?

This brief historical overview illustrates, among other things, the diversity of users of accounting and financial information. Like the character of Harlequin in the *Commedia dell'arte*, accounting serves more than one master, which inevitably creates tensions. We briefly present the most important of these users at this stage; the way that their conflicting requirements can lead to different choices of standards is addressed in chapter 3.

Shareholders. From owners of shares in the Genoese or Venetian "companies" of the fourteenth century to contemporary day traders,[7] shareholders rank first among users of financial information. The two principal uses of this information have barely changed over the course of six centuries. First, the availability of financial statements allows management performance to be overseen from a distance; second, they enable shareholders to evaluate the return on their capital with a view to sharing the profits among themselves, and they also enable comparisons among different companies with a view to optimizing investment decisions. This explains the particularly high level of importance of accounting for shareholders in public companies (i.e., those whose shares are listed on a stock exchange), because in such cases accounting data provide the only quantified information available to them to evaluate performance—whereas in non-listed companies, shareholders are less numerous and usually have more direct contacts with management, which gives them access to additional information. For shareholders, accounting data are mainly a key basis on which to estimate the value of the company, which they wish to be as high as possible. In the case of publicly listed companies, shareholders can also often rely on the opinions of equity analysts, whose task is to estimate that value on the basis of published information in order to give advice on purchase or sale of a company's shares. A particularly prominent role is played by large "institutional" shareholders, such as insurance companies, mutual funds, hedge funds, or pension funds, to which we come back in chapter 6.

Lenders and creditors. All parties to whom a company owes money have a potential interest in its accounting information. As we will see in more detail in chapter 3, however, their needs may not always be identical to those of the shareholders. What is important for lenders or creditors is not the company's value, which has no direct effect on their own wealth, but rather the risk of it defaulting on its debt, which determines the credit they are willing to grant and the rate of interest they can request. Here, too, a distinction can be made between two categories of players: on the one hand, commercial banks and other direct creditors of companies that can have an immediate contact with managers from whom they may receive more detailed information; on the other hand, holders of listed bonds and other debt instruments traded on the capital markets, for whom the public accounting data are often the only available source of information. They are seconded by credit rating agencies, which specifically evaluate the risk of default by companies on their listed securities. Beyond these agencies, credit research is growing alongside equity research as a distinct activity of financial research departments and firms.

Customers and suppliers. A company's trading partners are, to a certain extent, users of its financial information, either as creditors (in the case of suppliers) or for purposes of their business relationship. This is the case, for example, for large retailers wanting to know the financial situation of their suppliers in order to optimize their position for negotiating purchasing conditions. The same can be said of *employees*, for whom a precise understanding of the financial situation and the business of the company through its financial reporting facilitates an informed conduct of individual and collective negotiations, especially where an organized system of labor bargaining is in place.[8]

The State. Government agencies have become, particularly in the course of the twentieth century, a crucially important category of users of financial information. Tax authorities rely heavily (although differently from one country to another) on accounting information to determine or check the basis on which companies can be taxed. Separately, specialized supervisory authorities have the duty to protect the interests of customers in certain kinds of services involving long-term relations, such as banking, insurance, or public utilities; in the United States, such agencies include the Office of the Comptroller of the Currency, state insurance regulators, or public utilities commissions. These regulators may base their calculations, for example, of solvency ratios for banks or insurers or of electricity or water rates for utilities, on "regulatory accounts" which, as in the case of tax, may be more or less closely connected with companies' public financial statements. National statistical services are also users of accounting data, which they may aggregate into macroeconomic indicators. Finally, while not being users of financial data for their own purposes, securities regulatory authorities such as the SEC in the United States have become essential participants in all the debates concerning public accounting. It should be noted that unlike most of the users previously mentioned, government authorities often have the ability to gain direct access to internal company information, for example, when conducting inspections.

Corporate managers. This last category of users is not to be forgotten, even though different from the previous ones, as the managers' role is not only to use accounting information but also to prepare it. Accounting is an indispensable source of information for running a business. The distinction that used to exist in many places between public financial accounts, intended for external users, and management accounts or internal reporting, reserved for in-house controlling, has tended to partly fade in recent years. "External" and "internal" reporting are more frequently merging into one single information system in most companies, because of the growing complexity of large corporations, which makes it costly and risky to simultaneously maintain two parallel reporting systems, and because of the enabling effects of information technology solutions such as Enterprise Resource Planning (ERP) software packages. ERPs make it possible to centrally manage all the databases of the company, be it accounting, production orders, customer relationships, human resources, and so on. Increasingly, the same operational information serves as a basis both for internal management control systems and for the preparation of financial statements that are disclosed to external partners and, in the case of a publicly listed company, to the capital markets. In the end, managers have a double role as both preparers (exclusively) and consumers (along with the other users previously listed) of their company's financial information.

The uncomfortable reality is that all these participants have slightly different requirements regarding accounts, but that at the same time they wish to rely on a single financial picture of the company. With a single set of data being used to provide that picture, the feeling of objectivity is strengthened. For this latter reason, and for obvious considerations of cost and complexity, it would not be practical to have as many sets of accounts, using different rules, as there are categories of users: one for shareholders, another for creditors, a third for the government statistical services, and so forth. But some users' requirements can hardly be reconciled either, and therefore the opposite option, which would be a single set of accounts for all the different users, would be equally unrealistic. The result of these opposing constraints is that several sets of accounts have to be used simultaneously to accommodate the different users, but some categories of users nevertheless have to rely on the same accounts; the details of this compromise vary somewhat from one country to another. For example, in the United States, "tax accounts" (for the calculation of tax) and public financial accounts are largely separate systems, whereas in France, as we shall see in chapter 3, they have historically been very closely connected with one another.

In developed countries, the dominant perspective provided by public financial accounts is that required by investors and other economic partners or associates of companies; these are the ones referred to in shorthand as "financial statements" or "accounts." In a somewhat contorted way, the IASB explicitly recognizes investors as the primary users of its IFRS accounting standards: "As investors are providers of risk capital to the enterprise, the provision of financial statements that meet their needs will also meet most of the needs of other users that financial statements can satisfy."[9] It is, however, important to bear in mind that, along with this "financial information," other kinds of accounting can and sometimes do exist. Among these are the tax accounts and the already mentioned "regulatory accounts" used by sectoral supervision authorities such as in banking, insurance, or electricity. And, within companies, even though internal and external reporting systems are increasingly interlinked, managers may foster the use of other monitoring tools, for instance at the level of each business unit, which may in certain cases bear little resemblance to the public financial accounts.

The rest of this book is mainly concerned with public financial accounting, which applies particularly to publicly listed companies in their relationship to their investors. A history could also be written of tax accounting, of regulatory accounting, of management accounting, or of all the techniques used in noncapitalist economic systems. In the former Soviet Union, the State Planning Bureau (GOSPLAN) was well known for the length and complexity of the series of figures that it handled, which was a form of accounting even though it had nothing to do with a financial investor's viewpoint. The effort made by some countries such as France to unify various kinds of accounting into a single "general accounting" system, supposed to serve all users at once, has ultimately failed because it exacted too steep a price in terms of compromise between contradictory demands, particularly between investors and the government, and did not prove to be fully compatible with the requirements of vibrant capital markets. In the end, public financial accounting, because it is primarily directed toward investors, is the one variety that traces most directly its roots to the origins of double-entry accounting with the separation between investors and managers. It is also probably the most complex, as the needs of investors are arguably more all-encompassing than those of other users.

Financial Statements: A Primer

This section is intended as a brief presentation of the principal concepts of accounting as they are used in everyday business. Financially literate readers may wish to skim through these pages or skip directly to the next chapter; conversely, nonspecialists should not be concerned if some terms still seem a little obscure after their reading. It is not necessary to be a certified public accountant to be able to understand the underlying questions which this book attempts to address.

The "double entry" that defines modern financial accounting refers to the fact that every business transaction executed by a company is recorded twice, on the debit and on the credit side, in the company's accounts. Another essential distinction in accounting is that of assets, liabilities, and shareholders' equity, which forms the basis for the preparation of accounting balance sheets. These notions are subject to precise definitions. For example, in IFRS (which draws on concepts developed for US GAAP), an *asset* is defined as "a resource controlled by the enterprise as a result of past events and from which future economic benefits are expected to flow to the enterprise"; a *liability* is "a present obligation of the enterprise arising from past events, the settlement of which is expected to result in an outflow from the enterprise of resources embodying economic benefits"; and *equity* is "the residual interest in the assets of the enterprise after deducting all its liabilities."

In simplified terms, assets are what you have, and liabilities are what you owe to others. Cash or buildings, for example, are assets, and debts are liabilities. Shareholders' equity is a slightly less concrete notion, as it cannot simply be described as what a company "owes" to its shareholders. The particular status of shareholders' equity is to be both the property of the shareholders and the residual amount available to the company if it must repay all its obligations. For this reason it is also, in some situations, referred to as "net assets," that is, assets net of debts and other liabilities.

According to the double-entry principle, each transaction is registered as an exchange, by recording an identical amount as a debit on the one hand, and a credit on the other hand. For example, if the company incurs a debt of $100, its debts increase by $100 (in liabilities), but simultaneously its cash on hand increases by $100 (in assets). If the company sells products to a client for $150, its revenue increases by $150 (which increases earnings and thus also increases shareholders' equity) and accounts receivable from customers also increase by $150 (in assets). When the customer pays for the purchase, the latter receivable is cancelled and cash on hand increases by the same amount (by reallocation of amounts within assets). And so on.

Thus, every transaction of any kind, financial or operational, ordinary or extraordinary, shrewd or ill-advised, is expressed by a double entry that maintains constant equality between assets on the one hand and the sum of liabilities and equity on the other, like the two sides of a balance, whatever the size and complexity of the company. Luca Pacioli wrote that "you should not go to bed as long as the debit is not equal to the credit." The term "balance sheet," for the summary table of assets, liabilities, and equity, provides an apt image. The underlying idea is that each transaction is in its own way a balanced exchange, in other words, there is no economic transfer without compensation ("no free lunch"). Even in accounting for the most abstract transactions, double-entry accounting is always based on a philosophy of exchange between willing parties.

In addition to the balance sheet, which presents in summary form the elements of assets, liabilities, and shareholders' equity, the financial statements or "accounts" include an income statement (also called "profit and loss account," or P&L) presenting the company's

Table 1. Simplified Example of a Corporate Balance Sheet

Assets	($ millions)	Liabilities and Equity	($ millions)
Inventories	22	Loans	35
Accounts receivable	35	Accounts payable	36
Cash and cash equivalents	9	Accrued pension plan liability	15
Total Current Assets	66	Other liabilities	32
Trademarks	8	Total Liabilities	118
Goodwill	21		
Total Intangible Assets	29	Share capital	30
Land	5	Additional paid-in capital	10
Buildings	12		
Plant and machinery	45	Retained earnings	13
Total Tangible Fixed Assets (or "Property, plant & equipment")	62	Total Shareholders' Equity	53
Investments Available for Sale	18	Minority Interests	4
Total Non-Current Assets	109		
Total Assets	**175**	**Total Liabilities and Equity**	**175**

revenues and expenses over a given accounting period ending at the date of the balance sheet. The difference between revenues (e.g., sales of goods or services) and expenses (e.g., materials, wages, depreciation of assets, interest expense on loans, or taxes) constitutes the net income or earnings, which may be positive (profit) or negative (loss). The net income for the period is taken to shareholders' equity in the balance sheet in order to enable it to balance, as described above. The net income may later be partly distributed to shareholders in the form of dividends, depending on a decision by the annual general meeting of shareholders, with the remainder being accumulated in "reserves" or "retained earnings."

The balance sheet and income statement are accompanied by a third primary financial statement, the statement of cash flows, or cash flow statement. This is partly because not all revenue and cost items correspond to a flow of cash to or from the company. The purpose of the cash flow statement is therefore to explain the changes in a company's

Table 2. Simplified Income Statement (or Profit & Loss Account)

	($ millions)
Revenues	190
Sales	185
Other revenues	5
Costs of goods sold	(135)
Gross Margin	55
Selling, general and administrative expenses	(30)
Interest expense	(5)
Income from continuing operations	20
Income/(Loss) from discontinued operations	(9)
Net Income before tax	11
Corporate Income Tax	(4)
Net Income after tax	7

Note: The numbers in parentheses correspond to negative amounts, a commonly used convention adopted to avoid transcription errors.

cash position in a period, and to show how they relate to the balance sheet and income statement. For example, payments are deferred, debts are repaid, fixed assets are depreciated over a certain period. In the example above, the sale of goods to a customer for $150 is recorded under revenue in the income statement. The two other transactions—incurring a debt of $100 and the customer's payment for an earlier purchase—have no impact on income even though they have an impact on the cash position. In these two examples, the company derives no profit, in the economic sense of the word, because the variation in its cash on hand corresponds exactly to the variation in its assets and liabilities. Conversely, some entries in the income statement, such as depreciation charges or accrued future expenses, do not directly reflect immediate cash transfers but either correspond to past cash outflows whose economic effect still benefits the company (in the case of asset depreciation) or to a recognition of future likely cash outflows that have not yet materialized (in the case of accrued expenses). We will come back in chapter 2 to the distinction between revenues and expenses on the one hand, and cash flows on the other hand, seen from the point of view of the potential for fraudulent manipulation of this distinction.

In addition to the balance sheet, income statement, and cash flow statement, the financial statements include a set of "disclosure notes" that provide additional information on accounting policies and a series of specific items. In addition, depending on the system of accounting standards under which a company reports, other compulsory elements may be included in the financial statements, such as, under IFRS, a statement of changes in shareholders' equity, which makes it possible to better illustrate the impact of financial transactions which occurred in the period under consideration.

The depreciation of certain assets is another important notion: this is linked to the key accounting distinction between the purchase of goods or services used immediately, which are booked as expenses (or costs or charges), and other purchases that produce benefits over the medium or long term, which have to be considered to be fixed assets. The latter items are booked in the asset side of the balance sheet and may be depreciated over several years, or in some cases not at all. The depreciation charge is the decrease in the assets' value calculated according to a general formula, which is booked as an expense for each corresponding accounting period. Fixed assets themselves are divided into "tangible" fixed assets (property, plant, and equipment), "intangible" fixed assets (such as trademarks, proprietary technologies, or patents), and financial assets (such as loans or shares). The remaining assets, made up of theoretically less long-term assets (inventory, accounts payable, cash on hand), are often referred to as "current assets."

Shareholders' equity, for its part, is derived both from contributions from shareholders (successive capital increases, for instance) and from profits generated over time that are not distributed as dividends.

Liabilities include debts (financial, such as to banks and bondholders, and operating, such as debts to suppliers) and accrued liabilities, which can be for either certain amounts (in the case of goods received but not yet invoiced) or contingent ones. Accrued liabilities (or reserves) for contingencies represent amounts set aside to confront future risks or commitments that have been identified with sufficient precision to be quantified. This may be the case, for example, if the company is being sued and thinks that it will have to pay damages. Pension obligations, when they are assumed by the company, must also be entered as liabilities, in some cases reaching very substantial amounts.

The usual format of the income statement distinguishes between several categories of items: revenue and costs from operations, resulting in an operating profit; financial income (interest received on loans, minus interest paid on debt); and sometimes, "extraordinary" items connected to events so unusual they fall outside normal business activities.[10] Depreciation charges and accrued expenses appear as costs in the income statement, and are double entries to the corresponding variations of the related items on the balance sheet. Depreciation charges are decreases in fixed assets (thus, fixed assets are recorded on the balance sheet as "net" of depreciation); and expenses recorded on writing down inventories or "bad debts" (i.e., with a significant probability of default) correspond to decreases in the related assets, loans and receivables on the balance sheet.

All of the foregoing refers to "individual" or "company" accounts, those prepared for one single legal entity. In the more complex case of a group of companies, with several subsidiaries and cross-holdings, accountants have developed, since the late nineteenth century, a body of techniques for "consolidation," enabling them to summarize the accounts of all of a group's individual companies into a single set of financial statements, as though they were dealing with a single entity. Consolidation plays an important role in the preparation of accounts for large listed companies. It may involve some rather complex considerations, but its essential concepts can be summarized as follows.

When a company (a "parent") controls another company (a "subsidiary"), which is usually the case when it holds more than 50 percent of the latter company's shares, the assets and liabilities of the subsidiary are included in the accounts of the group ("consolidated accounts") for 100 percent of their value. The interests of other shareholders in the subsidiary appear on a line for "minority interests" on the consolidated balance sheet. This "full consolidation" permits the expression of the reality constituted by the control of a holding company over its subsidiaries. If the number of shares held is too small to exercise control (for example, if only a small percentage of the capital is held), then the parent company will merely record a line corresponding to the value of the shareholding. The amount of the asset will be equal to the purchase price or market value of the shares held, which means that such an interest, considered of a purely financial nature, is not consolidated (this manner of recording an interest in another company is referred to as the "cost method"). When the situation is an intermediate one, that is, when the parent company has a "significant influence" over a company in which it owns shares but does not exert sole control over it, then the method to be used is the "equity method." Under this method, the investing company initially records its investment in the other company at cost but, subsequently, records its share (e.g., 20 percent, 30 percent, etc.) in the profits or losses of the other company as an increase or decrease in its own profits. The double entry consists of increasing or decreasing the balance sheet amount of the parent company's investment in the "equity accounted" entity. Finally, in cases such as joint ventures, there may be a "proportionate consolidation" where all assets and liabilities of the partially held company are booked on the consolidated balance sheet of the parent, but only for a percentage of their book value equal to the proportion of total equity held by the parent—for example, 50 percent in the case of a joint venture.

The appearance of "goodwill" is one particular consequence of consolidation, which occurs whenever one company acquires another. Because assets and liabilities, for example in case of a full consolidation, are recorded on the balance sheet of the acquiring company at their book value (possibly modified by the revaluation of certain items at the time of acquisition), there is in most cases a difference between this book value and the price actually paid (in general, this price is higher than the book value even after revaluation). This difference is commonly referred to as "goodwill," and is the source of thorny accounting problems that will be analyzed in chapters 3 and 4.

Accounting standards, of course, must specify precise criteria for valuation and thresholds to determine which method is to be applied to each situation—that is, consolidation (full or proportionate), cost method, or equity method. Typically, if a parent company holds less than 20 percent of the voting rights, it is generally considered not to exercise significant influence, and the cost method is therefore appropriate. When holdings are between 20 and 50 percent, there is a presumption of significant influence and the equity method is generally applied. But other considerations, such as the way the directors of the company are selected, may also change the manner in which these general guidelines should be interpreted. Similarly, control is presumed to exist above 50 percent ownership, but there can be exceptions here, too. When this analytical framework is applied to all the subsidiaries and holdings in a group, it enables the preparation of consolidated accounts, which thus offer a summary of all the accounts of all the subsidiaries and direct and indirect shareholdings that constitute the "scope of consolidation."

It is easy to see that the rules determining which companies should or should not be included within this scope can have a considerable impact on the group's consolidated accounts. For example, in the late 1990s, Suez, a Paris-based conglomerate, controlled the Belgian electric utility Electrabel through a network of holding companies: specifically, in late 1997, Suez owned 63.5 percent of Société Générale de Belgique, which itself owned 48.9 percent of Tractebel, which itself owned 39.9 percent of Electrabel. The rest of Tractebel's and Electrabel's shares were in dispersed ownership on the Belgian stock market. Therefore, the economic interest of Suez in Electrabel was only 12.4 percent (= 0.635 × 0.489 × 0.399), but the cascade of controls meant that French accounting standards allowed Suez to fully consolidate Electrabel on its balance sheet, whereas this was not possible under US GAAP. Following its listing on the New York Stock Exchange in 2001, Suez had to publish two very different sets of accounts, one under US GAAP and the other under French standards. In 2002, for example, revenue according to French standards was €46 billion, whereas it was only €30 billion according to US GAAP, a difference of more than 50 percent.[11] This example and many other, similar ones illustrate how slightly different rules for the use of consolidation methods can have a material impact on companies' accounts.

CHAPTER 2

"CREATIVE ACCOUNTING" AND THE FAIRNESS CONUNDRUM

A few years later, Smoke & Mirrors, Inc., had again become the talk of the town. Joseph Smith had, in the meantime, had his term as Chairman and CEO extended for five years by a docile board of directors. But he was again in trouble. The fireworks manufacturer had issued two successive profit warnings and experienced a sudden and spectacular fall in its share price.

James Littleman, an individual shareholder who had just invested a vast amount of money in Smoke & Mirrors stock, was furious. One morning, he burst into Smith's newly (and lavishly) refurbished office.

"I'm a ruined man! And you are the one responsible for my ruin! Look at the newspapers' headlines last week: 'Doubts about the accounts of Smoke & Mirrors, Inc.' This article explains that you did some pretty dreadful things. It says that the competitive position of Smoke & Mirrors, in both industrial and commercial terms, has been going downhill for three years. This is not, however, what your accounts had stated. As it appears, during that time you've constantly engaged in some 'creative' accounting tricks that produced a far too optimistic picture of your company's operations. A very misleading picture. It seems, for example, that you sold your headquarters to yourself so that it disappeared from the accounts, which improved the debt ratio and profitability in a totally deceptive way. These accusations, Mr. Smith, are very serious. I expected to read a denial, but I've seen nothing. Now you must admit it: you committed fraud, and your accounts are false."

Smith remained calm. "Listen, our accounts tell no lies. Do you think our auditor would have agreed to sign off dubious numbers? He's a reasonable, professional family man. The accounts of Smoke & Mirrors are in order. Read our country's accounting standards—not the most fascinating reading, I'll admit—and you'll see that we have followed them to the letter, scrupulously. And I can assure you that the rules are very detailed."

"Your accounts may have been in order in the strict sense that you mean, following the rules. But they certainly have not given an accurate picture of the company, or fairly represented its operations."

"Oh, accuracy, a fair representation . . . compared to what? And in whose eyes? All of this is quite relative. I'll tell you a story. In March 2000, when we launched our website smokandmirrors.com, our shares were worth fifty times book value. The markets thought that our accounts did not provide a sufficiently upbeat picture of our business; in fact, they thought we were too modest. I remember: every week, people like you came to see me and accused me of setting up reserves, understating profits, using accounting methods that were too cautious or conservative, in fact the opposite of what you're reproaching me with today. So, accuracy, well . . .

"As for fairness, that's another empty word, if you ask me. The day someone can tell me what fair accounts are, I mean, the day that's defined in enforceable law, then I'll agree to talk about it. Fairness may be an interesting question for philosophers or moralists but not for business people like me. No, in the end, the only thing that really counts in accounting is compliance with the rules, I mean with the accounting standards. Believe me, I am an expert."

"Compliance with the rules . . . But what if there are flaws in the rules?"

"If there are flaws in the rules, that's not my fault. Go and ask the people who make the rules."

Visibly shaken, Littleman hesitated and wondered what he should think of Smith's line of defense. While he was pondering the matter, Smith took advantage of his distraction to escort him, courteously but firmly, to the door.

Although creativity is generally seen as a desirable trait, this is not true in the realm of financial reporting. The expression "creative accounting" generally means using flaws in accounting rules to "cook the books" and make the numbers say what you want them to say. The fact that Smoke & Mirrors was able to legally present positive earnings in spite of the deterioration of its performance is unquestionably an affront to common sense. And although this specific example is fiction, the practice itself is very real. By way of example, it is worth dwelling on what has appeared as "the mother of all accounting frauds": the Enron scandal, which led to that company's spectacular collapse in December 2001.

The importance of Enron's failure does not lie solely in the fact that it was the first major accounting scandal of this century. Enron was emblematic, not only because of the timing or the sheer scale of its default but also because it illustrated a systemic breakdown in the chain of control, from the auditors, through the board of directors, financial analysts, investment banks, and rating agencies, to government watchdogs. Using Enron's manipulations as a point of departure, the description of various possibilities for creative accounting will lead us to questions about the very meaning and limits of the notions of truthfulness, accuracy, and fairness of financial information.

Enron: "A Culture of Deceit"

The Enron scandal began on October 16, 2001, at a time when the United States was still in a state of shock following the September 11 attacks. On that day, the Houston energy-trading firm announced a third-quarter loss of $618 million, which included a one-billion-dollar extraordinary charge related to complex transactions with unknown companies located in offshore tax havens. The market was taken by surprise; some observers began to voice doubts, and after five days Enron's share price had fallen by 40 percent.

Until that point, Enron had been an impressive success story. It started in the mid-1980s as a local distributor of natural gas in the Houston area and had grown at a frantic pace to become a major player on the national energy stage. By late 2001, its scope included the production and transmission of gas and electricity, trading in gas and electricity markets—which had grown spectacularly in the late

1990s—as well as trading of raw materials, credit and weather risk insurance, the operation of a proprietary online trading platform, sales of broadband capacity, and even an unsuccessful attempt in the water distribution market.

Enron had become one of the most admired companies in the world. Between 1997 and the summer of 2000, its share price had quadrupled (thereafter and until October 2001, it had declined like most other stocks listed on the Nasdaq market). In 2000, *Fortune* had listed Enron seventh in its annual survey of large U.S. companies, giving its executives and employees first place for "quality of management" and second for "individual talents of employees." *Fortune* named the Houston firm "America's most innovative company" for the fifth year running. Enron was used as a prime example of an innovative corporation by major consulting firms, and as a case study of success in almost every business school. It seemed to be the very embodiment of all the best that capitalism could offer: growth, wealth, creativity, leadership, all in an energy market that was known to be of strategic importance but was traditionally not very open to innovation.

The fall was as spectacular as the rise. On October 22, 2001, the SEC announced the launch of an investigation of the company's accounts. On November 8, Enron disclosed that its profits for the years 1997 through 2000 had to be retroactively reduced by $569 million, or 16 percent of the published amounts, while its debt had to be increased by $628 million. On Wall Street, the stock had lost three-quarters of its value in three weeks. An attempted purchase by Dynergy, another energy trading company, was abandoned on November 28, when the three principal rating agencies lowered the credit rating of the company below investment grade, that is, to so-called junk status. A few days later, on December 2, Enron was forced to declare Chapter 11 bankruptcy. Ninety-eight percent of its share value, approximately $25 billion, had disappeared in six weeks.

Enron then began a long and painful process of restructuring. On January 17, 2002, Arthur Andersen, which had been accused of shredding documents after the opening of the SEC investigation, was dismissed as the company's auditor. A week later, Kenneth Lay, Enron's founder, resigned from his executive position; Andrew Fastow, the CFO appointed in 1998, had already been replaced on October 22, 2001; and Jeffrey Skilling, formerly chief executive, had left the company by August 2001. The board of directors was completely replaced. In 2002 and 2003, the company divested itself of sectors of activity that could be sold on acceptable terms. Energy trading activities were bought by UBS Warburg and were largely liquidated after a few months. A windmill manufacturing unit was acquired by General Electric. Finally, Enron transferred to a new company, CrossCountry Energy, all of its North American assets for the production and transmission of energy, which historically had been the core business of the company.

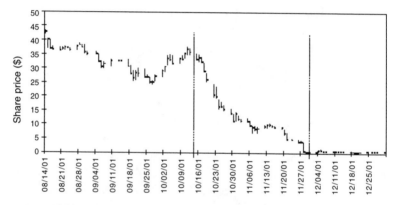

Change in Enron share price after the resignation of Jeffrey Skilling in August 2001. The first vertical line corresponds to the first earnings restatement on October 16, 2001. The second vertical line marks the date of the bankruptcy filing.

After a slow start, prosecutors eventually managed to overcome the difficulties in establishing individual charges against Enron executives, despite the extreme complexity of the case. In January 2004, Andrew Fastow, often considered the brain behind Enron's financial arrangements and subject to nearly one hundred court indictments, agreed to plead guilty. Kenneth Lay was indicted in July 2004, with special scrutiny placed on the period when he had directly taken over the role of Chief Executive following Skilling's departure in 2001. He and Skilling, who has also been indicted, are pleading not guilty. Their trial began in January 2006. Moreover, in January 2005, ten former Enron directors agreed to pay an unprecedented $13 million of their own money as part of a broader settlement.

Dissimulation as an Art Form

With more than four thousand subsidiaries, Enron had woven a tangled web of financial strands of astonishing complexity. To hide its debts and distort its balance sheet, Enron kept some subsidiaries outside the scope of its consolidated accounts by taking advantage of weaknesses in the US GAAP standards that allow for "deconsolidation," or sometimes by simply violating those standards. The Enron affair thus illustrates, among other things, defects in the design of some U.S. accounting rules, which offered unscrupulous executives various possibilities for abuse.

One main device used by Enron was to improperly exclude from consolidation certain subsidiaries in which debts and obligations that it wished to hide were recorded, thus improving the image of financial health presented in its consolidated balance sheet. For that purpose, the company created a number of special-purpose entities (SPE),[1] a practice that had spread rapidly in the 1990s and is used with complete legality by many companies around the world.

Special-purpose entities are used in particular for so-called sale-leaseback transactions, which is essentially what Smoke & Mirrors did with its head office building. In such a transaction, a company sells an asset to another entity specifically created for this purpose (hence the term "special purpose"), which immediately leases it back, often for a long period. The financing of the entity that purchases the asset is fine-tuned so that the criteria for consolidation do not apply; typically, one makes sure that some of the purchasing SPE's equity is held by third parties (at least 3 percent, according to US GAAP standards dating from 1990 and applicable until the collapse of Enron), and that the seller company is effectively relieved of the risks connected with the ownership of the asset. If the conditions allowing for deconsolidation are fulfilled, the seller can then remove the asset from its balance sheet, along with the corresponding debt. The advantage of the transaction is the reduction in assets, hence the improvement of certain financial ratios, but also an apparent reduction of indebtedness.

On several occasions, Enron went beyond the limits allowed under US GAAP for this kind of transaction. In these cases the SPEs did not fulfill the conditions required for their deconsolidation, either formally or substantively. Often, they were controlled by Enron's CFO

Andrew Fastow or by other employees in their own name, and Enron supplied almost all the financing. The rule that a minimum of 3 percent of the capital be held by outside parties, however apparently easy to satisfy, was not even always complied with. For example, one SPE called Chewco appears to have recorded funds provided by Barclays Bank in its accounts as shareholders' equity, whereas Barclays had recorded those same funds as loans in its own accounts, and rightly so as some of the funds were guaranteed by Enron (which is directly contradictory to the concept of shareholders' equity). As early as 1997, the failure to comply with rules concerning deconsolidation should probably have led the auditors at Arthur Andersen to refuse to sign off the accounting treatment of such entities on consolidation.

Another transaction illustrates the chain of events that precipitated Enron's fall. In 1998, Enron invested $10 million in an Internet access company, Rhythms Net Connections. In 1999, in the midst of the dotcom bubble, it wanted to record this holding in its accounts at its current stock value, which had grown to nearly $300 million; at the same time it wanted to protect itself against the risk of a fall in price (the simplest way to do this, selling the stock, was not a possibility as any straight sale on the market was barred by an agreement that Enron had signed with Rhythms). The purchase of a classic hedging device, such as an option to sell with a guaranteed floor price, would have been too expensive because of the limited liquidity and high level of volatility of the Rhythms stock. Enron therefore created in June 1999 an SPE called SwapSub and capitalized it by a fund partially controlled by Andrew Fastow, which sold Enron an option to sell the Rhythms stock for $104 million as well as a bill receivable for $64 million, in exchange for Enron shares valued at $168 million.

In appearance, the ownership of the option to sell protected Enron against the fall in Rhythms' share price, which indeed soon occurred. But the fragility of the arrangement was connected to the fact that the assets of SwapSub were almost entirely made up of Enron shares. The transaction thus amounted to a snake swallowing its tail: losses tied to the fall in Rhythms' share price were covered as long as Enron stock remained high; but if both Rhythms and Enron fell at the same time, then SwapSub would be unable to pay what it owed. The hedge was thus ineffective, and Enron in the end bore all the risk.

Enron set up similar arrangements with other investments, which it also guaranteed with its own shares. It thus created a house of cards whose collapse was inevitable once Enron shares were affected by the general decline in share prices that began in early 2001. Because the SPEs had hardly any assets other than those Enron shares, they eventually all became insolvent. Conversely, and ironically, if the bubble had not burst at that point, then Enron's fraud might never have been revealed.

It may be noted that Enron's complex transactions were also a substantial source of personal enrichment for several executives and their associates. In his plea bargain with the prosecution in January 2004, Andrew Fastow publicly admitted that he had, "along with other Enron executives, fraudulently manipulated the financial statements published by the company, set up arrangements in order to enrich [himself] and others at the expense of Enron shareholders, in violation of [his] fiduciary duty to those shareholders." His personal profit has been estimated to be at least $30 million.

Misrepresentation of Costs and Revenues

The improper deconsolidation of assets and liabilities is far from being the only fraud perpetrated by Enron in the years preceding its collapse. The costs of transfers of assets to special-purpose entities were often manipulated to present a distorted picture of the corresponding transactions. For example, if some assets were considered undesirable for the annual balance sheet, then Enron would sell them shortly before the end of its fiscal year to a nonconsolidated SPE, only to repurchase them a few months later at a different price. The sale price could be set arbitrarily, either because Enron exercised effective control over the entity and could thus force it to make an economically absurd decision, or because the transaction contained additional agreements, not accounted for on the balance sheet, that nevertheless changed its economic terms, or both.

For example, the accounts for 2000 and 2001 included a capital gain of $111 million on the sale of a business that distributed video programs on Enron's broadband telecommunications network. To do this, Enron had sold the business to an SPE for that high price, but the sales contract guaranteed future revenues to the purchaser and therefore effectively required the seller to assume all the economic risk. As a consequence, the apparent capital gain did not in fact reflect any real increase in wealth.

Enron also manipulated the way it accounted for long-term contracts on energy supplies. In accordance with US GAAP, these contracts must be booked as assets at "fair value" (see chapter 3). This value is normally determined by the observation of market prices, but for long-term contracts for which there is no reference market with sufficient liquidity, the value recorded on the balance sheet results from a calculation based on projected future energy prices. For this calculation, Enron chose overly optimistic assumptions, which enabled it to record asset values based on anticipated cash flows that later turned out to be completely imaginary.

As an example, in February 2001, Enron announced that it had signed a contract with the pharmaceutical company Eli Lilly for $1.3 billion over fifteen years, and immediately booked it on its balance sheet for the amount of future profits that it was supposed to produce. But Eli Lilly was located in Indiana, a state that had not deregulated its electricity market, and the company consequently did not have the right to purchase its electricity from Enron before the market was deregulated, which was expected but not guaranteed. In its valuation of the contract, Enron thus not only anticipated optimistic developments in energy prices over the following fifteen years but also included the assumption of deregulation of the Indiana electricity market. In practice, Enron used almost complete discretion to record the item at whichever value was most adapted to the tale it wanted to tell the markets at a given moment.

To lift itself to the rank of the seventh largest company in the United States, Enron used a manipulation of yet another kind. For this, it had to lie not only about its profits and balance sheet but also about its revenue. It did so by using the leeway available in the accounting rules for trading operations, which artificially inflated revenue on a massive scale.

The trading business involves connecting sellers and buyers for transactions on large quantities of goods. In some transactions, the trader bears the risk of reimbursement (i.e., the risk that the seller will not deliver or that the buyer will not pay) for only a very short time and does not own the goods involved in the exchange. For this reason, many trading activities are subject to accounting rules that prohibit the trader from booking as its own revenue the volume of goods exchanged. Only the margin realized, that is, the difference between the selling price (paid by the buyer to the trader) and the purchase price (paid by the trader to the seller), corresponds to a real economic risk and can be booked as revenue by the trader.

In order to specify the conditions identifying activities that should receive this particular treatment in the United States, the SEC and FASB had set out detailed criteria in two interpretive documents.[2] The first one specified that companies acting as intermediaries in a sale that do not bear the risks associated with ownership of the goods exchanged can book only the margin realized as their revenue. In the second one, the application of this treatment was imposed on all companies that do not have inventories of the goods they sell and merely transmit purchase orders to a supplier, as well as on those that receive a fixed commission on sales they conduct and do not assume a risk of price variation between purchase and sale.

Enron escaped these rules for its electricity trading business, which made up 90 percent of its turnover for the year ending December 31, 2000. This business was fairly new (it practically did not exist anywhere in the world before the 1990s), and those responsible for accounting standards, in the United States and elsewhere, were still uncertain about the rules that should be applied. In 1998, after considering the question for the first time, the FASB had decided to allow companies to choose the method of accounting for transactions resulting from contracts dealing with energy. Enron and other electricity trading companies took thorough advantage of the absence of clear and rigorous standards. It was not until October 2002, a year after the Enron scandal was triggered, that revisions of US GAAP abolished this room for interpretation.

The difference between the two accounting treatments (recognition as revenue either of the total amounts traded or only of the trading margin) has a spectacular impact, which can be observed also outside of the United States. For example, in the case of the energy trading business developed by France's state electricity company EDF since the late 1990s, French accounting standards authorized the posting of all volumes traded as revenue. When, in the second half of 2003, EDF decided to adopt IFRS (which do not allow such treatment) in most of its business, the revenue corresponding to the trading business was reduced to practically nothing. Specifically, revenue from trading fell from 15 percent of EDF's total revenue, in the originally published 2002 accounts, to 0.5 percent in the accounts for the same period but under the new IFRS rules, or a 97 percent reduction in amount.[3]

The conclusion is that Enron's manipulations involved virtually all aspects of the accounts, including the one that could seem at first sight the most objective of all, the revenue generated with the company's clients. Almost no component of assets or liabilities escaped from the ingenuity of the financial engineers and company accountants in Houston.

A System Failure

The enormous impact of the December 2001 collapse was not solely the result of the magnitude of the fraud that was uncovered and the extraordinary degree of cynicism displayed by some of Enron's executives. Even more, it was connected to the deficiencies that the scandal revealed among other parties involved, who were variously taken in, exploited, bribed, silenced, or recruited as accomplices by Enron. Almost all participants in the financial system had their reputations tarnished to varying degrees by the event, and some of them never recovered. In this way, Enron was not an isolated case, but the symptom of a widespread failure of a system of control whose effectiveness up to that point had seemed satisfactory to virtually everyone.

Auditors. Enron's audit firm, Arthur Andersen, was the first to come under fire. Its Houston office was responsible for the external audit of the company's accounts, but it also performed consulting services, notably the evaluation of risky financial schemes, for comparable or even higher fees than the audit work ($25 million for auditing and $27 million for consulting in 2000). After the first announcements of accounting restatements by Enron, Andersen reacted clumsily, to say the least, by destroying some documents after the SEC had announced the opening of an investigation. The ensuing trial was enough to cause the ruin of the entire worldwide Andersen network in the course of a few weeks.[4] The intervention of some of the most respected names in the international financial community, including Paul Volcker who had been Alan Greenspan's predecessor at the Federal Reserve Board, was not enough to save Arthur Andersen, a firm with 85,000 employees and branches in eighty-four countries around the globe, from complete collapse. In the United States, the network literally fell apart, and its local offices were absorbed one by one by rival firms. In other countries, each national firm of the Andersen network joined one of its competitors. Andersen's teams were absorbed by Ernst & Young in France and Germany, by Deloitte in the United Kingdom, and by PricewaterhouseCoopers in China and Hong Kong, thus further reducing the number of large global audit firms from five to only four (see chapter 5).

Directors. Enron's board of directors displayed a complete inability to prevent the crisis. And yet, this board had been set up as a model of corporate governance, with a separation established in 2000 between the roles of chairman and of chief executive officer, and with a large number of independent directors. The audit committee was headed by Robert Jaedicke, a respected professor of accounting and former dean of the Stanford Graduate School of Business. The example set by Enron vividly illustrates the fact that even the best-intentioned rules of corporate governance are not enough to grasp the complexity of the power relationships that make up the day-to-day reality of business. Eventually, directors were involved as well, as ten of them settled with shareholders in January 2005 for a total amount of $13 million.

Investment banks and consultants. Most major participants in the financial world were involved in Enron's manipulations. The list of companies prosecuted for Enron-related matters resembles a Wall Street directory: Citigroup, Credit Suisse First Boston, Deutsche Bank, Goldman Sachs, JP Morgan Chase, Lehman Brothers, Merrill Lynch, Bank of America, Barclays Bank, Canadian Imperial Bank of Commerce, and UBS. Of these, JP Morgan, Citigroup, Merrill Lynch, and Canadian Imperial Bank of Commerce paid the SEC more than $400 million in settlements reached during July and December 2003 (see appendix 2). McKinsey, one of the most prestigious global consulting firms, had been advising Enron for years and had on countless occasions boasted of the success of its client as representing the best possible use of its principles of strategy and value creation. McKinsey's reputation was correspondingly damaged by the scandal, even though there seems to be no indication that its partners or consultants had been directly involved in fraud or had known of it.

Analysts and rating agencies. Financial analysts in major banks (sometimes the same banks that made loans to Enron or advised it on its adventurous financial engineering) had almost unanimously recommended buying shares in the company, up to shortly before the collapse. For example, at Goldman Sachs—but this is far from the only such example—equity analyst David Fleischer publicly described Enron in February 2001 as "the most incredible growth machine there is." The same analyst published a study in which Enron was called "still the best of the best" after the first revelations about the fragility of the company, in October 2001. The same thing was true for the rating agencies, which, as we have seen, saw no clouds on the horizon until November 28. Only then, a few days before the default, did the three principal rating agencies—Standard & Poor's, Moody's, and Fitch—lower Enron to "junk bond" status.

Accounting standard-setters. US GAAP accounting standards turned out to be full of loopholes, permitting such practices as the undue deconsolidation of special-purpose entities and recognition of trading volume as revenue. After Enron's dealings came to light, US GAAP could no longer be automatically considered the best standards available, as had been the case before. As we shall see later, this had the effect of giving a temporary credibility boost to IFRS, including in the United States.

The U.S. Government. U.S. public agencies did not emerge untainted either. The principal U.S. securities regulator, the SEC, whose task is to protect the interests of investors in the capital markets, was unable to prevent the scandal by an appropriate examination of the accounts, and it reacted only after the fact. Congress, for its part, had confirmed in 2000, following heavy lobbying efforts from Enron and other energy companies, an exemption of electricity trading from regulations governing other raw materials and derivatives markets, which had been granted by a federal agency in 1993. Had this exemption been ended in 2000, as many other observers demanded, some of Enron's improper practices might have been detected and curbed earlier. Finally, the highest levels of federal government were accused of improper connections and complacency. President George W. Bush, when he was governor of Texas, had enjoyed excellent relations with Houston-based Enron and with Kenneth Lay, to whom he had given the nickname "Kenny Boy." On assuming office in January 2001, the Bush administration solicited the opinions of many Enron executives, particularly in the area of energy policy, and even recruited a few of them. Thomas White, who had spent eleven years at Enron and was head of one of its business units, Enron Energy Services, was appointed Secretary of the Army in May 2001, a position from which he did not resign until April 2003 for reasons with no apparent connection to Enron.[5]

All of these circumstances brought about an acute realization of the weaknesses of the controls inherent in U.S. and global financial systems. Shortly after Enron, a string of other scandals followed, at Adelphia, Tyco, Global Crossing, and many others, including, perhaps most spectacularly, the collapse of WorldCom in July 2002 which, bigger even than Enron, set the record as the biggest U.S. bankruptcy ever. *BusinessWeek* magazine, hardly a revolutionary firebrand in ordinary times, wrote in its year-end summary for 2002 that "the problems revealed by the scandals were systemic, not the result of a few bad apples. While only a few CEOs may go to jail for breaking the law, the breakdown was endemic to both the corporate and financial systems. Most CEOs, not just a few, were overcompensated for their success and protected from failure. Many, not just a few, accountants, analysts, attorneys, regulators, and legislators failed, to one degree or another, in ensuring the accuracy of financial statements and the free flow of honest data in the markets."[6] All of a sudden, it seemed that the "cockroach theory" was applicable to accounting scandals: when you see one in the kitchen, there are hundreds more behind the walls.

Among this multiplicity of corporate failures, Enron, the Houston giant with feet of clay, nonetheless retains an iconic status because of the pervasive "culture of deceit"[7] that prevailed among a large proportion of its headquarters employees. Even after revelations about many other fraudulent activities in the United States and Europe, Enron will probably long remain the symbol of "creative accounting" carried out with the greatest degree of deception and mendacity.

The Seven Pillars of Creative Accounting

Now, what exactly is creative accounting? In accounting, as elsewhere, the boundary between what is right and wrong is sometimes blurred. There has always been some scope for judgment in the preparation of accounts, and this room for maneuver is probably not only inevitable but necessary. No set of rules, however detailed and prescriptive, can cover all possible cases, particularly in view of the rapidity of innovations in financial matters. Judging the intentions of those who prepare accounts, particularly in the most complex situations, is no self-evident matter.

Regardless of intentions, several techniques for "managing earnings" or "cooking the books" are well known and can be listed with precision. Many years before Enron, Howard Schilit, by then a professor of accounting at American University in Washington, D.C., had published a book on the various ways of fiddling the accounts, which included a list of seven categories of "financial shenanigans."[8] This classification is useful as a way of organizing the various categories of manipulations that a creative accountant may use to his or her profit.

Professor Schilit defines these "shenanigans" as "acts that intentionally distort the figures for the financial performance and the financial position of a company. They range from the most benign (changes in accounting estimates) to the most reprehensible (fraudulent recognition of fictitious revenue)."[9] The seven specific categories that he identifies are the following.

Shenanigan number 1. Recognizing revenue too soon or of questionable quality. For example, recording revenue when future services remain to be provided, or before a customer's unconditional acceptance.

Shenanigan number 2. Recognizing bogus revenue. For example, recording cash received in lending transactions, or investment income, or supplier rebates tied to future required purchases, as revenue.

Shenanigan number 3. Boosting income with one-time gains. For example, selling undervalued assets, including investment income or gains as part of revenue, or reporting investment income or gains as a reduction in operating expenses.

Shenanigan number 4. Shifting current expenses to later or earlier period. For example, capitalizing normal operating costs as assets, or changing accounting policies and shifting current expenses to an earlier period, or amortizing costs too slowly.

Shenanigan number 5. Failing to record or improperly reducing liabilities. For example, failing to record expenses and related liabilities when future obligations remain, or reducing liabilities by changing accounting assumptions.

Shenanigan number 6. Shifting current revenue to a later period. For example, creating reserves and releasing them into income in a later year, or improperly holding back revenue just before an acquisition closes.

Shenanigan number 7. Shifting future expenses to the current period as a special charge. For example, improperly writing off some investments that are difficult to evaluate (such as research and development costs, which are entered on the balance sheet under most accounting standards), or accelerating discretionary expenses into the current period.

Enron's three principal tricks as described earlier fit rather well into this analytic scheme: concealing debts by transferring them to deconsolidated SPEs is a variation of shenanigan number 5; evaluating transferred assets at fictitious prices is an example of shenanigan number 3; and improperly recording trading volume as revenue fits into shenanigan number 2.

Another example of massive and notorious fraud is that committed by WorldCom (see also appendix 2). WorldCom had grown through aggressive acquisitions of telephone companies, including that of long-distance operator MCI in 1997. It eventually attempted to disguise disappointing operating performance by crudely concealing some of its costs and unduly boosting its apparent profit. Specifically, rents paid for the use of telecommunication transmission capacity were booked as investments in fixed assets and depreciated over several years, thereby reducing current expenses at the start of the corresponding period. This, of course, is a prime example of shenanigan number 4—but in this case, for a whopping amount of several billion dollars, in a maneuver that in retrospect looks more like a very bad joke than an Enron-like piece of sophisticated financial engineering.

For the record, it is tempting to add an extra item to Prof. Schilit's list, in the historical context of several European countries' accounting standards before the adoption of IFRS. This "shenanigan number 8" would consist of optimizing the scope of consolidation. French standards, in particular, used to permit a much wider-encompassing concept of "control" than permitted by US GAAP or IFRS for the consolidation of subsidiaries, which may have given rise to contentious interpretations. For example, the media-to-telecoms conglomerate Vivendi Universal consolidated in its 2001 accounts its mobile telephone subsidiary SFR, whereas it owned only 35 percent of the stock (44 percent of Groupe Cegetel, which itself owned 80 percent of SFR). As a consequence, Vivendi Universal communicated to the markets consolidated EBITDA[10] figures that included the whole of SFR's

EBITDA, whereas in fact the holding company had no direct access to SFR's cash flows, as became apparent in mid-2002 when the company came close to a liquidity crisis. Recording these cash flows proportionally to Vivendi's economic interest would have resulted in an EBITDA of €3.5 billion in 2001, as opposed to the €5 billion publicized by the company, a difference of 43 percent. Fortunately, consolidation practices are more strictly controlled now that consolidated accounts of listed European companies are published according to International Financial Reporting Standards, but some scope for this kind of misrepresentation can remain.

Some shenanigans lead to an artificial overstatement of current profits, whereas others understate them to improve profits in future years. The most obvious example of the latter is the "clean sweep" or "blank slate" approach that every newly appointed CEO long felt entitled to adopt. This consisted of accusing the previous management team of having performed worse than disclosed until then, that is, a series of inevitable costs had not been anticipated and it was therefore necessary to accrue a massive amount of future expenses in the year the new management took over. If those accruals later proved excessive, then profits in the following years, on the basis of which the new management would be judged, would be correspondingly improved.

The same thing is true for restructuring liabilities, booked at the time of the announcement of planned layoffs or closures of facilities. In the recent past, before accounting rules were tightened first in the United States and then in Europe, restructuring could be recorded for an oversized amount without shocking analysts (who have become used to the idea that restructuring is expensive but always better than lack of action). The results of later years could then be artificially improved, as costs proved less steep than initially booked. In such cases, and cynically enough, the restructuring seems justified after the fact to the inattentive observer, as improved performance has followed a large restructuring announcement.

In summary, clever and unscrupulous use of the seven shenanigans and their variants may make it possible to "manage" the accounts for a given year by making them say almost anything one pleases. Only in the longer run can recurring distortions prove unsustainable.

A quintessential example of "earnings management" was provided by the accounts of Xerox between 1997 and 2000. Xerox desperately wanted to satisfy the financial analysts. To this end, its financial statements were distorted to produce earnings per share identical to the "consensus," that is, the average of forecasts made by analysts before publication of the quarterly or yearly results. In a somewhat perverse reversal, pursuit of a good reputation had led Xerox into fraud. The SEC analyzed the case in detail and filed a complaint on April 11, 2002, which is based on the following statements:

- For 1997, earnings per share according to a proper application of US GAAP would have been $1.65, while Xerox had artificially inflated this figure by 18 percent to $2.02 in the published accounts.

- In 1998, earnings per share under US GAAP should have been $1.72, but they were inflated by 26 percent to $2.33.

- In 1999, earnings per share should have been $1.48, but they were inflated by 24 percent to $1.96.[11]

The interesting fact is that the consensus of analysts, as measured by the financial data firm Thomson FirstCall for those years, was, respectively, $1.99, $2.33, and $1.95. In other words, the overstatement had the sole purpose of aligning, with almost-perfect accuracy, published figures with market expectations. To do this, Xerox had used a whole range of fraudulent techniques which, according to the SEC complaint, included the anticipated recognition of revenue not yet realized (shenanigan number 1), misrepresentation of financial profits as revenue (number 2), misrepresentation of borrowings as sales of assets (number 5), and the arbitrary cancellation of liabilities that had been improperly accrued (number 6). The most extraordinary aspect was that Xerox kept correct accounts internally, which enabled the SEC to indicate in its complaint what profits would have been if accounting standards had been properly applied. In April 2005, KPMG, which had been Xerox's auditor throughout the period in question, reached a $22.5 million settlement with the SEC, including $10 million in fines.

True and Fair Accounts: Any Such Thing?

After this catalogue of fraud and improper behavior, there are grounds for feeling discouraged. Can accounting really be anything other than fraud and deception? Numbers can lie, as the preceding examples amply demonstrate; but is it inappropriate to expect them at least sometimes to tell the truth?

The legal base of financial statements can give no definitive response to these questions, as its key criterion, as we shall see, is the compliance of such statements with accounting standards, which govern the calculation of revenues, profits, and all other accounting information, and necessarily give considerable importance to human judgment. Therefore, and as harsh as this statement may sound, objectivity is intrinsically impossible to attain in preparing the financial statements of any large and complex business.

Accounting Legislation and the Interplay between Fairness and Compliance

In the United States, there was no federal legislation on financial reporting until the Securities Act of 1933.[12] The 1933 act introduced the requirement that investors have access to financial and other significant information concerning securities being offered for public sale, along with the prohibition of deceit, misrepresentations, and other fraud in the sale of securities.[13] Shortly afterward, the Securities Exchange Act of 1934 first gave legal status to the expression "generally accepted accounting principles":

> Every issuer (. . .) shall make and keep books, records, and accounts, which, in reasonable detail, accurately and fairly reflect the transactions and dispositions of the assets of the issuer, [and] devise and maintain a system of internal accounting controls sufficient to provide reasonable assurances that (. . .) transactions are recorded as necessary to permit preparation of financial statements in conformity with generally accepted accounting principles or any other criteria applicable to such statements.[14]

The same act placed the enforcement of this provision in the hands of the SEC, thus entrusting it with preparation and updating of US GAAP as has been described in the previous chapter.

Thus, the U.S. legislation states both that the accounts must be "fair," and that they must conform to US GAAP. The crucial question of whether fairness can be assessed independently from compliance with US GAAP, however, has not received a clear answer. The standard wording of audit reports in the United States, as codified by the American Institute of Certified Public Accountants since 1939 in the so-called Statement of Auditing Standard (SAS) No. 69, maintains the ambiguity on this matter by stating that "the audited financial statements present *fairly*, in all material respects, an entity's financial position, results of operations, and cash flows, *in conformity with generally accepted accounting principles*" (our emphasis). To avoid unwarranted judgments about what is fair and what is not, the same SAS 69 text specifies that fairness is not an independent concept and "should be applied within the framework of generally accepted accounting principles"; it also mentions that "application of [GAAP] almost always results in the fair presentation of financial position." The only exception to the prevalence of compliance with rules over any other consideration is, again in SAS 69, that "an auditor should not express an unqualified opinion if the financial statements contain a material departure from [GAAP], unless, due to unusual circumstances, adherence to the pronouncements would make the statements misleading."[15] In other words, except for "unusual circumstances," which almost never happen (and indeed, accounting practice has not defined any significant scope for such circumstances that would allow divergence from applying the usual standards), fairness is reduced to the strict implementation of US GAAP.

Thus, in the United States the only requirement on financial statements that can be realistically monitored and enforced is their compliance with US GAAP rules. In spite of the differences in legal systems, this is also, essentially, the case in most other developed countries. The United Kingdom is a special case, where tradition and legislation give a key importance to the concept of "true and fair view" that the financial statements must give of the financial position of a company (as can be noted from previous quotes, the adjective "true" is entirely absent from the corresponding U.S. texts).[16] The "true and fair" concept was enacted in European Union framework legislation in 1978 ("The annual accounts shall give a 'true and fair view' of the company's assets, liabilities, financial position and profit or loss."),[17] even though, as usual in Europe, there is an additional complexity of interpretation due to the translation into different languages. For example,

French or Spanish translations of the 1978 directive, and corresponding national legislation, do not retain the reference to "true" view and
only refer to a "faithful image" (*image fidèle, imagen fiel*).

There is a debate whether the European notion of "true and fair
view" leads to differences with the United States in the quality of accounts and the responsibility of corporate managers vis-à-vis their
shareholders as regards financial information.[18] In most instances the
practical use of the "true and fair view override" (i.e., departure from
the strict application of existing accounting standards in particular
cases where these standards are deemed not to lead to a true and fair
view) seems to be rather limited, and the few examples of jurispru-
dence that exist on this issue seem to indicate that when asked, the
law courts tend to adopt the accounting standards as the essential reference for assessing "truth and fairness."[19] The conclusion is that
while fairness has been a requirement on financial statements
throughout the developed world for many decades, there still is no
clear way to define what it means apart from the application of the
legally enforceable accounting standards that exist in each country.

Truth in Cash Flows?

As profit manipulation seems to be possible under all systems of
accounting standards, one temptation is to simply get rid of the complex computations of accrual accounting and to rely on cash flows instead. A consolidated income statement is based on a complex set of
assumptions about the future and of easily distorted calculations. By
comparison, cash flows may appear much more objective. "Profit is
an opinion; cash is a fact," the saying goes. If the analysts who praised
Enron in 2001 had had a closer look at its cash flows, they would perhaps not have uncovered all the fraudulent engineering, but they
would at least have recognized that it was not the huge and successful
company it pretended to be.

But unfortunately, things are not that simple. The difficulty is in
knowing which cash and which flows are being talked about. Pure
cash accounting, in fact, does not provide very useful information,
and rapidly reaches its limits. The reason for this is that most corporate transactions give rise to obligations that are deferred in time.
When you sell a product to a client, he generally does not pay you at

once. When you incur debt, you oblige yourself to repay amounts of capital and interest for several years to come. When you receive payment for a sale, you do not immediately pay value-added tax to the tax authorities, and so on. Accrual accounting serves to bring consistency into the recording of such deferred transactions. One definition of accrual accounting is that "the effects of transactions and other events are recognised when they occur (and not as cash or its equivalent is received or paid) and they are recorded in the accounting records and reported in the financial statements of the periods to which they relate. Financial statements prepared on the accrual basis inform users not only of past transactions involving the payment and receipt of cash but also of obligations to pay cash in the future and of resources that represent cash to be received in the future. Hence, they provide the type of information about past transactions and other events that is most useful to users in making economic decisions."[20]

Abandoning the use of accrual accounting would mean that no distinction could be made between a loan and a capital increase, or between an expense and capital expenditure; the view of the company would be obscured rather than clarified. In practice, only public authorities, including most national governments, still use primarily cash accounting—and even they generally distinguish between operating expenses and investments. Moreover, the inadequacy of such cash-based public accounting is frequently, and rightly, criticized. For example, the European Union's member states have agreed on a "stability and growth pact" under which they may incur penalties when their budget deficit is superior to 3 percent; but this threshold applies to the difference between tax receipts and a heterogeneous sum of investment and operating expenses, with little economic value. No wonder, then, that the rule has been criticized not only by profligate EU member state governments but also by a growing number of serious economists.

In order to more directly illustrate the ability of companies to generate cash, financiers and analysts have increasingly developed the use of so-called pro forma (i.e., nonstandardized, or "non-GAAP") measures of corporate performance. But these ratios, which are not defined by legally enforceable standards, have little to do with crude cash flows, and much more to do with accruals-based operating income and profit figures. Probably the best known of these pro forma measures of performance is EBITDA (earnings before interest, tax, depreciation, and amortization), which has been alluded to earlier with reference to Vivendi Universal's past consolidation of its holding in the mobile phone operator SFR. EBITDA can supplement the picture of the company given by (standardized) financial statements, but it would be thoroughly deceptive to consider it as a measure of cash flows "not subject to manipulation." As it is calculated on the basis of accrual accounting, it is almost as susceptible as net profit to the various types of accounting shenanigans used by Enron or others. The same can be said of "free cash flow," another figure that is generally calculated by subtracting tax payments and recurring capital expenditure from EBITDA. Free cash flow can shed useful light on the strategic margin of maneuver available to a company for new purchases or investments, and it also corrects certain distorting effects of EBITDA, which presents too favorable a picture of highly capital-intensive industries that must maintain a constant flow of large investments. But just as EBITDA, "free cash flow" in no way corresponds to the difference between instant cash in-and-out flows, and is also subject to the possibility of manipulation inherent to any calculation made according to the accrual accounting principle.

In practice, EBITDA and other ratios that eliminate the effects of the depreciation and amortization of assets have sometimes been used by some executives to hide their management failures rather than as a means of increasing transparency. This is because the charges taken for depreciation and amortization, which cannot be seen in the EBITDA or free cash flow, convey information that can be very important to shareholders. For example, some huge asset write-downs recorded in 2001–2002, following acquisitions during the technology bubble, were improperly played down by corporate managers on the pretext that they were "non-cash" items, while in fact they gave the right information about acquisitions that had been overpaid. Here again, Vivendi Universal is a good illustration: Jean-Marie Messier, then the company's chairman and CEO, tried to reassure Vivendi's shareholders as he disclosed in March 2002 an eye-popping (and for France, record-setting) yearly loss of €13.6 billion for the 2001 financial year, mainly due to a write-down of €15.7 billion on past acquisitions. "It's just an accounting technicality," he explained with a smile to the financial analysts, "it's not about cash, it's not value destruction." He contrasted these "purely accounting" figures to the "reality" of the company's business which, according to his expression that at the time became famous in the French business community, "is doing better than well."[21] In fact, as far as "reality" goes, the restriction of value destruction to instant cash expenses is not defensible. Cash expenditure to pay for the acquisitions, or the dilution in value of existing shares in the case of acquisitions by exchange of shares, had already taken place in earlier years and had not been recognized in the income statement because of the high value attributed to the companies acquired. The decrease in this estimated value, following changed market conditions, unambiguously had an impact on the financial well-being of Vivendi Universal as a whole. In short, "calculated expenses" such as depreciation, amortization, impairments or accruals are as necessary for financial analysis as a detailed account of cash flows. The sometimes-heard idea that one could do without accrued or calculated accounting entries could be described, at best, as a kind of utopia, created in the minds of some observers by ignorance of the complexity of real-world corporate finance. At worst, it can reflect in certain cases a desire to deceive.

EBITDA and similar tools used by companies in their financial communication have a further weakness: they are not subject to standardization and are thus open to manipulation on the part of companies seeking to adopt the most favorable definition at any given moment. On both sides of the Atlantic, securities regulators have warned against the promotion of pro forma figures in the financial disclosures of listed companies, insisting that "information given to the public should be accurate, precise, and comparable over time."[22]

In the end, both forms of analysis, of cash flows and of accounting profit and loss, are necessary and complementary. The cash flow statement, as defined by accounting standards, provides indispensable additions to the information on performance supplied by the income statement. In systems of accounting standards such as US GAAP or IFRS, the cash flow statement has the same importance as the balance sheet and the income statement as a component of financial statements. Cash flows and accruals-based accounts are two equally indispensable tools to analyze corporate activity.

What in all cases is naïve and misleading is the idea that one single figure, be it earnings, cash flow, or whatever else, could be sufficient to give a consistent measure of company performance. Many of the flaws attributed to accrual accounting stem in fact from excessive reliance of many market participants on the observation of net income (or earnings per share). In reality, the business of a corporation cannot be summed up in a single number, however cleverly calculated it may be. The net income certainly has relevance as an analytic tool when a company's business is well defined and recurring. But it becomes much less useful when the scope of consolidation changes frequently, when the business model evolves at a rapid pace, or when the company uses complex financial engineering techniques. The fact is that the diversity and complexity of the business of today's large companies is no longer—if it ever was—satisfactorily expressed by net income or earnings per share. Instead, it is increasingly necessary to consider a whole set of accounting and non-accounting data to form an opinion about any business.

"On a Balance Sheet, Everything Except the Date Involves a Judgment"

The above quotation is not from a heinous accuser of the accounting profession, but from Roman Weil, professor of accounting at the University of Chicago's Graduate School of Business and an internationally recognized expert in the field.[23] Accounting is not an exact science; it is rather a discipline that constantly requires its practitioners to make choices and frequent, non-obvious assessments. The way accounting standards frame these choices is certainly a driver of the quality of accounts, but that quality can never be taken for granted. In other words, in the absence of perfect knowledge of past, present, and future, accounts can only rely on assumptions and approximations.

Past, present, *and future*: in fact, one surprisingly common misrepresentation of accounting is that it deals only with the past. There is probably no better illustration of this than that most basic tool of accrual accounting, depreciation. The choice of the period over which fixed assets are depreciated involves a judgment as to whether you are going to use them for, say, five, ten, or twenty years. Consideration of the past may help to make this kind of decision but cannot be the only criterion. For example, depreciation policies for assets that have a long life or are subject to technological advance may be subject to changes over time. In the first half of 2003, EDF, the French electricity company, extended by a third, from thirty to forty years, the depreciation term for its nuclear power plants, in view of the progress that had been made in the operation and maintenance of these plants since they had been built. This accounting change instantly added almost two billion euros to EDF's net income; even though it was opportunely timed (making it possible to compensate the write-down of goodwill related to foreign acquisitions and thus to record a profit at a politically sensitive moment), the move was generally accepted in the financial community because the new depreciation period seemed reasonable considering the changed context of nuclear power, where reactors can now be planned to operate for fifty or even sixty years.

The conclusion of all this is that assumptions, expectations, beliefs, intent, and judgment all play an essential role in accounting, and therefore that fairness is not something that can be objectively assessed when it comes to preparing financial statements. This, again, strengthens the importance of accounting standards. If the practice of accounting does not make it possible to mechanically attain accuracy or even to guarantee fairness, what remains is the requirement for compliance with the standards, which in any case must remain a primary criterion for evaluating the quality of accounts. In other words, in light of the imperfections of human judgment in general, and of the judgment of accountants in particular, well-conceived accounting standards are indispensable to buttress, insofar as possible, the relevance of accounts. This gives decisive importance to debates about standard-setting, which we consider in more detail in the following chapter.

CHAPTER 3

STANDARD-SETTING AND ITS CHALLENGES

James Littleman, the disappointed shareholder in Smoke & Mirrors, Inc., was nothing if not persistent. A few weeks after his conversation with Joseph Smith, he succeeded in arranging a meeting with one of the leading members of the National Accounting Standards Board, the publicly sponsored accounting standard-setter of the country of not so far, far away. Littleman was still eager to find someone responsible for his ruin.

"I'm in disarray," he exclaimed, holding out Smoke & Mirrors' latest annual report. "These accounts were a damned set of lies. The figures said nothing about the true situation of the company. That was bad enough; but now they tell me that these lies were made in perfect compliance with your rules. So you and your colleagues must be the ones responsible for my losses. I invested in a company whose accounts were deceptive because of you."

"What are you saying, sir?" the other replied. "Please make an effort to understand the simple facts of life. I'm not surprised that you hold a self-centered, naïve viewpoint typical of an individual shareholder. But shareholders are not alone in this world. You need to make some compromises when, as we do, you are working for the public interest."

"The public interest against shareholders? What do you mean?"

"Let me give you an example. You mention Smoke & Mirrors, Inc: I know that company all too well. The fireworks industry was in serious trouble ten years ago; at that time, I remember, many companies considered laying off most of their staff and shifting all their operations overseas. The guys in the industry, led by your new friend Joe Smith, went to Parliament and everywhere to complain of unfair competition from foreign rivals who published their accounts according to Oceanian Accounting Standards. The truth was that these Oceanian standards made it possible to take a charge for 'risk of future powder dampness,' a rather peculiar rule indeed, that in fact lets companies manage their results at their convenience. Well, we had to act. The survival of the whole fireworks industry was at stake, and at the time there were many members of Parliament who said the fireworks industry was of utter strategic national importance. Of course, we were not that enthusiastic about adopting the same rule about future powder-dampness liabilities, which I agree makes little sense in principle; but the government insisted, and you know, they are the ones who sign our paychecks in the end. So the rule is now an integral part of our accounting standards. Thus was the fireworks industry rescued."

"I cannot believe it. I had thought accounting standards were supposed to realistically reflect the economic position of a company. Now you tell me they can be used to save jobs, to help the competitive position of domestic companies. . . . I feel lost, really. What remains of the requirement for fairness? I thought that was an article of faith for you."

"Do you think saving hundreds, thousands of jobs is less noble than your view of fairness? Welcome to my world, Littleman. Accounting standards are part of national economic policy, period. By the way, I'm more than a little worried that the guys in Europe and Canada have given up their jurisdiction to establish standards to a private body, the IASB, with no guarantee that it will operate in the true public interest."

Double-entry accounting mixes some straightforward notions with others that are not intuitive at all. On the one hand, revenues and costs are seemingly easy-to-grasp concepts, and once they have been properly defined, it seems common sense to calculate the net income as the difference between them. On the other hand, some accounting notions such as goodwill or even shareholders' equity are less transparent to the untrained.

In fact, accounting is two things at once, a defined logical system and a set of conventions. It is firstly a defined logical system: US GAAP, for example, includes seven "Statements on Financial Accounting Concepts" published between 1978 and 2000,[1] which provide rigorous definitions of each and every important concept used in subsequent standards, and with which all standards are supposed to comply. Similarly, the IASB issued in the late 1980s a "Framework for the Preparation and Presentation of Financial Statements" (commonly referred to as the "IASB Framework"), which serves a similar purpose. But accounting is also a set of conventions, with the inevitable whiff of the arbitrary. For example, there is no inescapable reason why some changes in the value of financial assets are recorded in the income statement, while some others (for example, changes in the value of assets classified as "available for sale" under IFRS) have no impact on the income statement but are only booked through the balance sheet. Distinctions such as this one abound, and there is often no obvious reason why the standard-setters have chosen one option rather than another. Accountants therefore have to rely on conventions to ensure that financial statements of different companies can be compared with one another, and many of these conventions are somewhat arbitrary. Tellingly, the "IASB Framework" has not been revised since its original drafting, and many of the more recent IFRS rules depart from its definitions; but the IASB seems largely unbothered.

We have already seen in chapter 1 that the public standardization of accounting rules was a direct consequence of financial crises. Specifically, the 1929 crash was the source of the first comprehensive legislation that eventually gave birth to US GAAP and other sets of accounting standards. Even in times when there are no major crises, the work of establishing accounting standards is a constant struggle against the ingenuity of abusers and misleaders. This work is unfinished, because there will always be clever financiers who find new ways to get around existing standards—just as in the "struggle between the sword and the shield" in the arms race, where the progress in offensive weapons technology unendingly brings about advances in defense technology, and vice versa.

The fight against fraud is not, however, the only purpose of setting accounting standards. One must first look at what constitutes, in principle, a high quality set of accounting standards, before considering to what extent they are suited to the diverse needs of their many users.

What Makes Good Accounting Standards?

Accounting standard-setters often assert their determination to develop standards "of the highest quality." For example, the mission statement of the International Accounting Standards Board (IASB), which develops the IFRS, is to "to develop, in the public interest, a single set of high quality, understandable and enforceable global accounting standards that require high quality, transparent and comparable information in financial statements and other financial reporting to help participants in the world's capital markets and other users make economic decisions."[2] But what does quality mean in the case of such an essentially conventional and abstract product? In fact, the notion refers to different and sometimes divergent aims.

Accounting Standards, for What Purpose?

As we have seen in chapter 1, relevance, reliability, and comparability have been the principal characteristics expected from financial information since the origins of accounting in the late Middle Ages, when shareholders and managers were first separated. From their beginning, accounting standards have had to ensure the satisfaction of these requirements, even though that is not necessarily easy to do.

Relevance. In the first place, information has to be relevant to be useful. Relevance of accounting information is necessary to make good decisions: an investor who buys or sells a stock, a lender who finances or refinances a loan, a shareholder who approves the payment of a dividend, a judge who approves a restructuring plan, a lawmaker who votes on new regulations, a banking supervisor that authorizes a bank to do business—all these users of accounting information, and many others, need information enabling them not to make mistakes in these difficult decisions. Accounting standards must therefore reflect, insofar as possible, their respective concerns.

Reliability. Second, the information should be reliable, in that the standards should have the purpose of avoiding, to the extent possible, any risk of fraud or manipulation. For some data, this can be fairly simple: for example, in many businesses, revenue is easily verified by consulting the amounts billed (although the Enron case showed us that misrepresentation was possible even there). But when it comes to assessing the value of a business unit that may be subject to a write-down on the balance sheet, reliability becomes a much taller order, because the valuation depends on numerous assumptions involving, for example, forward-looking business plans, future interest rates, and other data that are in large part a matter of opinion. In other words, the only information that is perfectly reliable, that is, verifiable and neutral, is information concerning the past. Because accounting necessarily brings together observations of the past with assumptions about the future, perfect reliability cannot in most cases be attained.

Comparability. One of the aspects of this third requirement is stability over time: one must be able to compare the accounts of a single company over the course of several financial years and to describe separately each factor of change in the business. But comparability between different companies is also indispensable to a capitalist system that relies on the allocation of capital to the companies where it can perform best. An investor wants to be able to choose, and to choose not only among several companies in the same industry but also among companies in different sectors and, if possible, in different countries. Ideally, the investor wants to be able to put any company to the test—say, a Swedish bank, a Californian clothing manufacturer, an Egyptian cement maker, or an Indian software firm—in order to find out which one can provide the best return in relation to the risk she or he is willing to accept. For that purpose, and even if ambitions are scaled back from this ideal scope, comparability is necessary (although not always sufficient), and only precise and well-enforced accounting standards can guarantee it.

Once these three goals of relevance, reliability, and comparability are set out, however, difficulties begin. The problem is that they are only partially compatible with one another.

Relevance and Reliability. The most intractable conflict is probably between relevance and reliability. Albert Einstein is said to have hung a sign in his office at Princeton with the text, "not everything that counts can be counted, and not everything that can be counted counts." There is an uncomfortable truth in the fact that the data that can most certainly be verified are not necessarily the most interesting for economic and financial analysis and for investment decisions. Conversely, the most decision-relevant indicators can be difficult to establish in a reliable way. For example, intangible fixed assets such as

patents and trademarks have gained considerable economic importance over the past few decades and now form a substantial part of
many companies' wealth, in industries as wide-ranging as financial
services, media, information technology, life sciences, and consumer
goods. But how can the value of such intangibles be reliably assessed?
The valuation is possible in isolated cases, for example when a patent
has been purchased and therefore given a reference price, but no un-
questionable method provides a generally accepted response. However, a proper analysis of intangible assets is highly relevant to the financial analysis of companies, for which accounting information is
expected to provide the main materials.

Relevance and Comparability. These two do not always fit well together either. An accounting method appropriate for one kind of business may be less appropriate for another. This is the reason that has
been given in countries such as France, which, for decades, maintained specific standards for certain industries such as banking, insurance, and agriculture. In these countries, until the recent adoption of
IFRS, it was virtually impossible to compare, say, the accounts of a
bank with those of a manufacturing company. Such industry-specific
standards also make the preparation of consolidated accounts difficult for a company involved in both financial and nonfinancial activities—for example, companies that provide credit services for their
clients, such as retailers or auto manufacturers. Financial services accounted for 37 percent of French carmaker Renault's operating profit
in 2001. Even in US GAAP or IFRS, there are a number of sector-
specific or situation-specific provisions, which potentially diminish
the comparability of accounts across industries. For example, buildings are not accounted for in the same way, dependent on whether
they are owned for the purpose of real estate development or for corporate operations. This means that two companies that own the same
set of buildings may have different accounts, because they use them
for different purposes. This is justified in terms of relevance but is
hardly satisfactory in terms of comparability.

Comparability and Reliability. Finally, the simultaneous pursuit of
comparability and reliability can also create dilemmas. Consider geographical comparability, that is, the ability to compare the accounts of
companies located in different countries, which is one reason for the
increasing adoption of IFRS in Europe and in many other developing

or developed countries around the world. In fact, some kinds of information can be reliably obtained in some countries but not in others. The reference to market value for listed securities, for example, assumes that capital markets are efficient—that they offer sufficient depth and liquidity. This may be considered an acceptable assumption in most developed economies but not in all emerging markets. In a country in which capital markets have little liquidity and trading is limited, a reference to market value may be less relevant and reliable than a reference to historical acquisition cost. Application of identical accounting standards in different countries, although justified in principle by the aim of comparability, may thus work against the reliability of accounts.

Of course, these are particular cases, and the principles of relevance, reliability, and comparability often work together. But when conflicts arise, as in the examples mentioned, the aim for the standards to be of "high quality" requires some kind of compromise between the divergent requirements. This may additionally be based on a fourth consideration: the cost of accounting to companies should not be unduly high, a consideration that may act as a deterrent against the temptation of looking for ever more detailed information. Finally, and despite the technical nature of the questions considered, the standards must be understandable for their users, an aim which frequently runs counter to the increasing complexity of corporate operations.

Neutrality Is Not an Option

The discussion of what constitutes a high quality set of accounting standards would not be complete without addressing the question of their economic neutrality.[3] Theoretically—and leaving aside the exotic realm of quantum physics—the reality being measured does not depend on the measuring device. Therefore, accounting standards should have no effect on the life of companies and the decisions of their managers. A corollary of this point of view, which is defended by some observers,[4] is that the conventions around which financial statements are constructed are irrelevant, and that only the raw information disclosed to the market is important, not the way that accounting ratios are calculated. In other words, from this point of view accounting standards serve only one useful purpose, that of guaranteeing transparency. But this supposes that analysts and other users of financial information efficiently carry out all kinds of recalculations in order to derive from the published accounts, whatever the standards used for their preparation, the figures or ratios they need. Analysts and investors would thus care little what net earnings are per the accounts, because they calculate profits or value in their own way according to their own view of the company, on the basis of the published raw data.

However, this theory of the neutrality of accounting standards is not confirmed by observation of the facts. If it were, it would be difficult to explain why debates about standards provoke so much controversy, for example in the case of stock option expensing in the United States, or the adoption of IFRS by the European Union. In fact, the ability of users to reprocess information is limited, for down-to-earth reasons that include the fact that budgets available for financial analysis and research are limited. The technical competence and rationality of observers fall short of absolute perfection. Moreover, investors and financial analysts often operate in emergency conditions. They do not have enough time and cannot analyze exhaustively all the information contained in the accounts and footnote disclosures. Finally, for investors, the partially collective nature of market behavior, which does not always respond only to rational analysis by individuals, gives additional importance to accounting data. Accounts are generally the only information available to everyone in the market, and have a prominent influence on the least sophisticated investors, who typically calculate a price-earnings ratio on the basis of published earnings (not having an independent ability to reprocess information) and make investment decisions accordingly. And since there are many such "unsophisticated" investors in the market, the other investors must take them into account, which in turn influences market prices.

The reality of accounting standards' influence on investment choices is reflected in the behavior of companies themselves, which anticipate the reactions of markets and tend to concentrate on optimizing the profit shown in the accounts, even in some cases when this course of action may not involve making optimal business decisions. According to a study published a few years ago, the hedging of profits for accounting purposes has about the same level of priority as the hedging of cash flow in the implementation of risk management strategies through the use of derivatives. Specifically, 55 percent of German executives surveyed reckoned that the principal purpose of their hedging instruments was to minimize the variability of accounting profit, well above hedging cash flows (34 percent) or value (12 percent). In the United States, while the most widespread purpose was the hedging of cash flows (49 percent), hedging GAAP earnings was a close second (44 percent).[5] As a result, the way in which profits are calculated according to accounting standards has a direct effect on management decisions. Stock options are another example. A study of the transition to IFRS in Europe has shown a spectacular drop in the proportion of executive incentive awards represented by stock options. This proportion fell from 36 percent to 21 percent, in the year of transition toward the requirement to expense stock options under the IFRS 2 rule (on which more later).[6] There is little doubt that the change in accounting standards was a key factor in this shift.

Put simply, the economic neutrality of accounting standards is a fiction. Many standards have, to some degree, an effect on corporate decisions and on the economy. The real question therefore is not whether these induced effects exist, which they do; but rather whether they should enter into consideration in judging the quality of the standards, as politicians would typically tend to see it, or whether the only thing that counts is reaching the goals of relevance, reliability, and comparability in any particular measure adopted, as accounting professionals would prefer. In all cases, this means that accounting standard-setters have a responsibility as de facto economic policy makers, even though they may tend to view this responsibility as accidental. The relationship between standard-setting and public policy objectives will be explored further in the second part of this chapter.

Of Principles and Rules

It has already been noted how Enron removed debts and potential losses in very large amounts from its scope of consolidation, while retaining most of the associated risks, and that to do so it took advantage of the possibilities provided by the detailed rules set out in US GAAP accounting standards. Following the shock of Enron's default, many observers proposed shifting to standards more clearly based on general principles rather than on detailed rules: making them "principles-based" rather than "rules-based," in the jargon of the profession.

In general, the more detailed and prescriptive a rule, the easier it is to invent "creative" ways to get around it. Enron took advantage of the rule of 3 percent of the capital to be held by third parties in SPEs and deconsolidated entities in which those holdings, while higher than 3 percent, remained small. The formulation of a precise limit, in this case as in others, facilitated evasion of the initial purposes of the rule. In contrast, the most "robust" rules are often those expressed in the most general but concise terms.

Accounting debates frequently refer to the distinction between principles-based and rules-based standards. After Enron, the IASB, which develops the IFRS with what it calls a principles-based approach, tried to push its advantage and to present its standards as more reliable than the US GAAP for this reason. In testimony to the Senate committee investigating Enron on February 14, 2002, David Tweedie, the chairman of the IASB, stated: "The IASB has concluded that a body of detailed guidance (sometimes referred to as *bright lines*) encourages a rule-book mentality of 'where does it say I can't do this?' (. . .) Put simply, adding the detailed guidance may obscure, rather than highlight, the underlying principle." Many observers then tried to contrast "virtuous" IFRS based on principles, to "pernicious" US GAAP based on overly prescriptive rules.[7]

An important milestone in this debate has been the study conducted by the SEC on "the adoption by the United States Financial Reporting System of a principles-based accounting system," which was published in July 2003 (this study was mandated by the Sarbanes-Oxley Act passed in July 2002 following the Enron and WorldCom scandals). It concluded that the movement toward principles-based or, as the SEC calls them, "objectives-oriented" accounting standards is indeed desirable, and it identified possible ways to get there in addition to the steps already taken.[8] However, the SEC study also highlighted that the contrast between US GAAP and IFRS in this respect is less clear-cut than sometimes claimed. The rules-based nature of U.S. accounting does not reflect a deliberate choice; on the contrary, the original intent of the US GAAP standards was to have them based on an analysis of the economic reality of a company rather than on formal considerations. The drift took place gradually, as the ingenuity of companies in getting around existing rules provoked reactions from the FASB, which resulted in the proliferation of detailed rules. The U.S. legal system, which fosters a high number of court actions, has also contributed to the detailed character of the rules that have accumulated over time. Hence, the volume of US GAAP standards has skyrocketed. There are now about 150 FAS (Financial Accounting Standards) rules compared with about 30 of them twenty years ago, and a significantly higher number of supplemental provisional and interpretive documents that are also part of the body of US GAAP.

Conversely, the IFRS benefit from their relatively recent origin, as their development started about forty years later than did US GAAP. Most importantly, they have given rise to much less litigation and interpretation, because so few major international companies used them before 2005. And even so, in its report the SEC ironically points out that despite the claims of the IASB, the IFRS are far from the "objectives-oriented" or "principles-based" approach that is called for:

> As they currently stand, the IFRSs do not embody the objectives-oriented approach to principles-based accounting standard setting. Indeed, a careful examination of the IFRSs shows that many of those standards are more properly described as rules-based. Other IFRSs could fairly be characterized as principles-only because they are overly general. Accordingly, we reject the notion that IFRSs constitute a model for principles-based accounting standards.[9]

On the particular question of the fraud perpetrated by Enron, after trying to assert the higher quality of its own standards, the IASB was eventually forced to recognize that they perhaps would not have been enough to prevent the abuses.[10] And as a consequence of the mandatory adoption of IFRS, which started in 2005 for thousands of (for now, mainly European) companies, it will be necessary to clarify certain issues with more detailed rules in order to reduce the legal insecurity that may arise from their application. The volume of IFRS and their interpretive rules, some of which are already rather long, is therefore likely to grow and eventually reach a level that might become of the same order as the volume of US GAAP. As an example, the IAS 39 standard is already 170 pages long, not counting the accompanying "basis for conclusions" and "implementation guideline"—not exactly the best example of concise "principles-based" drafting.

In theory, clarity and the expression of simple principles remain essential goals of accounting standard-setting. But in practice, it appears unfortunately inevitable that there be enough detailed rules to guarantee minimum legal security and uniformity of implementation, to fulfill the already discussed requirement for comparability. The opposition between principles-based and rules-based standards provides a useful analytical framework, but it is insufficient to describe, let alone resolve, the real dilemmas of accounting standard-setting.

Accounting as Translation

Quite apart from the debate on principles and rules, another important feature of accounting is that it aims to reflect ever more precisely the underlying economic reality of transactions and companies, while gradually downplaying their apparent legal structure. This principle, generally described in English-speaking countries as "substance over form," is integral to both US GAAP and IFRS. The IASB expresses it the following way: "If information is to represent faithfully the transactions and other events that it purports to represent, it is necessary that they are accounted for and presented in accordance with their substance and economic reality and not merely their legal form. The substance of transactions or other events is not always consistent with that which is apparent from their legal or contrived form."[11]

An analogy can be established between this distinction and a well-known way to contrast two different attitudes to translation, depending on whether it focuses on the source language or on the target language. The analogy is not surprising: an accountant is indeed a translator, insofar as he translates the operations of a company, as they are expressed by oral or written contracts, orders and billings, and sundry dealings, into a common language that can be understood by users of accounts such as the company's investors. Accountants can take for themselves, word for word, Umberto Eco's description of translation as the result of a "process of negotiation" in which all participants end up "with a feeling of rational and mutual satisfaction on the basis of the golden rule that you cannot have everything."[12]

In the essential distinction between source-oriented and target-oriented translation, each attitude expresses in a different way the same concern for fairness to the original text. What differentiates them is the nature of that fairness. For "source-oriented" translators, what is most important is to transmit the structure of the original text, not necessarily paying attention to the perception a reader may have of it. As Chateaubriand proudly claimed about his own translation of Milton's *Paradise Lost* into French, the goal is to "trace" the translation over the original.[13] Conversely, "target-oriented" translators are concerned primarily with the reader's perception and attempt to communicate to him the deep content of the work without reference to the formal structure of the original version. Some degree of "targeting" is in fact always necessary considering the gaps between structures and formulations in different languages. For example, one would not translate "hot dog" into French as *chien chaud.*

The contrast between source and target orientation in translation recurs in the distinction between two possible conceptions of accounting: one being formalistic, in the sense that it aims to "trace" the results of contracts and commitments as they are expressed in the company's documentation; and the other being more economic, in the sense that it aims to convey the substance of transactions rather than the way they have been legally expressed. A source-oriented translation would correspond to a concern to transcribe the legal operations of a company in the form represented by signed contracts. Conversely, the target-oriented approach finds its analogy in the notion of accounts transmitting to the user a relevant idea of the underlying reality of a company's business, which may involve a reformulation of some legal connections. In this latter approach, the original structures, that are constructions of language in translation and legal "form" in the case of accounting, should not necessarily be visible in the end result.

The treatment of leasing contracts, a commonly used financing technique, provides an example of the contrast. In past accounting practice (including, in most of continental Europe, until very recently), such contracts enabled companies to use a plant or equipment while not including it on their company balance sheet. From a contractual point of view, the lessor maintains ownership of the equipment until the expiration of the contract, and the lessee pays it annual rent in exchange for its use for its business. When the contract expires, ownership is transferred back to the lessee, but at that point the equipment has been depreciated and its repurchase thus does not affect the balance sheet. In the "source-oriented" version, the execution of the contract is translated into accounting terms by an operating cost (the rent for the lease) but has no direct impact on assets or liabilities.

By contrast, accounting standards such as FAS 13 in the United States (introduced in 1976 and revised several times since) and IAS 17 in IFRS (introduced in 1982, revised in 1997 and 2003) have introduced a distinction between capital (or financial) leases and operating leases on the basis of an economic analysis of the distribution of risks. IAS 17 specifies that the distinction between these two possibilities "depends on the substance of the transaction rather than the form of the contract" (§ 8). When a contract of this kind results in the effective transfer of the economic use of the equipment to the company that leases it, the standard requires an accounting adjustment. The equipment is recorded as an asset on the balance sheet at an amount corresponding to its value in use, and a debt of the same amount, corresponding to the financial obligation assumed, is recorded as a liability. The accounting treatment of leasing rentals is also changed to distinguish between the amount corresponding to interest and that corresponding to repayment of the initial obligation. In other words, the contract is entirely reinterpreted in the accounts, as if it were a purchase of equipment financed by debt. With such standards, and unlike in the "source-oriented," formalistic approach, leasing agreements cannot be used to artificially slim down the balance sheet and thereby reduce the apparent level of debt.

In accounting, the requirement of "substance over form" means that when the source-oriented approach is incompatible with the target-oriented approach, the latter should prevail. But, as in translation, too radical an approach can be dangerous. A company can be reduced neither to the text of the contracts that it has signed, nor to its cash flows. The economic (as opposed to narrowly legalistic) view is certainly more relevant for business decisions, but it often involves making assessments about the future that can easily verge on the arbitrary. Each individual has his or her own view of the future, which may also change over time. In attempting to provide an accurate economic picture of a company, accounting always runs the risk of being governed by subjectivity and short-lived judgments. Take the example of the manager newly appointed to head a company, who immediately sets aside large provisions for the restructuring of the operations conducted by his predecessor, which are suddenly deemed unsustainable. The economic approach of accounting has difficulty in supporting either the approval or rejection of such accounting choices, which appear improper, or not, depending on whether the observer shares the strategic vision and intent of former or current management.

The Conflicting Interests of Accounts' Users

The principle that fixed assets are depreciated over time is one of the most elementary and universal accounting conventions. But what does it look like from the perspective of each of the users of accounts?

Shareholders, looking for a "fair" view of the company, want to see a so-called economic depreciation, reflecting the actual decrease in value resulting from the "consumption" of fixed assets. In the case of a car, this could consist of booking each year as depreciation the loss of blue-book value; this is not likely to result in constant depreciation over time. For some kinds of assets (e.g., intangible or financial), it is even possible to imagine that the depreciation would sometimes be negative, in other words, the asset's net value increases over time. This can be the case, for example, for certain brands or historical buildings. In such cases, depreciation would have to be replaced by revaluation.

The tax authorities, by contrast, want the simplest possible method in order to minimize the risks of fraud, specifically because the amount booked as depreciation affects the profit that is subject to corporate income tax. Therefore, its calculation is one of the factors in determining the actual amount of tax payable in any given year, and in most cases, unlike for cars, there is no objective reference value on which everyone can agree (indeed, if the blue book were to be a basis for tax calculation, it would probably become subject to a number of distortions). Thus, the tax authorities generally favor the method of straight-line depreciation, whereby the value of the asset is reduced by the same amount each year until it reaches zero at the end of the depreciation period. Typically, buildings can be depreciated over twenty or thirty years, machinery over three to ten years, computers over two to five years. This method has the great advantage of simplicity, even though it can lead to very different results from those derived from a calculation of economic depreciation, if only because, as proven by a quick look to eBay, the value of many assets in fact never comes down to zero even after the end of the "depreciation period." The picture is further muddled by the fact that the government may also have concerns other than tax receipts. For example, it may seek to foster capital expenditure by authorizing "accelerated" depreciation, where depreciation is higher in the years immediately following the acquisition of fixed assets, thus correspondingly reducing income tax and stimulating investment.

Company executives, for their part, may have yet another view about depreciation. In some cases, they may wish tax depreciation to be as high as possible, in order to minimize tax payments. But in other cases, the corresponding decrease in net income is not necessarily to their benefit, such as when their bonuses are directly related to profits.

Accounting standards may aim to reconcile these various and partly contradictory requirements. One lazy solution is to allow companies to choose among several methods, or "options" in accounting jargon. The proliferation of options, however, causes problems of its own, not least because it contradicts the principle of comparability. Two identical companies that choose different accounting options can publish different financial statements to describe identical operations, which is not satisfactory. Another solution is to issue different standards for different users: in this example, depreciation rules in tax accounts are generally different from those in public financial statements, even though the discrepancies vary from one country to another. But, as previously mentioned, there is a limit to the number of different accounting systems that a company can simultaneously maintain.

The important fact to remember is that regardless of the clarity of the guiding principles chosen, accounting standard-setting is never a matter of mere deductive reasoning. It also has to be seen as the result of the respective priorities given to different users, which themselves reflect the respective powers of different economic agents in a given financial ecosystem. Behind almost any discussion about accounting standards, there are interests at stake; ultimately, some win and others lose. Recognition of these interests is essential for an understanding of the debates about accounting and standards.

An Illustration: Government-Mandated Standards in France

France provides a perfect example of the interrelation between the structures of an economic system and the standards used in accounting. Under the Vichy regime following the 1940 defeat inflicted by Nazi Germany, and even more during the "reconstruction" years after liberation in 1945, the state took a leading role in organizing the economy. At the same time, it directly supervised the establishment of the first French national accounting standards and quickly identified them as one means of implementing its policy objectives. The widespread use of accounting as an instrument of government economic policy has been described by some scholars as "accounting Colbertism."[14]

In the United States, accounting standards had been established by an act of Congress that assigned the task to the SEC, which in turn immediately delegated the responsibility to a private body. By contrast, until the adoption of the IFRS in 2005 the French government never considered giving up its control over accounting standard-setting. The successive overhauls of the accounting standards in 1947, 1982, and 1999 all had the status of government regulations.

The National Accounting Board (Conseil National de la Comptabilité or CNC), which was first established in 1957 and is often presented in shorthand as the standard-setting authority in France, in reality has only an advisory role to the Ministry of Economy and Finance. In practice its views are usually adopted, but it has no decision-making authority of its own. In 1996, the makeup of the CNC was changed to give more representation to accounting professionals and other market participants, but soon thereafter a new body was established, the Accounting Regulations Board (Comité de la Réglementation Comptable or CRC), which is effectively controlled by government representatives.[15] In practical terms, the establishment of the CRC introduces another layer in the filtering of proposals coming from the CNC before any formal decision by the government. The very structure of the CNC confirms its advisory rather than decision-making role as it has no fewer than fifty-eight members (it had one hundred and three before the 1996 reform), as opposed to seven for its United States and German counterparts, and ten in the United Kingdom.

The connection between tax accounting and public accounting is perhaps the most striking among the many consequences of this particular institutional arrangement, which still is a special French feature. The rules for corporate taxation, like those for accounting itself, must establish a balance among several sometimes contradictory demands. They must be economically sensible, eliminate as much as possible the risk of manipulation, and simultaneously ensure a measure of fairness among companies of all sizes from all industries. These requirements, however, are far from equal in importance. For tax authorities, fighting fraud is the number one priority, and the information underlying the calculation of the tax base must be completely verifiable from a company's documentation and not rely on assumptions that might be used by management to reduce the amount of taxes to be paid. Hence, as in the previously discussed case of depreciation, the tax authorities are inclined to favor the use of simple formulas based on documented evidence rather than economic calculations on value, which are inherently less objective and appeal more to human judgment. In this light, the requirements for relevance and comparability have much less importance than reliability in setting rules for tax accounting. This simple fact has led many tax authorities, including the U.S. Internal Revenue Service, to build their own systems of tax accounting rules, with no direct link with public accounting standards such as US GAAP. But France, since the Second World War, has constantly strived to maintain a close connection between the rules for determining the tax base and the accounting standards. This link was expressly set out by law in a 1965 decree. Of course, it makes the work of the tax authorities all the easier as there is relatively little processing to be done in shifting from "general" (financial) accounting to tax accounting, and therefore accountants in a sense pave the way for the tax collector. This is so much the case that common parlance in France often uses the expression *liasse fiscale* (the yearly corporate income tax returns) to refer to a company's accounts, particularly for small- and medium-sized businesses.

The connection between accounting and tax rules is not absolute: it would be too impractical. Some changes (including for the above-mentioned possibility of accelerated depreciation) have to be made between the two sets of numbers. Furthermore, some tax-related rules have an effect only on individual accounts and are eliminated in the preparation of consolidated accounts, which are of the most interest to investors. Finally, the many changes made to French accounting standards in recent years have progressively reduced their differences with their main international counterparts. However, the dominance of tax considerations over financial ones in setting accounting standards and preparing accounts is still deeply rooted in French practices, and until the adoption of IFRS this has often created tensions with other points of view, especially those of investors.

The preparation of national statistical accounts is another government function that has exercised heavy influence over the development of French accounting standards, along with the "tax/accounting connection." This is linked with the long-standing use in France of the concept of a "General Chart of Accounts" (in French, *Plan Comptable Général* or PCG). This concept was initially developed in the 1920s by a German university professor, Eugen Schmalenbach,[16] and was adopted before the Second World War by heavily state-controlled economies, such as the Soviet Union in 1930 and Nazi Germany in 1937 in the form of the so-called Goering Plan, as a way to organize the handling of supplies and the buildup of a war economy (at the same time, Schmalenbach was persecuted because of his Jewish origins). In 1942–43, France's Vichy regime followed suit and adopted the first PCG as a variant of the German National Chart of Accounts, but the unraveling of the regime soon occurred, allowing time for implementation only in the aircraft industry. In the period immediately following the war, France undertook economic and social reconstruction, and for the first time instituted consistent tools of "national accounting," making it possible to monitor key macroeconomic indicators such as growth, inflation, exports, and investment. The PCG, therefore, was developed as a common basis for both company accounts and national accounts, a framework for corporate data that could be aggregated at the level of the entire national economy. The first peacetime version of the PCG was adopted in 1947 and was initially reserved primarily for state-related companies. Its use was extended to all companies, however small, in the 1960s. The PCG itself was revised in 1957, 1982, and 1999, but its structure remained essentially unchanged and even after the 2005 adoption of IFRS for consolidated accounts, the updated PCG is still mandatory for all French companies' individual accounts. This now constitutes a "French exception," with very few equivalents outside France and its former colonies and protectorates, even though the French PCG also had some influence on the accounting systems of countries such as Belgium, the Czech Republic, Greece, Romania, and Spain.[17]

The PCG assigns a place in the general chart of accounts to every accounting item, whatever its nature, and assigns it a four-digit identification code that is the same for every company, regardless of size or activity (or almost regardless: as already mentioned, there are special sectoral charts for some industries, such as banking, insurance, and agriculture). For example, code number 2138 designates "infrastructure work," a subcategory of code 213 "construction," included in turn under code 21 "tangible fixed assets,"[18] itself enclosed under class 2 "fixed assets." The PCG thus has five "classes" of balance sheet codes (1 to 5) and two classes of income statement codes (class 6 for expenses and class 7 for revenues), as well as a class 8 for miscellaneous items that do not fit under the first seven.

The PCG has the advantage—a considerable one for statisticians—of making it possible to add together, without any further processing, data from all the companies in the country to determine macroeconomic aggregates. For example, the sum of code 2138 for all companies provides the total of fixed infrastructure assets for the entire French corporate sector. The same purpose explains the structure of the income statement according to French standards, whereby expenses are presented "by nature" (e.g., materials, labor costs, depreciation, and such) rather than *par destination* or "by function" (cost of goods sold, sales and marketing, research and development, general and administrative expenses), as is the case in most other countries. This particular way of presenting things greatly facilitates the calculation of national aggregates on the basis of individual company accounts, even though it makes it difficult to calculate a gross margin, which is defined in English-speaking countries as revenue less cost of goods sold.

The PCG has other advantages. It enables all companies to share the same conventions for the preparation of accounts, and thus facilitates the teaching of accounting and the mobility of accounting professionals between companies. And of course, it simplifies the preparation of tax returns. The PCG's major drawback is the excessive rigidity inherent in this kind of system, the value of which is also diminished by the fact that the codification of certain entries can still vary from one company to another because of differences in the interpretation of categories. One can apply literally to the *Plan Comptable Général* the words used by political scientist Pierre Rosanvallon to describe what he calls the "French political culture of generality":

> The prism of generality softens the harsh edges of the world in order to shape it so that it is as transparent as our concept of it. By dismissing any relation to particularity, the law creates an imaginary world. This is the source of the distrust of executive power, identified with specific actions, that has weighed so heavily on French political life.[19]

In almost every other country in the world, most notably in English-speaking countries, each company decides on its chart of accounts according to its own priorities. Not so in France. As noted by Alan Roberts, a researcher at the University of Canterbury (Christchurch, New Zealand), "an Anglo-Saxon observer might see the PCG as being bureaucratic, inflexible, over-formal, unnecessarily prescriptive in its detail and an unreasonable intrusion into business affairs. On the other hand a French observer of the accounting scene in New Zealand would be astonished to discover the absence of an accounting plan in a country so populated by SMEs [small- and medium-sized enterprises]. He or she would be equally bemused to find that the construction of national financial reporting rules was, effectively, in the hands of a non-state body, the accountancy profession."[20]

By means of its broad institutional control over the setting of accounting standards, the French state, more than in most other developed countries, made itself the arbiter among the various interests involved in those standards. It is not surprising that it frequently used this power to advance its own agenda—but, as the next examples will show, the link between accounting rule making and economic policy making is by no means unique to France.

Accounting Standards as Industrial Policy

Accounting rules can be used more directly by governments (or with their approval) to support a particular sector of activity or type of economic conduct, and not only for fictional fireworks manufacturers such as Smoke & Mirrors, Inc. In this respect, the United States has arguably gone further than most other countries, including France, in using accounting standards to advance perceived interests of its corporations, sometimes at the price of some deviation, at least temporarily, from the requirement for "fairness" of the accounts.

Stock option accounting provides the quintessential example of this interference between accounting rules and economic policy, thus also illustrating the lack of neutrality of accounting standards that was mentioned earlier in this chapter. One could even argue that the spectacular development of stock options as a form of compensation for executives and other employees over the last two decades has largely been made possible by decisions on accounting standards made first in the United States and subsequently in the rest of the world.

In publicly listed companies, the granting of stock options makes it possible to compensate executives according to future increases in the share price. Options are granted at no cost with a "strike price" usually close to the current market price. After a "vesting" period, which typically ranges from one to five years, the holder has the right to "exercise" the option, that is, to buy shares from the company at the strike price. If at that time the market price is higher than the strike price (which is often the case, because stock prices generally tend to increase over time even though some may fall), the option holder pockets the difference as a capital gain; if the market price is not higher than the strike price, he does not exercise the option, and thus gains nothing but loses nothing either. Therefore, in no circumstances does the beneficiary of the option run the risk of losing money, except if he were to hold on to the shares after exercising the option and their price were to fall below the strike price. This feature makes stock options attractive to the beneficiaries; but the interesting thing is that they generally have also been painless for the companies issuing them, as long as these were not required to record stock options as expenses in their income statement. In effect, until the widespread adoption of IFRS and changes in US GAAP in 2005, no significant system of accounting standards had mandated the recognition of the cost, or "expensing," of stock options in the income statement of listed companies. Consequently, stock options have spread quickly over the course of the past twenty years.

It is difficult to justify economically the claim that stock options cost nothing. As the saying goes, there is no such thing as a free lunch. Double-entry bookkeeping is, as we have seen, based on the principle under which every transaction is balanced—at least, accounting-wise. Employees who are given stock options receive an advantage, as the popularity of the practice clearly shows. As for the company, it is obliged to sell shares to the beneficiary when he or she exercises the option. Depending on the details of stock option plans, the company either buys these shares on the market, or issues supplementary shares at the strike price. In the first case, the company incurs a capital loss (because the strike price is lower than the market price). In the second, there is no cash loss, but the company issues shares at a cut-rate price and therefore dilutes the value for existing shareholders, that is, it diminishes their respective share of future profits. In other words, as intuition suggests, in every case shareholders pay for the advantage granted to recipients of stock options. The options create the equivalent of a financial flow from investors to their recipients, hence compensation for the latter and a cost for the company. To quote the characteristically plain language of Warren Buffett, the legendary investor: "If stock options are not a form of compensation, what are they? If compensation is not an expense, what is it? And if expenses shouldn't go into the calculation of earnings, where in the world should they go?"[21]

Why have the US GAAP so long permitted companies not to book stock options as an expense? The defenders of this seemingly absurd situation have often based their arguments on a technical difficulty. When granted, an option is not a firm promise of future gains as it is contingent on future market developments. There is no question that the assessment of the corresponding option value is a tricky exercise, as is well known to financial theorists and capital market professionals alike. Calculation models usually used, such as the Black and Scholes formula or the binomial model, require in particular an assessment of the anticipated volatility of the share price, which introduces substantial uncertainties into the calculation. But even so, an approximate evaluation of the cost of stock options, imperfect though it may be, is certainly more "fair" than the practice of counting them as no cost at all. In addition, there are other items just as complex as stock options (or even more so), such as pension liabilities or financial derivatives, that have to be evaluated in financial statements. The distortion created by the US GAAP rules on options opened a hole into which companies literally rushed headlong, enabling managers to compensate their employees, and themselves, with large sums with no effect on the company's income statement. We quote Warren Buffett again: "In effect, accounting principles offer management a choice: pay employees in one form and count the cost, or pay them in another form and ignore the cost. Small wonder then that the use of options has mushroomed."[22]

The permissive accounting treatment of stock options was essentially motivated by what can be called considerations of industrial policy, as has been amply illustrated by public arguments on the corresponding accounting standards. Stock options are an important device for start-up technology companies, which themselves are widely considered one of the key drivers of long-term growth in the United States. Such companies often lack sufficient immediate resources to pay their employees in cash, but they enjoy a high growth potential and therefore the prospect of considerable value creation for shareholders. This allows them to entice and motivate highly qualified employees with stock options rather than salaries. In the matter of a few years in the 1980s and 1990s, stock options became a nearly universal device in technology companies to offer the prospect of sometimes serious wealth to employees, while not imposing any apparent burden on company profits. By closing its eyes and even encouraging this accounting trick, the U.S. government gave to rapidly growing technology companies a de facto advantage over the rest of the economy. Because the advantage of not expensing stock options was disproportionately benefiting technology companies, these companies also had most to lose in the new requirement for expensing. It is estimated that the negative impact of options expensing would have been a moderate overall reduction of corporate earnings, by 4.4 percent, for all 500 companies composing the S&P 500 stock index, but that the average impact on those companies in the index that are primarily active in the high-tech sector would have been as much as a 19 percent reduction of earnings.[23] Thomas Friedman, a *New York Times* columnist, expressed the concerns of technology companies when he complained in an article on China that "at a time when China is encouraging its new companies to offer employees stock options to get Chinese innovators to stay at home and start new firms, the Bush team has been mutely going along with a change in accounting standards that will force U.S. companies to expense stock options by June 2005. This is likely to dampen the growth of our own high-tech companies and encourage U.S.-educated Indian and Chinese techies to go back home."[24]

This interventionist, "industrial-policy" view on the accounting treatment of stock options was graphically illustrated in 1994, when the FASB, the body to which the SEC delegates responsibility for preparing the US GAAP accounting standards, made a first attempt to require companies to expense stock options. This attempt was perfectly legitimate, and even overdue, under the requirement for relevance (or of "fairness") of financial reporting. But it met extraordinary opposition from politicians, especially those from areas with many high-technology firms such as Northern California. Arguments were developed by corporate lobbyists against stock option expensing, sometimes with a bizarre rhetoric of spontaneous value creation.[25] Congress eventually threatened to cut off the FASB's funds if it stood by its proposal. Confronted with this threat, the FASB and the SEC ingloriously gave up the fight, and the resulting FAS 123 standard made the expensing of stock options an option rather than a requirement as initially envisaged. As a result, before 2002 only two companies, among the thousands listed on U.S. markets, had chosen the option of expensing; for all others, stock options were booked at no cost.[26]

The accounting scandals that have come to light since 2001 have provided ample proof of some unfortunate effects of stock options. In some cases, the holding of large numbers of options has encouraged corporate executives to make decisions that had the short-term effect of artificially inflating share prices at the time the options could be exercised, in order to maximize their gains, even if it meant a subsequent collapse of the stock once the manipulation was revealed. Paul Volcker, the former chairman of the Federal Reserve Board and a highly respected figure within the financial community, was not alone in concluding that "stock options are subject to abuse and temptation in a way that's almost irrefutable. I think we ought to get rid of them."[27]

In this context, one might have thought that the accounting oddity of not expensing stock options would immediately have been ended. But even after the scandals, requiring that stock options be expensed proved to be a long and controversial process, and would perhaps not have happened if the European Union had not in the meantime announced its intention to adopt the international standard IFRS 2, which mandates expensing. Indeed, the FASB waited for the IASB to publish IFRS 2 in February 2004, and only then, in April 2004, published Declaration 123 R, which modifies the FAS 123 rule and makes the expensing of stock options an obligation. But the same interests as a decade earlier were still willing to fight against this. A sense of the atmosphere can be found in the title of a conference organized by the American Enterprise Institute, a conservative think tank, on January 8, 2004: "Expensing Employee Stock Options Looks Like a Major Mistake." In the course of that conference, one of the five SEC commissioners, Paul Atkins, expressed (in a personal capacity) his doubts about the appropriateness of expensing options:[28] by then, opposition to the expensing of stock options extended to within the regulator itself. Finally, the SEC, under its then-chairman William Donaldson, stood firm by the FASB rule even though it conceded an extension of the implementation deadline for some companies. But the controversy had been intense, and questions still linger on the methodologies to be used in valuing the options-related expense.

The accounting treatment of stock options is an emblematic example of a powerful economic incentive policy carried out exclusively by means of accounting standards. Technology start-ups and other corporations have probably gained from this policy as well as a number of managers who benefited greatly from stock options, but conversely, many shareholders have paid a price, usually without even being aware of it.

Stock options are far from the only example of accounting standards playing a role that can be described as industrial policy. Another graphic illustration is the "pooling of interests," a method for the preparation of accounts following acquisitions through exchange of shares. The "pooling" method allows the inclusion of the target company's equity on the balance sheet of the acquirer at an amount equal to its book value rather than at the acquisition price. It therefore makes it possible to avoid recording any goodwill of the target in the assets of the acquirer, whose balance sheet bears no indication of the actual cost of the transaction—however high this may be. This generally improves the future profits of the merged entity by avoiding any write-downs (or impairments) of goodwill, which caused so much trouble, for example, to AOL Time Warner, Vivendi Universal, and France Telecom in 2002. Crucially, the pooling of interests also leads to higher apparent ratios of return on equity. This can run directly against the interests of existing shareholders. Similar to the case of stock options, the pooling method in fact conceals the true impact of the acquisition on the existing shareholders' return on equity, as their holding is diluted in proportion to the acquisition price.

To be sure, no accounting method is fully satisfactory when it comes to dealing with the problem of goodwill. Accounting takes into consideration "external goodwill" (the difference between the acquisition price of the company and its book value, net of debt and after revaluation of individual assets), but not "internal goodwill," which would represent the creation of value connected with the normal business of the company. This element is sometimes very significant; one indication of this is the fact that most listed companies, except during major market slumps, have a market capitalization higher than their net asset value. Unfortunately, it is impossible to measure internal goodwill in a reliable and rigorous way, which makes it inevitable that it will be treated differently from external goodwill. As a result, a company will necessarily have different balance sheets depending on whether it has developed a business on its own or has acquired the same business through the purchase of another company. A related problem is the great difficulty of assessing the correct amount of goodwill to be impaired (if at all) in the years following the acquisition. This highlights a fundamental limitation in the capacity of accounting to provide a relevant and comparable picture of companies.

The bottom line, however, is that the pooling of interests is a questionable method from the standpoint of "fairness" of accounts. That said, this method offers other advantages that have nothing to do with the principles of accounting, namely, fostering mergers and thereby accelerating the movement of consolidation that in the 1990s helped to strengthen and modernize entire industries in the United States. The method had long been accepted in the United States in circumstances specified in a US GAAP rule of 1970. It was also made possible in France by a 1999 accounting regulation, allowing its use in several large mergers concluded during that year, such as those between TotalFina and Elf, or BNP and Paribas. The impact on financial ratios is huge. For example, in 2001, TotalFinaElf (now Total) recorded a net profit of €7.7 billion and shareholders' equity of €33.9 billion according to French standards, using the pooling method. If that method had not been applied, the profit figure would have been lowered by €1.4 billion (−18%) and the assets increased by €39.6 billion (+117%). Pretax return on shareholders' equity, a key indicator for financial analysis, would have been under 9 percent, instead of 23 percent as published, an enormous difference in perceived performance.

Finally, the excesses of the merger and acquisitions craze that characterized the late 1990s led the U.S. authorities to reconsider the pooling of interests method and eventually to end its use in July 2001. The IFRS, for their part, never permitted the use of pooling except in severely restricted circumstances, and have now prohibited it entirely (only companies that have used pooling in the past are authorized not to make retroactive adjustments when they make the transition to IFRS). But before these changes, many companies have taken advantage of the pooling method, and some mergers would probably not have taken place if this method had not been permitted, even though it is impossible to estimate their precise number.

Accounting Standards and Financial Stability

Another concern of public authorities, apart from promoting economic interests through actions that may be described as industrial policy, is ensuring financial stability and preventing crises through what is generally referred to as prudential supervision of financial firms. Specifically, banking and insurance are subject to particular requirements for caution, which do not apply to other sectors. This is because the bankruptcy of a large bank or insurer may affect not only their own shareholders and creditors but also the depositors and/or people insured, and beyond that, the public's confidence in the financial system as a whole. History illustrates the disastrous consequences of this kind of shock, whether in Germany in the 1920s or Argentina much more recently. To avoid such catastrophic events, governments intervene beforehand by supervising financial activities. This task, which essentially consists of monitoring the major financial firms to track the risk of a crisis prompted by a sudden loss of confidence in one of them, is generally given to central banks or specialized agencies such as the United Kingdom's Financial Services Authority or the U.S. Office of the Comptroller of the Currency.

Such prudential supervisory agencies typically ascertain that credit institutions are solvent by requiring that the ratio of their equity to their outstanding loans be at least 8 percent. This solvency ratio is calculated in every country following uniform rules, established by consensus in the framework of the "Basel Committee," which includes the central banks and supervisory authorities of thirteen large developed countries.[29] Similarly, insurance regulators (which in the United States exist only at state, not federal, level) make sure that insurance companies are able to honor their commitments to the insured. For that purpose, they analyze the balance between insurance liabilities representing those commitments and the assets held by each company.

In some countries (France, again, is an example), the work of prudential supervisors is in large part based on the public accounts disclosed by banks and insurance companies. Hence, in those countries public financial accounting and regulatory accounting have been somewhat blended together, which has given rise to an uneasy coexistence between the principle of prudence directed toward the supervisory authorities and the principle of "fairness" or "true and fair view" directed toward shareholders. Here again, the two competing principles are not always quite compatible. In France as in other such countries, public regulators in the financial sector have often exercised a strong influence on accounting standards in order to carry out their policy of prudential supervision, sometimes at the risk of distorting the picture given to other users of the accounts. This can be by allowing "safety cushions" in the form of provisions for broadly defined risks that cannot be described as the accrual of a specific future liability. This is not the case in other countries, such as the United States, where regulatory accounts prepared for the purpose of prudential supervision are markedly different from public financial accounts (in IFRS as well, considerations of prudential supervision have limited influence). Even in these countries, however, banks' and insurers' public accounts have an impact on the perception of their financial strength and therefore on trust in the financial system as a whole. In fact, the tension between the prudential approach and accounting transparency will always raise difficult questions. As we have seen, the integrity of accounting standards is often threatened by special business interests. But financial stability is a concern of general, not special, interest, and many observers, including some central bankers, fear that accounting standards might have the effect of threatening that stability even though they otherwise rigorously conform to the requirements of relevance, reliability, and comparability. This is still an undecided issue, as most present standards on financial instruments, such as FAS 133 in US GAAP and IAS 39 in IFRS, are rather recent and it is too early to fully assess their long-term consequences on financial systems.

Creditors and Shareholders

Let us now turn away from questions of public policy and consider the way in which the interests of the principal contributors of external financing to companies, that is, lenders (creditors) and shareholders, are involved in the setting of accounting standards.

As has been already noted, the distinction between creditors and shareholders is not the only relevant one. A distinction may be made between, on the one hand, those operating in the framework of organized capital markets, that is, owners of listed shares, bonds, and other listed securities; and on the other hand, investors who act outside these markets, such as family shareholders or owners of "private"—read unlisted—equity, for example, venture capital or leveraged-buy-out (LBO) funds, as well as commercial banks making loans alone or as part of a banking syndicate.

Participants in public capital markets are usually much more dependent on public financial information than those operating outside those markets, who have more opportunities for direct contact with the management of the companies where they have invested their money. This distinction does not necessarily affect the principles governing accounting standards, particularly in striking a balance among the goals of relevance, reliability, and comparability. But it at least has the logical result of increasing the demand for transparency whenever the interests of participants in the public capital markets are taken into consideration.

In the United States, strictly speaking, US GAAP rules are imposed only on listed companies, even though in practice many other companies also apply them. Similarly in Europe, only companies issuing listed securities (stocks and/or bonds) have to apply IFRS for their consolidated accounts, at least for now. This is also the reason why countries with a long tradition of organized capital markets, such as the United States and the United Kingdom, have for a long time required more transparency from their listed companies than has been true in the countries of continental Europe or Asia.

Nonetheless, lenders, whether banks or bondholders, commonly make demands not necessarily made by shareholders. These demands often display a tendency toward prudence in considering accounts, which is the accounting equivalent of "a bird in the hand is worth two in the bush." According to the IASB's definition, prudence means "the inclusion of a degree of caution in the exercise of the judgements needed in making the estimates required under conditions of uncertainty, such that assets or income are not overstated and liabilities or expenses are not understated."[30] In other words, even if a gain is highly probable or even certain but not yet realized, it should not be booked in the accounts; whereas it is enough that a loss be probable for it to be booked.

This principle of prudence appears well adapted to the interests of creditors because they are mainly concerned as to whether future cash flow will be sufficient to reimburse outstanding debts. The primary concern of creditors is the analysis not of value but of risk: the rate of interest that is appropriate for loans to a company is essentially determined by its risk of default of payment. If a company has a very high value but a high risk of failure, as can typically be the case for technology start-ups, it may have no access to credit and can find external financing only in the form of equity.

Hence, application of the principle of prudence tends to play down the profitability of a company in a way that is suited to the needs of creditors who are primarily interested in avoiding undue optimism. But by the same token, such excessive pessimism may lead to a departure from a "fair" view, as prudence may distort the economic analysis of a company by systematically adopting pessimistic estimates, even if they are not the most likely ones. For their part, shareholders tend to be primarily interested in the analysis of value rather than of risk. Their primary goal is to maximize the value of their investment, taking into consideration all future capital gains and dividends. The accounting principle most specific to them is thus not prudence but "fairness," as it is important for them to have at any given moment the most accurate picture possible of a company. The IASB, whose approach puts investors (and, implicitly, shareholders) first, is careful to specify as much, immediately following its definition of accounting prudence quoted above by the following caveat: "However, the exercise of prudence does not allow, for example, the creation of hidden reserves or excessive provisions, the deliberate understatement of assets or income, or the deliberate overstatement of liabilities or expenses, because the financial statements would not be neutral and, therefore, not have the quality of reliability."

The difference in approach between shareholders and creditors also brings out the ambiguities of the previously highlighted requirement for relevance, as this latter implies that the accounts provide information relevant to economic analysis, but the particular kind of economic analysis involved remains to be defined. If the aim, as for creditors, is to conduct an analysis of risk, particularly the risk of default, then the goal of relevance may sometimes lead to an emphasis on the principle of prudence. But if what is at stake is primarily an assessment of value as needed by shareholders, then the principle of prudence should have less impact.

In addition, it has already been noted that the requirement for relevance cannot always be fulfilled simultaneously with the two other key requirements of reliability and comparability, which are also essential for shareholders. Investors are as attentive as other users to the reliability of financial statements, because they need to be sure that the information available to them has not been manipulated. Even a slight suspicion of uncertainty about the reliability of accounts can be enough to cause a slump in stock price, as was the case for IBM in June 2003 or Adecco, a temporary-work firm, in January 2004. Moreover, the requirement for comparability is crucial for shareholders, because one of the essential roles of financial information is to enable a rational choice for the allocation of capital among different companies. It doesn't do a shareholder much good to be familiar with and fully understand the accounts of a given company if he cannot compare its performance with that of other companies in which he might also invest.

The gaps between the interests of various users of accounts make it possible to explain many differences among various national accounting standards. In France and Germany, shareholders, particularly those who participate in public capital markets, have long had much less influence than the large commercial banks, which have been the primary sources of corporate financing for several decades. It is therefore not surprising that the principle of prudence has historically occupied a prominent place in French and German accounting standards. Conversely, in the United States, capital markets, particularly stock markets, have occupied a much more prominent position, and the "equity culture" is much stronger. Unsurprisingly, requirements for transparency have historically been more developed in the United States than in continental Europe, and the principle of fairly representing economic activity is omnipresent, whereas the principle of prudence plays only a minor role in the setting of standards. The same is true for IFRS, which are very similar to US GAAP in this respect.

Accounting Standards and Labor

Like other economic agents, employees may also be concerned by changes in certain accounting standards—even when they are not recipients of stock options. A good example of this interaction is provided by the accounting treatment of health care and other commitments made by large U.S. companies to their future pensioners.

In 1993, the FASB instituted a new US GAAP rule (FAS 106) requiring U.S. companies to change the accounting treatment of these commitments known as "post-retirement benefits other than pensions" (for example, medical and dental insurance, or life insurance). Such benefits had until then been widely granted by companies to their pensioners, which was at least partly explained by the accounting treatment as the benefits were booked as current expenses, that is, they had to be recorded not at the date on which they were contracted but at the date of actual payment, often in a distant future. For an employer, granting generous retirement benefits at the time of hiring thus had no effect on profits until a long time had elapsed.

The new FAS 106 rule required that those rights would accrue as liabilities as soon as granted. Following its adoption, commitments had to be booked at their discounted present value as soon as corresponding contracts were signed. In addition, the present value of all existing commitments already made to employees also had to be recorded as expenses. Because of the demographic structure of labor and the fact that the use of this form of deferred compensation had increased over time, future commitments made by companies were often much larger than current payments, and the adoption of the new rule therefore had the effect of reducing profits in many companies.

Some companies that were particularly affected reacted quickly, by abandoning the benefit policy they had adopted until then toward their employees and pensioners. For example, in 1992 the financial services company Primerica (now part of Citigroup) used the new accounting rule to justify ending the provision of medical coverage for pensioners, beginning in January 1993. The decision affected future pensioners as well as employees who had already retired and whose coverage by the company was not contractually guaranteed. The latter were given the option of signing up for insurance for which they would have to pay an extra price. An employee court challenge to the decision was unsuccessful.

Similar measures were taken by several dozen large U.S. companies, including such blue chips as McDonnell Douglas and Unisys. In every case, court action by employees was unsuccessful, despite severe consequences for pensioners and particularly those aged below sixty-five, the age of Medicare eligibility. In reaction, Congress in 1994 passed the Employee Retirement Income Security Act to standardize the rules applying to medical coverage for pensioners, notably providing for more disclosures to employees. However, this did not have the effect of restoring previous benefits.

Similarly, although to less brutal effect, the shift in 1993 toward

recording pension commitments as accrued liabilities under US
GAAP contributed to the decision of many U.S. companies to give
up defined-benefit pension plans for their employees in favor of
defined-contribution plans. In the former, the company commits itself to a pension amount to be paid to the employee, whereas in the
latter, the only commitment relates to the amounts to be paid to the
pension fund for the employee, but the employee bears all the risk
of a possible fall in the rate of return that would mean a decrease in
his pension. In 1979, 28 percent of employees were covered by
defined-benefit pension plans, compared with 7 percent for defined-
contribution plans. By 1998, five years into the change in the US
GAAP rule, these figures had been almost exactly reversed, to respectively 7 and 27 percent.[31]

In both cases, the new accounting standard, by forcing companies
to make a quantified estimate of its long-term commitments, gave
them an incentive to transfer as much risk as possible to their employees. This consequence took place despite the absence of any new expense. The standard had no effect on the amounts the company
would have to pay in the future, and furthermore, no new information was given to the market because information on future benefits
had already been included in disclosure notes before the adoption of
the new standards. But because of the new rule of calculation, companies anticipated a negative reaction by investors to what they would
possibly interpret as a decline in profitability, and therefore gave up
compensation practices they had willingly adopted in the past.

The Shift to "Fair Value" Accounting

The problems that may arise in the debate about accounting standards, because of the divergence of interests among users, are well illustrated by the vivid controversies over fair value accounting that
developed in Europe (extending well beyond the accounting profession) around the adoption of IFRS in 2005, and which are also developing in the United States.

The principle of "fair value" accounting involves the accounting
treatment of certain assets and liabilities in reference to market sig-
nals. The SEC defines fair value as "the amount for which an asset
could be bought or sold, or a liability could be incurred or settled, be-

tween willing parties, other than in a liquidation"; the IASB's definition is almost identical. To understand what this means in practice,
one can refer to the explanations given a few years ago by a group of
national standard-setters in anticipation of changes in international
accounting standards:[32]

- First, observable market exit prices for identical instruments are to
  be used if available (this is often referred to as "mark-to-market");

- If such prices are not available, market exit prices for similar financial instruments are to be used with appropriate adjustment for
  differences;

- Finally, if the fair value of a financial instrument cannot be based
  on observable market prices, it should be estimated using a valuation technique that is consistent with accepted economic pricing
  methodologies. Such a valuation technique should incorporate estimates and assumptions that are consistent with available information that market participants would use in setting an exit price
  for the instrument (this situation, which entails the construction of
  a financial valuation model generally involving discounting future
  cash flows, is often referred to as "mark-to-model").

The concept of fair value is common in US GAAP and extensively
used in IFRS, to a much greater extent than in pre-existing accounting
standards applicable in most continental European countries. Under
these pre-existing standards, different accounting methods were applied to different types of assets or liabilities, either fair value (for example, for listed securities held for a short duration), or historical cost
(for example, for certain securities held over a long term or for real estate investments), or not recording them at all in the financial statements (as in the case of many financial derivatives). Therefore, in
these countries the transition to IFRS has meant a significant increase
in the use of fair value accounting, which has not been easily accepted. Somewhat similarly, an extension of the scope of fair value accounting in US GAAP has been proposed by the SEC in a comprehensive new report in June 2005, and has sparked some controversy.[33]

In Europe, the IAS 32 and IAS 39 standards covering financial instruments (which are part of IFRS) have been vehemently criticized
by several banks and insurance companies, eventually leading to the

"carve-out" (i.e., deletion) of certain provisions of IAS 39 in the version endorsed by the European Union in late 2004. Specifically, the heated discussions surrounding the adoption of IAS 39 have focused on the treatment of banking assets, particularly deposit accounts (which do not bear interest in several continental European countries) and other accounts with regulated interest rates, such as savings plans for house purchases, for which presentation in terms of fair value poses some thorny problems. Some of the discussion has dealt also with the use by many banks in continental Europe of the technique of block hedging of certain risks, known as "macro-hedging." On these seemingly obscure issues, politicians involved themselves at a senior level: President Jacques Chirac of France personally wrote to the European Commission in July 2003 to express his fear that the adoption of IAS 39 would lead to "an increased dependence of the economy upon finance (*une financiarisation accrue de notre économie*), and to methods of corporate management giving too much emphasis to the short term," with "harmful consequences for financial stability."[34] In this discussion, the IASB has frequently been caricatured as a group of accounting ideologues wanting to impose "full fair value" accounting, that is, the recording of all financial assets and liabilities at their fair value. In reality, the position of the IASB was far from "full fair value": IFRS, like most European standards they replaced, are based on a hybrid model in which only some financial instruments are booked at fair value (however, the proportion is larger under IFRS than under most pre-existing standards). And in many cases, alternatives to fair value, for example, recording at historical cost, provide no greater guarantee of protecting the interests of users of accounts. It is easy to identify some shortcomings of fair value accounting, but it is much more difficult to find an alternative method that would generally be preferable.

The amount of controversy generated by fair value accounting is a perfect illustration of the divergent interests of the various users of accounts, and of the way in which choices of standards arbitrate among those interests. The principle of fair value generally favors shareholders, as they are interested above all in the value of a company and its various assets and liabilities. That probably explains why fair value has been the focus of so many of the debates about changes in accounting standards: fair value has become the symbol of the priority given to investors and shareholders in the newly adopted IFRS. Nonetheless, fair value accounting does not necessarily favor the interests of other users. Creditors, as we have seen, are more inclined toward the principle of prudence; so are banking and insurance supervisors, as we have seen earlier in the discussion on accounting and financial stability, and not by coincidence the Basel Committee of supervisors has been one of the harshest critics of IAS 39 in the European debate. Perhaps most decisively, corporate managers lose some leeway with the adoption of fair value accounting. Senior executives of continental European bank and insurance companies, especially, had many tools to "manage" their earnings and hide some risks from the financial statements before the adoption of IFRS, which are no longer available under the IAS 39 standard. Thus, far from being primarily a technical debate about the best ways to resolve hard accounting problems (and even though this dimension has been present, too), the European debate on fair value accounting has in reality been essentially a struggle about which interests accounting standards should take most into consideration. Its current outcome, the adoption of the bulk of the IAS 39 rule less the few "carved-out" provisions, is a compromise that is likely to be temporary, as pressure will build up from investors to eventually endorse the full rule, or perhaps a quasi-identical variant that would allow all parties involved to save face. And the U.S. debate on fair value accounting, following the above-mentioned SEC report of June 2005, is likely to develop along similar lines.

Accounting standards emerge from this analysis as being far from simply the result of rational, abstract considerations. Like a mirror of capitalism, they reflect the respective influence of various participants in the life of companies and their financing. While standards aim at limiting the risk of manipulation by preparers of accounts, they also impose their own biases.

But accounting standards are only one of the determinants of financial statements. Their enforcement by auditors and regulators, and the way accounts are used by various capital markets participants, are just as important. All things considered, in cases such as Enron, Parmalat, and others, the standards themselves were less at stake than bad audits and weak monitoring and use of information by financial intermediaries, investors, and regulators.

Global capitalism is currently undergoing rapid changes that affect all the species that live together in the "financial ecosystem." The role of financial information has been changed by this transformation, which has in turn raised important questions about the collective organization and supervision of capital markets, both in the United States and in Europe. While keeping in mind the choices and limits of accounting standards, the second part of this book is therefore devoted to recent and current changes in the preparation, use, and regulation of financial information.

PART II

THE CHANGING WORLD OF FINANCIAL REPORTING

CHAPTER 4

CAPITALISM IN FLUX

I t is only recently that financial reporting has become widely acknowledged as a matter of public interest. It has arguably been debated more often since 2001 than over the whole of the previous two decades. Why now? Today, as in the 1930s, the spark has been a fall in the stock market, this time the bursting of the "technology bubble," which exposed manipulation and fraud that would have gone unnoticed had there been no market crisis. But accounting scandals have roots that go beyond the market slump, and they should not be seen as isolated events. The controversy over the accounting treatment of stock options in the United States began as early as 1993, before the beginning of the technology bubble, which is usually dated from the initial public offering (IPO) of Netscape, Inc., in August 1995. And the European decision to adopt International Financial Reporting Standards (IFRS) was made in early 2000, before the beginning of the market downturn and well before the collapse of Enron.

The newfound interest in financial information, whether linked to corporate scandals or to controversies about standard-setting, can be interpreted as the mirror image of a wider transformation of market capitalism, which can be observed in all developed economies. The unprecedented accounting scandals of the early 2000s are, in this sense, a telling symptom of a deeper change. To understand the present and future stakes of financial reporting, we need to broaden our perspective to include structural trends affecting today's corporations. As it would be overambitious, and ultimately impossible, to aim at presenting here a comprehensive picture of all current changes in global (or only Western) financial systems, we concentrate on the typologies that can be used to characterize relations among the various participants in the system. We then develop some items that are particularly relevant for the future of financial reporting, such as the increased speed of change of corporate boundaries through mergers, acquisitions, and restructuring; technological and financial innovations; and new patterns for the compensation of senior executives.

The Shifting Fault Lines of Financial Systems

In the 1980s and 1990s, an influential school of thought succeeded in describing the various incarnations of capitalism in different countries by concentrating on differences inherited from history and differing political institutions, or "varieties of capitalism" as termed by Peter Hall and David Soskice.[1] A stylized version of this description was the influential book published in the early 1990s by Michel Albert, a French economist, under the title *Capitalism vs. Capitalism*. The book presented a stark geographical contrast between two systems for financing business. On one side was the "Rhine model," referring to West Germany as an exemplar of this tendency, with all-powerful commercial banks, a dense network of small- and medium-sized family companies, and widespread employee participation in decision making. On the other side was the "Anglo-American model," with all-powerful financial markets and an obsession with short-term profit. The popularity of Albert's book on both sides of the Atlantic reflected its relevance at the time, in the context of the German and (even more strikingly) Japanese manufacturing successes of the late 1980s, of the recent memories of the 1987 U.S. stock market crash, along with the collapse of the Polly Peck business empire in the United Kingdom, all soon to be followed by other corporate disasters involving BCCI and the Maxwell Group. In the early 1990s, it seemed that some national models of capitalism were more efficient than others, and that reliance on public markets was not necessarily positively correlated with a high level of business efficiency.

After a decade and a half, however, Albert's sharp geographical contrast probably no longer corresponds to today's reality. The two countries presumed to embody the two opposite models of capitalism, Germany and the United States, both have undergone spectacular changes, and each of them has arguably adopted part of the features of the other.

In Germany, the erstwhile figurehead of the "Rhine model," the privileged links that bound companies to banks have been gradually weakened. Banks began in the 1990s to shed their large holdings in the country's major industrial concerns, and the government accelerated this trend by removing related tax advantages. Deutsche Bank, the former flagship of the "Rhine model," founded in Berlin in 1870 (almost simultaneously with Bismarck's German Empire) to counter the influence of London-based institutions, has lost most of its specific German features and now essentially resembles the large U.S. investment banks. Other leading German banks have disappeared or lost much of their stature. Dresdner Bank was swallowed by the Allianz insurance group in 2001. Bayerische HypoVereinsBank (HVB) was acquired in 2005 by Italy's Unicredito. Commerzbank has been considered a likely takeover target for several years. And the system of public regional banks (*Landesbanken*) lost crucial federal government guarantees in 2005 following a ruling by the European Union's competition authorities. Since the creation of the euro in 1999, most of the powers of the Bundesbank, the country's once all-powerful central bank, have been transferred to the European Central Bank which, although located in Frankfurt, has Germany as only one of many stakeholders. The decision centers of major industrial companies are also less exclusively concentrated in Germany. In the late 1990s, the iconic Daimler-Benz group transformed itself into a German-American company with one foot in Michigan through its merger with Chrysler; Daimler's former aerospace subsidiary DASA (Deutsche Aerospace AG) became one component of the European Aeronautics Defence and Space company (EADS); Mannesmann was acquired by Vodafone; and chemistry giant Hoechst merged with Rhône-Poulenc to form Aventis, which later lost whatever remained of its German identity when it merged with France's Sanofi and its headquarters were transferred from Strasbourg to Paris in 2004. In early 2005, the CEO of Deutsche Börse, Germany's national stock exchange, was ousted from his job by London-based hedge-fund shareholders in what was described by *BusinessWeek* magazine as an "amazing coup." As if those were not enough, the codetermination (*Mitbestimmung*) system, which enables elected employee representatives to participate in strategic decision making, is going through a major crisis exemplified by the scandals at Volkswagen in mid-2005, and its earlier image as an exemplary social arrangement has been severely eroded.

A similar story can be told for Japan, which Albert put alongside Germany as a variant of the same broad institutional pattern. Japan experienced several banking collapses, Nissan's restructuring by Renault's Carlos Ghosn, Sony's appointment of a non-Japanese CEO, and the waning of influence of the Ministry of Economy, Trade and Industry (METI, formerly MITI, Japan's main economic ministry). But it is only part of a broader picture. At least equally interesting is what has happened in the United States during the same period, and which can in many ways be described as a growing prevalence of features that Albert and others once attributed to the "Rhine model." In today's America, business networks have arguably acquired a degree of power that contradicts certain characteristics usually attributed to "Anglo-American capitalism." At the top, links between government and large companies, an essential "Rhine" hallmark, may have grown stronger than at any time since the 1929 crash. This is evidenced by the influence of corporate lobbyists on policy, as well as by the career of many of the current administration's main figures who came to Washington, D.C., from previous positions as corporate CEOs—be it Vice President Dick Cheney at Halliburton, Treasury Secretary Paul O'Neill at Alcoa and his successor John Snow at CSX, or Commerce Secretary Carlos Gutierrez at food producer Kellogg.[2] As more specifically regards corporate financing, the rise of private equity and venture capital also increases the Rhenish flavor of the U.S. economy. In this form of financing, relations between individuals are of major importance and specialized funds play a role for technology companies, which is in some ways comparable to that of banks for family enterprises of the German *Mittelstand*. Moreover, in these technology companies the distribution of shares among all employees contributes to a corporate culture of consensus which, although very different from the German *Mitbestimmung* system, also marks a new kind of relationship between managers and employees. At the same time, a spectacular series of mergers has been taking place in the banking sector. Citicorp merged with Travelers in 1998 to form Citigroup, Bank of America merged with FleetBoston in 2003 and purchased MBNA in 2005, and JP Morgan Chase merged with Bank One in 2004. It is too early to tell how the emergence of these banking giants will affect the U.S. economy, but what is sure is that the landscape of commercial banking in Albert's time, with strong players in Germany and fragmented ones in the United States, has been spectacularly reversed.

The United States, Germany, and the other developed countries now display mixed characteristics. They are neither totally "Rhine" nor totally "Anglo-American," following Michel Albert's patterns, but blend elements of the two systems, depending on the company, the sector, and the point in the business cycle. In the industrialized world at least, the geographical approach no longer seems the best way of characterizing the structure of the economy.

Possibly more relevant for the present time than geographical contrasts is a comparison between two distinct dynamics that simultaneously exist within each large developed economy, the terms for which we borrow from Raghuram Rajan and Luigi Zingales.[3] On one side are "relationship-based" financing systems, in which relations between individuals, typically established in school or through social or political connections, play the key role in the allocation of external financing of companies. On the other side are what Rajan and Zingales call "arm's-length" financing systems, in which personal relations are not decisive and economic decisions are made in an impersonal or downright anonymous manner. This is the case, for example, when an investor on the public markets chooses to buy or sell stocks or bonds without cultivating any personal relationship with the companies in which he invests. According to this analytic framework, organized capital markets are representative of "arm's-length" capitalism, whereas financing by commercial banks, private equity funds, or the government, are characteristic of "relationship-based" capitalism.

As Rajan and Zingales demonstrate, neither of these two models is superior to the other in absolute terms. Rather, their respective strengths and weaknesses show up in different contexts. For example, in circumstances of capital shortage, prevalence of small- or medium-sized companies, legal systems offering low levels of protection, limited openness of borders, and a relatively low level of innovation, relationship-based capitalism is generally more effective. Conversely, where there are more developed markets, larger and more organized companies, more effective systems of legal protection, and more frequent and radical innovations, arm's-length capitalism offers better results.

This difference in performance is due in particular to arm's-length capitalism's greater capacity for what economists since Joseph Schumpeter (1883–1950) term "creative destruction." In the case of a sudden change in the environment, due for example to the emergence of new technologies, relationship-based capitalism devotes excessive resources to the defense of doomed companies and too few to newly formed ones that may be more suited to the new context, whereas arm's-length capitalism basically has no problem with the incumbents' disappearance from the stage and can generously finance better-adapted new entrants. By way of comparison, in circumstances of fairly regular growth in a stable, reasonably closed environment, the complex and costly legal and financial arrangements that make an arm's-length financing system possible may not be justified, and a relationship-based system is likely to be economically more effective.

France, in a somewhat surprising way, exemplifies the (unfinished) transition from a relationship-based to an arm's-length system. In the period following the Second World War, it broadly followed the relationship-based model.[4] The penurious circumstances of reconstruction strengthened the role of the large banks, stable family stock ownership, and the state, in a way similar to what happened simultaneously in Germany or Italy. Powerful business empires were created by entrepreneurs with privileged access to ministries and (state-owned) banks. This happened in industries dependent on the state because of public procurement or regulation (Dassault in fighter jets, Bouygues in construction and later media and telecoms, Lagardère in military procurement and media), or even in nonregulated industries: the state-owned Crédit Lyonnais played an instrumental role in the creation of LVMH (Luxury) by Bernard Arnault and of PPR and Casino (retail), respectively by François Pinault and Jean-Charles Naouri. And, true to Rajan and Zingales's characterization of relationship-based systems, the state and banks wasted enormous resources in huge corporate bailouts, such as the steel industry in the

1970s, carmaker Renault or paper mill La Chapelle-Darblay in the 1980s, Crédit Lyonnais itself in the 1990s, and Alstom, the engineering group, in the 2000s.

However, things have been changing enormously since the early 1980s, and the French economy has largely opened itself to market mechanisms. In less than twenty years, the number of individual shareholders has nearly quadrupled to reach a total of close to six million, or one-tenth of the population.[5] The market capitalization of companies listed on the Paris stock exchange has increased from an average of less than 12 percent of GDP in the 1970s to 16 percent in the 1980s (in spite of the nationalizations of 1982–83), 45 percent in the 1990s, and 97 percent in the early 2000s.[6] Simultaneously, government ownership has been sharply reduced. Among the twenty largest French companies in terms of market capitalization, two-thirds are either companies that have been or are in the process of being privatized or the product of mergers in which a privatized company was a major component. The "hard cores" of shareholders, which had been put in place during the first wave of the first privatizations in the mid-1980s to stave off foreign takeovers, have been almost completely dismantled, and the proportion of foreign shareholders in large listed companies has grown spectacularly during the same period—from around 10 percent to above 40 percent. In parallel, the powers of the securities regulator have been considerably increased, and the judicial system, though far from perfect, has become somewhat more reliable.

The bottom line is that all major industrialized economies now present a mix of relationship-based and arm's-length systems, in Rajan and Zingales's classification (while most emerging economies, such as China, remain almost entirely relationship-based). The cultural attitudes of the business community remain starkly influenced by the past, more arm's-length in the United States and more relationship-based in Germany, Japan, or France; but the underlying economic realities are much more similar across the developed world than they were even as recently as one decade ago. In the realm of financial reporting, the symbol of this unification has been the adoption of IFRS in the European Union, that is, of a system of accounting standards that does not differ considerably from what existed previously in the United States and the United Kingdom. And this sense of unity also means that most developed economies feel the same impact of the more recent transformations of capitalism, to which we now turn our attention.

New Forces at Play

The late 1990s and early 2000s are likely to be remembered as times of tremendous changes in the developed world's corporate and financial landscape. As previously mentioned, we focus here on only a few traits of these transformations in the business environment, which have a distinctive impact on the way companies prepare and report their financial statements.

A Flurry of Mergers and Acquisitions

Since the early 1990s, the pace of mergers and acquisitions (M&A) among large companies has reached fever pitch, and even the bursting of the technology bubble has barely slowed it. In the United States, the yearly flow of M&A activity has risen from an average level of $225 billion yearly in the decade 1985–1994 to almost $900 billion on average over 1995–2004. Even if one excludes the "bubble" years from 1997 to 2001, the yearly average is still a staggering $563 billion, or a +150 percent increase on the decade before.[7] And six of the ten largest European market capitalizations are the products of mega-mergers that occurred in the past decade: BP (merger with Amoco and Arco, 1998–99), Vodafone (merger with Mannesmann, 1999), Total (merger with Fina and Elf, 1998 and 1999), GlaxoSmithKline (merger between GlaxoWellcome and SmithKline Beecham, 2000), Novartis (Ciba-Sandoz merger, 1996), and Sanofi-Aventis (created in 2004, and the two components of which themselves resulted from almost simultaneous mergers in 1998).[8]

These spectacular combinations are only the tip of the iceberg. Perhaps even more important are the constant changes of boundaries that affect most large multinational companies. Vivendi Universal, now mainly a media and telecoms group, is an example of such frantic moves. Under the successive leaderships of Jean-Marie Messier and Jean-René Fourtou, it bought media groups Havas in 1999 and

Seagram-Universal in 2000, then sold most of its interests in publishing, cinema, and entertainment in 2003; bought the U.S. publishing company Houghton Mifflin in 2001 and sold it in 2002; from 1999 on, established a diversified—but never profitable—group of commercial Internet sites, and then sold or liquidated most of them; since 2000, spun off the former global business of Générale des Eaux in water, energy, urban transport, and waste treatment, renamed Veolia Environnement in 2003, now France's twenty-fifth-largest company by market capitalization; and in 2005 became the majority owner of Maroc Telecom, Morocco's dominant phone operator. Although this may seem an extreme example, most large companies are now subjected to constant waves of expansion and restructuring, which result in unending modifications of corporate borders through mergers, acquisitions, divestitures, spin-offs, or joint ventures.

This perpetual change of the boundaries of large corporations means the scope of consolidation never remains stable, and therefore, from one year to the next, consolidated financial statements refer to different sets of businesses. As a result, accounts are increasingly difficult to compare over time, in the sense that financial statements do not let investors well understand changes in performance of continued operations of a stable entity or group of entities.

To compensate for this, companies do release some information in addition to the standardized financial statements, through what are known as pro forma accounts, giving a retrospective picture of what the figures for preceding years would have been under the current scope of consolidation, thus providing a basis for comparison. But in most cases, these pro forma figures are not subject to accounting standards and are not subject to audits, as the variety of possible configurations would be too great to be encapsulated in one uniform rule or would lead to an excessive burden in terms of calculation. In other words, pro forma figures may help to better understand business dynamics, but they are also inherently unreliable because of the absence of standardization. We take again the example of Suez, the French-Belgian diversified group. In its annual report for 1999, with accounts compared to 1997 and 1998, it published revenue for its waste-management unit of €2.22 billion in 1997 and €3.53 billion in 1998; but in the 1998 annual report, the published figures of revenue from waste management had been, respectively, €3.46 billion for 1997 and

€5.12 billion for 1998. The difference is due to different scopes used for the calculation of pro forma figures between one annual report and the next. Examples of this kind are innumerable. Moreover, the hundreds of companies that constitute large multinational groups often exchange financial flows with one another, which are eliminated on consolidation. This has an additional impact when they enter or leave the scope of consolidation. In short, constant changes in the scope of consolidation necessarily diminish the legibility of accounts and the external observer's ability to assess performance in the medium term. There is no simple solution to this problem.

Another important consequence of the proliferation of mergers and acquisitions is the appearance of massive amounts recorded as goodwill on the asset side of corporate balance sheets. Goodwill, as has been mentioned earlier, is the difference between the price paid by an acquiring company and its share in the net asset value of the target at the time of purchase. When the price paid is hefty, the goodwill can weigh heavily on the balance sheet of the combined entity. For example, on the balance sheet of France Telecom at the end of 2001, goodwill amounted to €35 billion, or one-third of the total fixed assets of €104 billion, following the acquisition of Orange, a wireless phone operator, and of other companies at the height of the market bubble. The problem is that each component of goodwill, once recorded on the balance sheet, may change every year in a largely un-predictable way. Under IFRS and US GAAP alike, these items must be evaluated annually, and written down if a loss in value is identified. In 2002, AOL Time Warner thus wrote down goodwill for a whopping $99.8 billion, thereby recording the largest loss ever by a U.S. com-pany. Even several years after the collapse of the technology bubble, goodwill amounts remain far from negligible. For companies in-cluded in France's SBF 120 stock index, the average recorded goodwill was equivalent to 54 percent of shareholders' equity as of December 31, 2002.[9] This introduces a degree of volatility into financial state-ments that is difficult to control.

An Outburst of Disruptive Technologies

Information technology (IT) has a huge impact on financial report-ing. On the one hand, accounting rules must adapt to the accelerated pace of the development of new technology-related activities in companies. On the other hand, accounting practitioners are themselves heavy users of IT, which has transformed their profession in a variety of ways.

IT-intensive businesses often raise difficult questions with regard to the preparation of their financial statements. For example, the dematerialization of exchanges conducted on the World Wide Web sometimes makes it difficult to unequivocally assign revenue to a given location. Take the example of a global company that displays advertising banners on a website consulted by Internet users from all around the world, and bills advertising customers through different national subsidiaries. Should the revenue be recorded in the country where the users are, or where the advertisers are based, or where the banner-distributing servers are located, or in the place (supposing there is a single one) where the site was created? There is no single answer, and the lines between the different options can be blurred. Moreover, these questions are not limited to the realm of financial information, and they have their equivalents in tax matters. For example, the U.S. tax authorities have not yet fully determined their response to the special challenges posed by the Internet, which has enjoyed a regularly renewed moratorium on sales tax after a landmark 1992 Supreme Court decision (which some states would like to see reversed today). A similar choice was also made on a global scale for customs duties on electronic data transmission.

Non-cash transactions, such as the bartering of services between companies, provide another illustration of the accounting challenges posed by Internet-based operations. This kind of transaction has existed for a long time in the media. For example, a radio channel may promote a new movie and receive in return the appearance of its logo on the movie poster, with no exchange of cash. The essential requirement for this kind of transaction is that the marginal cost of production be very small, which is frequently the case for Web-based operations. Internet media offer a multiplicity of advertising platforms that can disseminate information at a negligible cost, and their commercial conditions have tended to be quite volatile, at least until recently, which generates multiple opportunities for barter transactions. The snag is that the accounting treatment of such transactions is difficult to control. The price attributed to the bartered services is arbitrary, because there is by definition no exchange of cash in the transaction. Several Internet companies, including, so it seems, AOL in its early days, have therefore abused the possibilities offered by barter and attributed an excessive price to the advertising space exchanged in their accounts. They could therefore arbitrarily inflate their revenue, and because at the time of the dot-com bubble many evaluations were made by applying a direct multiple to revenue, this had a significant impact on what many analysts saw as these companies' intrinsic value. In one single transaction between AOL and the online job-offer website www.monster.com, the overestimation of revenue is said to have reached some $100 million.[10] As with Enron's accounting for its trading revenue, this kind of accounting trick does not change the profit realized but gives a misleading picture of revenue. The telecommunications operator Qwest went even further by destroying the symmetry between the two sides of the barter transaction. The revenue was immediately recorded into the accounts, but the corresponding charges were spread out over several years. The company thus recorded an entirely artificial profit in the first year, balanced by losses in subsequent years. The total fictitious revenue booked by Qwest, according to the SEC, amounted to approximately $144 million in 2000 and 2001.[11]

In this example as in others, accounting irregularities have been made possible by the emergence of new economic activities on the Internet for which there was no pre-existing accounting standard. Ill-intentioned executives could then distort the picture provided by their company's accounts by freely choosing whichever accounting policy best suited their aims. In other words, the accelerated pace of technological innovation means that accounting standard-setting institutions have to react much more quickly in order to limit as much as possible the opportunities of misrepresentation.

New technologies have also led to the recording of many intangible items in the assets of companies, in addition to the goodwill from acquisitions as previously discussed. These intangible assets, such as patents, in-house developed software, or new brands, raise delicate questions of evaluation for accountants. As their proportion in the value of companies increases as an inevitable consequence of the dissemination of IT and other new technologies, the preparation of financial statements that are both relevant and reliable becomes ever more difficult. No one has yet found a general and unchallengeable method for the evaluation of intangibles, the value of which is as volatile as their name suggests. To quote Georges Barthès de Ruyter, a former chairman of the IASC (the IASB's predecessor body), "The situation has become disquieting. Companies record more and more hot air on their balance sheets, and on this hot air the wind blows ever faster."[12]

In addition to the difficulties it creates in the preparation of accounts, the spread of IT has a different kind of impact: such technologies are widely used by financial information professionals themselves. The combination of the use of databases and of the Internet makes possible a considerable increase in the volume of financial information published by companies and in the ability of various market participants to process that information. Thanks to IT, the preparation of financial information is in the process of evolving from craft to mass production.

The use of databases and of Enterprise Resource Planning (ERP) software has already led to some convergence between financial and management accounting, which had long stayed at least partly separate. Now, in most large corporations, essentially the same sets of data now feed the published financial information on the one hand, and that used for internal controls and cost analysis on the other. This also means that the auditors' work increasingly consists of verifying not only the data themselves but also the IT systems that collect, aggregate, and process them. More recently, the Internet has had a profound impact on the way financial information is disseminated, as listed companies now can (and in many cases must) make accessible online almost all their publications and financial notices, and much more. Downloadable broadcasts of shareholders' meetings and presentations to financial analysts are more widespread, thereby increasing the quantity of information available to the financial community and the general public, while simultaneously decreasing the cost of access to it.

Moreover, this represents only a first stage. In the near future, accounting and financial reporting may become much more extensively "automated" and disseminated on the Internet in the form of computerized databases rather than printed or downloadable text. Already, most companies store all their financial information in databases, and users of accounts also create series of data and spread-sheets for the purposes of financial analysis. The missing link is a standardized interface. This gap is likely to be closed soon, thereby enabling analysts to carry out their number-crunching much more easily than before. One such interface has been under development since 1999 by a consortium that now brings together more than two hundred large companies under the name XBRL (eXtensible Business Reporting Language, referring to the XML Internet protocol that enables the online exchange of information structured in the form of databases). XBRL permits the automated treatment of accounting data according to a reference framework (known as "taxonomy") tailor-made for each set of accounting standards, for example, IFRS or US GAAP.[13] The prospect for a generalization of such tools in the next few years is high.

The availability of financial information in an easily usable form has the potential of enabling anybody to conduct self-designed processing and analysis, somewhat in the way that the use of automatic translation devices partially reduces the need for professional translators. Of course, as suggested in this parallel the change will not be complete, at least in a first phase—anyone who has used translation software knows that human intervention remains necessary. It will nonetheless have consequences for the uses of financial information and on the organization of the accounting and financial research professions.

The new uses of IT may also affect the periodicity of financial disclosures. The European Commission encountered stiff resistance in 2002–2003 when it proposed to mandate quarterly publication of financial statements for listed companies, as has long been the case in the United States, and the proposal finally had to be withdrawn at the end of 2003. However, an increase in the frequency of publication is an inevitable consequence of the spread of real-time information systems inside companies. There will inevitably be pressure from investors in the future for more disclosure than the current quarterly pace of publication, gradually approaching real time at least for certain categories of data.

There is a legitimate question as to how much an increased frequency of disclosure may change corporate behavior. Some observers, both in Europe and in the United States (Bill Crist, the former chairman of CalPERS, is an example), claim that too-frequent releases of intermediate results may foster a myopic form of management, which focuses only on short-term profits rather than long-term interests. This debate often verges on the emotional, between advocates of transparency on the one hand, and accusers of the alleged short-termism of financial markets on the other. In any event, there is little doubt that information technology will in the future enable an almost real-time availability of current financial data with little effort, and that many investors will claim interest in this kind of information.

An Outbreak of Financial Engineering

The extraordinary growth of financial engineering over the last few years would have been difficult to imagine only two decades ago. With the deregulation and growth of financial markets, financial innovation has flourished, and increasingly complex tools and schemes are provided to companies by banks and by sundry consulting and advisory firms. New financial techniques, partly referred to under the obscure category of "structured finance," enable companies to slim down their balance sheets by simultaneously eliminating some elements of both assets and liabilities, with the effect of modifying their debt and/or return on equity ratios. Some already mentioned practices, such as leasing, sale-leasebacks to special-purpose entities, or securitization,[14] fall into this category. As illustrated by Enron, such schemes have been used by some to distort their financial statements, but they also have many legitimate uses. They may result in greater efficiency through the optimization of financial costs or because of their risk-sharing effect, such as in the case of securitization. Thus, asset-backed financing can reduce the risk for lenders and thus lead to a lower interest rate than would have been possible with an ordinary bank loan. These techniques have spread considerably in recent years. For example, the volume of securitization transactions in Europe alone has increased tenfold from the early 1990s to the early 2000s.

Another rapidly expanding activity is the use of financial derivatives, which enable the contractual transfer of exposure to specific risks. These contracts, which are either standardized or negotiated on a one-to-one ("over-the-counter") basis, are generally entered into for prudential or insurance purposes. Frequently hedged risks include fluctuations in interest rates, stock prices, currencies, or commodities and raw materials prices. More recently, more complex instruments have appeared, such as credit derivatives, which cover the risks of a debtor's default, or weather derivatives, for the purpose of protection against meteorological risk. Futures contracts (i.e., future purchases and sales), options, or combinations of contracts such as "swaps," "caps," "floors," and so forth, are more and more commonly used. In its June 2005 quarterly report, the Bank for International Settlements estimated that risks covered by derivatives around the world amounted to $300 trillion, 20 percent higher than one year before. This is a mind-boggling amount, as becomes clear if it is compared, for example, to global gross domestic product ($40 trillion in 2004) or global market capitalization ($40.4 trillion at the end of March 2005).[15]

Here, too, accountants often find themselves ill-equipped to describe the complexity of all such transactions, whose valuation is notoriously difficult and whose recording on balance sheets has long been optional or even prohibited in many countries, just as for stock options in the United States. The overall impact of derivatives is made less easy to assess by the fact that it goes in two opposite directions. On the one hand, their growing use spreads risks within the financial system and may thus increase its overall stability. In his speech accepting the Nobel Prize in Economics in 1997, Robert Merton stated that derivatives "had improved the efficiency [of the financial system] by increasing opportunities for sharing risks, by reducing transaction costs, and by lowering information and agency costs."[16] Federal Reserve Chairman Alan Greenspan has also supported the idea that credit derivatives provide a positive contribution to financial stability, for example by diluting the effects of large corporate defaults like those of Enron or WorldCom. On the other hand, derivatives, like all complex devices that are difficult for the layman to understand, can also be misused by unscrupulous executives or may simply lead to mistakes in judgment because of their technical complexity. In any event, their use introduces another layer of intricacy, not to say illegibility, into corporate financial statements. Experience has shown that derivatives, although originating in a desire for insurance to hedge against financial risks, have in many cases been poorly controlled and become themselves the source of very significant risks. This was sadly illustrated by Procter & Gamble in 1993 ($150 million lost); Orange

County, California, in 1994 ($1.7 billion lost); Barings in 1995 (more than 800 million pounds lost by a single trader, Nick Leeson, leading to the absorption of this 230–year old institution by the ING group); or French reinsurance company SCOR in 2002. Warren Buffett had some reason to famously call credit derivatives "financial weapons of mass destruction" in his annual letter to Berkshire Hathaway shareholders in March 2003.

With every advance in financial engineering, a new challenge is thus posed to accountants and standard-setters, who must determine how to deal with such innovations. The Enron case illustrated the difficulties of avoiding improper uses of deconsolidating arrangements. Stock options are another example in which the technical difficulties posed by their accounting treatment served as a pretext to maintain the strange status quo in which a significant expense was not expensed at all. The recording of derivatives at their fair value also has been an important aspect of the controversy over the European Union's adoption of IFRS, and most specifically, the IAS 39 standard on financial instruments. Just as it struggles to keep up with the pace of technological innovation, accounting practice often finds it difficult to adapt swiftly to financial innovation, which has been constant for decades and has no prospect of slowing down in the coming years.

An Explosion of "Infectious Greed"

"An infectious greed seemed to grip much of our business community. Our historical guardians of financial information were overwhelmed. Too many corporate executives sought ways to harvest some of those stock market gains. As a result, the highly desirable spread of shareholding and options among business managers perversely created incentives to artificially inflate reported earnings in order to keep stock prices high and rising. (. . .) It is not that humans have become any more greedy than in generations past. It is the avenues to express greed had grown so enormously."

In his semi-annual congressional testimony on July 16, 2002, Federal Reserve Chairman Alan Greenspan, probably the most influential figure in the world financial community at the time, pointed with unaccustomed clarity to the disease he identified as having attacked the U.S. financial system. Indeed, the thoughts and actions of higher executives around the developed world seem more and more determined by their compensation schemes, as these have become more sophisticated and have increased the opportunities for large-scale enrichment, to the extent that the buildup of these compensation schemes has become a key factor in the transformation of capitalism.

Here again, stock options are at center stage. In the preceding chapter, we saw the difficulties and controversies surrounding their accounting treatment in corporate income statements. But the reason for stock options appearing in the first place is that this tool, together with similar share-based compensation mechanisms, both establishes a direct financial link between the financial interests of management and the company's share price, and at the same time provides the possibility of large financial gains for its beneficiaries.

By apparently aligning the interests of management with those of the shareholders, stock options were supposed to guarantee that the former would make the best possible decisions for the benefit of the latter. This alleged feature had drawn unqualified enthusiasm from some observers who candidly imagined that stock options could provide the "silver bullet" to what economists call the agency problem, namely, the potential divergence of interests between shareholders and managers. The agency problem is at the root of all the debates about corporate governance, and is as old as capitalism itself. It was described (in hindsight with a little exaggeration) by Adam Smith in a famous passage of the *Wealth of Nations*, which refers in particular to the eventful bankruptcy of the South Sea Company in 1720:

> The directors of such [joint stock] companies, however, being the managers rather of other people's money than of their own, it cannot well be expected that they should watch over it with the same anxious vigilance with which the partners in a private copartnery frequently watch over their own. Like the stewards of a rich man, they are apt to consider attention to small matters as not for their master's honour, and very easily give themselves a dispensation from having it. Negligence and profusion, therefore, must always prevail, more or less, in the management of the affairs of such a company. It is upon this account that joint stock companies for foreign trade have seldom been able to maintain the competition against private adventurers.[17]

Michael Jensen, a Harvard economist and one of the most enthusiastic advocates of stock options, famously justified stock options in
the early 1990s by asserting that "on average, corporate America pays
its most important leaders like bureaucrats. Is it any wonder then that
so many CEOs act like bureaucrats rather than the value-maximizing
entrepreneurs companies need?"[18] But in the real world, stock options
seem to have led a large number of executives to abandon prudence,
to focus on short-term targets, and to implement highly aggressive accounting policies. In short, the incentive device turned an incentive
into fraud. Managers were effectively encouraged to use all possible
means to get the share price to a very high point at the precise moment they could exercise their options, rather than over the longer
term. With the opportunity to acquire considerable wealth in a single
transaction, which in many cases could insure them a comfortable living for the rest of their life, more than a few managers lost the concern
to take care of the future of the company that was in their custody. In
fact, empirical evidence seems to confirm that earnings management
(measured as the shifting of expenses or profits from one year to another) is correlated with high levels of distribution of stock options to
executives. Even more disturbing, this distortion is particularly pronounced in years in which the options are exercised.[19]

In the United States, the value of stock options held by executives and
managers was still $80 billion by the end of 2002, in the midst of a mar-
ket slump.[20] Some individual grants have been staggering: the stock option compensation awarded for the sole year 2000 to Sanford Weill, the
CEO of Citigroup, amounted to $224 million, and other executives re-
ceived amounts of the same order.[21] In such circumstances, it should not
come as a surprise that a sense of "there is no tomorrow" did develop—
all the more because, at the same time, risks of takeover bids and high
rates of turnover at the top of U.S. companies did not encourage executives to display a long-term commitment to their employer.

The debate on executive compensation is certainly one of the most
difficult among those that have arisen recently to define the business
environment. The link between compensation and performance is far
from being straightforward, as good executives are often justly re-
warded, but also bad executives tend to be greedier. The *Financial
Times*, not customarily inclined toward anti-business demagoguery,
calculated in July 2002, in a sample of twenty-five companies that had

gone bankrupt in the United States since January 2001, that executives had collectively accumulated more than $3.3 billion in salary and stock options in 1999, 2000, and 2001.[22] Anger against "fat cats" has become a recurring theme on both sides of the Atlantic. There seems to be a disquieting overall correlation between the weakness of shareholders, the level of fraud, and the amount of executive compensation. One empirical study concluded that companies that had experienced difficulties with the SEC over their accounts paid their executives on average 69 percent more than other companies of comparable size and sector of activity.[23] Another study focused on the growth of executive pay between 1993 and 2003 and found that it was most rapid at companies with weak governance and few shareholder rights.[24] The same study found that the aggregate pay to the top five executives rose from an average 5 percent of consolidated earnings in 1993–95 to about 10 percent in 2001–2003 in U.S. listed corporations, leading *New York Times* columnist Nicholas Kristof to speak of "hijacking of corporate wealth by top managers," calling them "captains of piracy."[25] And average total CEO pay packages in the United States, after a drop in 2002 and 2003, have started rising again in 2004, with no more obvious correlation than in the previous period between pay increases and improvements in corporate performance.[26]

All this has a direct effect on the preparation of accounts. As Alan Greenspan stated in his testimony, misconceived incentive schemes can drive corporate executives to manipulate and distort their company's financial statements. A large number of accounting frauds, from the almost harmless to the downright disastrous, can be traced back to a wish to optimize an element of personal compensation, which in turn is often linked to the ownership of shares or stock options. The apparently irreversible development of share-based compensation (which continues to spread even in companies that, like Microsoft in July 2003, have given up the use of stock options as such) has therefore introduced an additional risk factor affecting the reliability of corporate financial reporting.

A Transformation of the Financial Ecosystem

Seen in the light of these new features of the business environment, the accounting scandals of the early 2000s take on a clearer significance. They were not only a temporary disorder due to the inflation of stock prices but also a set of symptoms of Western capitalism's adjustment crisis in the face of the many transforming influences to which it was, and still is, subjected. The accelerated rate of change of the boundaries of corporations, of technological and financial innovations, and of managers' incentives through the spread of share-based compensation, are some of these shocks, the effect of which has been a profound transformation of the financial ecosystem.

Whether this is unqualified bad news is another question. For doomsayers, capitalism has spun out of control; its mechanisms have become structurally unstable and are fatally undermined by the contradictory interests of its participants. But a less pessimistic view would point out that, in response to the rapid changes, the financial system has already developed some defense mechanisms against the principal risks of distortion and fraud. In part through regulations, in part through self-regulation and social control on the behavior of executives, these risks could be gradually mitigated and lose their systemic nature.

The capital markets have shown their resilience in the face of scandals as much as in the face of the geopolitical shifts following the September 11 attacks. Even though the shock was severe, the collapse predicted by some did not actually take place. But the financial system of tomorrow will be very different from that of yesterday. To further our understanding of this changing landscape, we now move from the preparation of accounts in corporations to their verification by external auditors, which is the topic covered in the next chapter.

CHAPTER 5

AUDITORS UNDER SCRUTINY

Financial information is crucially dependent on accounting standards, but if those standards are to have any effect, there must be people to enforce them. This is the essential function of external auditors, who assure shareholders and the general public that a company's financial statements "fairly present its financial position"—even though others also play a backup supervisory role, notably government regulatory authorities.

Auditors have been struck full force by the accounting scandals of the early 2000s, of which they have been victims and also, ironically enough, beneficiaries. The Enron bankruptcy led to the disintegration of Andersen, which in the United States alone had 26,000 employees, more than Enron's 20,000, an astonishing "collateral damage" with deep and long-lasting consequences as this chapter will illustrate. And in late 2003, revelations about the Italian food-processing company Parmalat and its brazen manipulations made it clear that flaws in auditing systems were by no means specific to the United States. Audit firms have been durably weakened by these and other developments. Simultaneously, they have also benefited: new regulations such as the U.S. Sarbanes-Oxley Act of July 2002 have increased the demand for their services and boosted their revenue.

Audit is a strange business. Because of the highly specialized skills it requires, it is largely inaccessible to the uninitiated. As a result, the members of the audit profession have acquired the habit of taking care by themselves for both drafting the common rules for their profession and organizing their enforcement. But at the same time, the quality of the accounts of publicly listed corporations is legitimately considered a matter of public interest—at least since the 1929 crash, as we have seen—and the public therefore has a right to know whether audit tasks are properly performed. This tension between a technical specialization that fosters self-regulation and the common interest that makes auditing a matter of public policy lies at the heart of the organization of the profession. Another equally fundamental tension, of course, is the one between the audit firm and the audited company. The auditor provides a service to its clients and simultaneously acts as a watchdog of these same clients' conduct. As former SEC Chairman Arthur Levitt once wryly remarked, the role of the auditor is "sublimely unique": "In most professions, the customer is always right. But auditors are required to tell their customers when they're wrong."[1] Auditors have sometimes been compared to policemen, whose task is to enforce law (i.e., accounting standards) and order in corporate accounting. But they are policemen with neither weapons nor handcuffs, and whose paymasters are the very people they are supposed to control.

In the aftermath of the Enron collapse, self-regulation of the audit profession was essentially replaced by a variety of models of public oversight, most notably in the United States as a consequence of the Sarbanes-Oxley Act. But beyond this obvious change, many unresolved questions remain about the responsibility and usefulness of auditors, which Parmalat and other cases have since cast in a harsh light. At the same time, the paradoxical relationship that exists between companies and their auditors has shifted, and the questions raised by the concentration of the auditing of large companies among four global accounting firms have become increasingly urgent.

The End of Self-Regulation

Self-regulation is a usual way in which specialized professions enforce discipline in their ranks. For the legal profession, in most places bar associations are private organizations that take full responsibility for drafting ethical rules and enforcing compliance with them. The same is true (though less in the United States than in many other countries) of other professions, such as doctors, engineers, or architects. At the same time, competition constantly helps to informally regulate the profession and marginalize bad practice. To attract customers, a good reputation is essential, precisely because of the highly technical nature of the services. If this scheme of self-regulation functions effectively, direct government intervention can be minimal.

Until the 2000s, this self-regulatory framework was also the one that governed most of the developed world's accountants and auditors. They essentially controlled the bodies charged with developing their rules of professional conduct, commonly known as auditing standards to distinguish them from accounting standards which, as we have seen, have generally been subject to direct government oversight for decades. To be precise, financial information professionals cover not one, but two professions: accounting and auditing. The profession of accountant can be exercised either inside a financial department (corporate accountants) or in an external firm, whereas the auditor is always external to the company audited and, in the case of listed firms, has a wider responsibility to the public. In practice, the initial training is identical, and the same professionals and firms may, depending on the client, operate as accountants or auditors—but the two activities cannot be carried out simultaneously for the same client because an auditor would then have to review his own work as an accountant, a clearly unsustainable conflict of interest.

In varying ways in different countries, the same division of duties used to be found in the organization of the profession. In the United States, the American Institute of Certified Public Accountants (AICPA), established in 1887, traditionally supervised both accountants and auditors. Until March 2002, its semi-autonomous Public Oversight Board, established in 1977, was in charge of the professional discipline of auditors of listed companies. However, also up to 2002, peer review to monitor this discipline was conducted on purely contractual terms between auditing firms, without any direct intervention by the AICPA. The profession's organization was comparable in the United Kingdom, where the principal professional organization is the Institute of Chartered Accountants in England and Wales (established in 1870 and given a royal charter by Queen Victoria in 1880), which also has an Auditing Practices Board (established in 1991 and reformed in 2002) more specifically charged with supervising the quality of auditing practices. In France, two independent institutions still coexist: the Ordre des experts-comptables for accountants, created in the 1940s, and the Compagnie nationale des commissaires aux comptes (CNCC) for auditors, established in 1969, with many professionals simultaneously belonging to both organizations. There, the self-regulation of auditors has never been as complete as it used to be in the English-speaking world. The CNCC was created by government decree, and its oversight of professional audit practices has been partly exercised jointly with the national securities regulator since the mid-1990s. But even then, inspections and reviews have been conducted exclusively by peer firms, which largely amounted to self-regulation in practice if not in principle. Until the early 2000s self-regulation also prevailed among auditors in most other developed countries, under different forms but always primarily involving peer review to ensure the respect of professional ethics.

The Enron and Andersen debacle put a brutal end to this old and nearly universal arrangement. Soon after Enron's default in December 2001, the entire auditing profession found itself under pressure. The AICPA reacted clumsily by stonewalling against any kind of reform, thus seriously undermining its own credibility. In an atmosphere of crisis, the Public Oversight Board decided to disband in January 2002, and its chairman, Charles Bowsher, testified in March of the same year that "the disciplinary system is not timely or effective. (. . .) I've come to the conclusion that the voluntary self-regulatory program needs to be replaced because it has failed to keep pace with challenges faced by the profession. More troubling is the resistance of the profession's trade association, the AICPA, and several of the Big 5 firms to major reform."[2] Andersen was indicted for obstruction of justice in March 2002, and convicted in June by a federal jury in Houston. And when the WorldCom collapse revealed yet another massive accounting manipulation, adding further outrage, the profession was not in a position to resist the calls, by Senator Paul Sarbanes and others, for the introduction of direct public oversight of the audit profession. As a consequence, the Sarbanes-Oxley Act in July 2002, aside from its many other significant provisions, such as increasing the criminal liability of executives of listed companies and requiring them to personally certify the accuracy of accounts and the quality of internal controls, abolished the principle of self-regulation of the audit profession. It established an audit regulator under the authority of the SEC, with the austere name of Public Company Accounting Oversight Board (PCAOB, nicknamed "Peekaboo" by facetious Brits). The PCAOB, a five-member board appointed by the SEC and which has its own staff and budget, has taken over many tasks that had until then been left to the profession itself. It may at any time require any kind of information from audit firms, subject them to inspections, and impose penalties in cases of misconduct. It is also charged with establishing auditing standards, a task which it can, however, delegate to the profession. At the same time, and as a consequence of the conflicts of interest that had been observed between Andersen and Enron, the Sarbanes-Oxley Act extended the list of activities incompatible with the conduct of an audit, thus severely restraining the range of consulting services that firms can propose to their audit clients.

An additional impact of the Sarbanes-Oxley Act is that it extends beyond the borders of the United States. Consciously or not, Congress gave the PCAOB extraterritorial authority: it has jurisdiction over the auditors of all companies listed in the United States, including the numerous companies for which the United States is only a secondary location for listing and the auditor is foreign-based. In other words, the auditors of the likes of DaimlerChrysler, France Telecom, Toyota, or China's Sinopec, all of which are listed on the New York Stock Exchange, are as much subject to Sarbanes-Oxley provisions as are the auditors of General Motors or IBM. They therefore have to be duly registered with the PCAOB, which has the power at any time to launch an inspection of their offices, including outside the territory of the United States.[3] The extraterritorial authority of the PCAOB under Sarbanes-Oxley explains the remarkable speed with which the Europeans have followed suit in putting an end to auditors' self-regulation in their own jurisdictions. European governments were immediately concerned with limiting the direct authority of the PCAOB on their territory. For this, it was essential they be able to argue to their U.S. counterparts that they had a comparable and equally effective regulator at home, with which the PCAOB could then make cooperative agreements. Hence, the creation of the PCAOB indirectly but very quickly led to the establishment of (usually public) national bodies to oversee the audit profession in Europe. The European Commission accordingly proposed a framework legislation (the Directive on the statutory audit of annual accounts and consolidated accounts, also known in euro-jargon as the "8th Directive" and adopted in 2005), which would mandate the creation of such bodies. But many European countries have not awaited the adoption of this directive to act on their own. In France, the already existing components of public supervision were overhauled, and new legislation enacted in August 2003 created the Haut Conseil du commissariat aux comptes (High Council for Statutory Audit), a twelve-member council which, like the PCAOB, has a minority of representatives from the accounting profession; similar developments have been introduced in other European countries. In practice, thus, the PCAOB has been able to develop a policy of partnerships with national regulators to avoid the politically awkward effects of its extraterritorial jurisdiction, even though this setting may prove only temporary if the partner regulators' efficiency is found to be insufficient.[4] This sequence of events, with virtually all Western economies shifting almost overnight from self-regulation of the audit profession to its regulation by a government body, provides a striking illustration of the challenges posed to national regulators by the interconnectedness of global capital markets, to which we come back in chapter 7.

The concrete significance of this legal change is, however, still difficult to evaluate. The establishment of a regulatory framework is one thing, but its practical impact is quite another. For securities regulation, twenty-seven years elapsed in the United States (and eight years in France) between the adoption of legislation criminalizing insider trading and the first successful prosecution under the legislation; and yet, it is unlikely that virtue had been universal in the meantime. Similarly, it will take some time to evaluate the real effects of the creation of the PCAOB and related regulatory initiatives on the way in which audits are conducted.

More Change Than Meets the Eye

The end of self-regulation may be the most visible event of recent years for the audit profession, but it is far from being the only one. A wave of transformations has swept over auditors, affecting their business model and even more profoundly the nature of their relationship with their clients. To understand this, one needs to take a closer look, particularly at the "Big Four" global firms who, since the demise of Andersen, are almost the exclusive players in the business of auditing large international companies.

A Business Model Turned Upside Down

All major accounting firms are partnerships in which, unlike in corporations, there is no clear separation between managers and shareholders. The partners manage the company and divide the profits among themselves, with no external shareholders. In most countries, this also has the consequence of relieving them from having to publish their accounts. It is one of the small paradoxes of the financial world that the audit firms, which are charged with ensuring the transparency of others companies' financial reporting, are themselves subject to no requirement of financial disclosure. For this reason, it is impossible to assess precisely how much their profitability has changed in recent years. Nonetheless, the little information that is available suggests that the audit firms' business model has been undergoing significant changes.

Until the Andersen collapse, auditing in the strict sense was far from being the main source of revenue, let alone profits, of the so-called global audit firms, which in fact derived most of their fees from work other than auditing, such as consulting or tax advice. According to the Investor Responsibility Research Center (IRRC), a private research firm, the share of non-audit services was as high as 72 percent of total fees in 2002.[5] And if one could look at profits rather than revenue, the contribution of audits would probably have been even smaller, because the consulting business is known to be more profitable than auditing (on the other hand, audits have the advantage of being less vulnerable to economic downturns). For this reason, there were great incentives to develop consulting services in parallel with audit work, including, if the opportunity arose, for the same clients.

Long before 2001, the reciprocal dependence between auditing and consulting had cast a suspicion of conflict of interest over the Big Five firms, but Enron proved to be the last straw. Andersen's involvement in devising the structure of Enron's SPEs had earned it several million dollars in consulting fees, and it had then validated the same adventurous arrangements as part of its audit work. This proved fatal to its reputation, even though Andersen has never been technically convicted of fraud in the Enron case. For all of the year 2001, Andersen billed Enron more for consulting work ($27 million) than for audit ($25 million)—and this was even after its IT and strategic consulting branch (formerly Andersen Consulting, now renamed Accenture) had already been spun off in 2000. The accusation of systemic conflict of interest was inevitable.

Since 2001, the Sarbanes-Oxley legislation, its equivalents in various countries, and the firms' own concern to safeguard what was left of their reputation has led them to shed large swathes of their consulting business. Thereby, they lost a significant source of revenue and even more of profit. The above-mentioned study by IRRC shows a plummeting of the share of non-audit services in the large firms' revenue, from 72 percent in 2002 to 55 percent in 2003 and only 42 percent in 2004. Even activities that for a long time had seemed to be very closely associated with auditing, such as legal and tax advice, have in certain cases been separated or spun off. In particular, law firms related to auditing networks have scaled down or closed their operations in many countries.

Moreover, accounting scandals have inflicted high legal costs on audit firms and have increased their insurance expenses. These extra costs are difficult to quantify (firms are not transparent on this), but they are likely to have altered the audit firms' cost structure. Particularly in the United States, the burden of litigation, and of staving it off, has become a significant element of the business model of the accounting profession. Added to this is a long-term downward trend of hourly fees, accentuated by the increased use of bidding procedures for the selection of auditors, even though the particular post-Sarbanes-Oxley context of high demand for audit services has often enabled firms to increase their total volume of fees.

Indeed, as already mentioned, there has also been some rather good news for auditors. At the same time that the new legislation forced the Big Four to give up some of their revenue sources, it also opened new markets. With U.S.-listed clients, the verification of internal control procedures to comply with section 404 of the Sarbanes-Oxley Act has proved a highly lucrative by-product of Enron for the surviving firms. Extra expenses for compliance with section 404 have been evaluated as representing as much as 20 percent of audit revenues.[6] And in Europe, the preparation for the transition to IFRS in 2005 has also led to a windfall in revenue for the major firms.

In view of the almost complete lack of public information about the profitability of audit firms, it is impossible to quantify the overall impact of all these changes. But it is nonetheless quite clear that the Big Four's business model, and to an extent their corporate culture, has been profoundly changed by the loss of most of their consulting business. This loss, together with the reputation damage inflicted by scandals, may have temporarily impaired the firms' ability to attract bright new graduates and especially to recruit specialized industry skills, which the consulting business allowed them to maintain in-house. And a similar shift may now happen with tax advice, following the revelations of KPMG's involvement in unlawful tax-shelter schemes that generated a total of $124 million in fees between 1997 and 2001.[7] For a profession that relies primarily on the technical expertise and credibility of its practitioners, effects of this kind are far from negligible.

The Growing Auditor/Audited Gap

Change is not only within the firms. The relationship between auditors and their audit clients is also going through a profound transformation.

In this respect too, Andersen's disappearance has had a lasting effect on firms' behavior. Andersen had grown too close to its clients' interests. And Enron had not been a unique example: in June 2001, six months before Enron's bankruptcy, Andersen had agreed to pay a $7 million civil fine, then a record amount for an accounting firm, after having been accused by the SEC of "knowingly or recklessly" issuing false and misleading audit reports for Waste Management, Inc. Waste Management's earnings had been improperly inflated by more than $1 billion between 1993 and 1996, which the press at the time had labeled the "largest accounting fraud in history"—not knowing how much larger the next frauds would be. Here too, the relationship had grown too stable to stay at arm's-length (Andersen had been auditing Waste Management's accounts since 1971), the audit partners and the client's senior executives had grown excessively close, and the combination of both audit and consulting services had proved a highly unhealthy mix. This precedent helps to demonstrate why Andersen collapsed so quickly in early 2002: Waste Management and other cases had already badly damaged its reputation, and it could not be given the benefit of the doubt.[8]

Auditors got the message. Since 2002, they have gradually altered their attitude vis-à-vis their clients. Whereas cooperation and in many cases consensus had been the unwritten rule of the relationship, it now tends to be based on a more structured discussion in which the audited company must increasingly justify its accounting choices and figures. The interests of companies and those of their auditors have in many cases ceased to converge. As Dennis Nally, the chairman of PricewaterhouseCoopers' U.S. business, said in an interview, "the stress levels between [companies] and their auditors were at an all-time high [in 2005]."[9] In the most extreme cases of disagreement, auditors are increasingly likely to resign instead of yielding to client pressure as they often did before 2002. In 2004, the Big Four resigned from 210 public companies, up from 152 in 2003 and 78 in 2002.[10]

The implications of this changed relationship are manifold. Not so long ago, an auditor would have been called to the rescue for delicate questions of interpretation of accounting standards, or to handle new difficulties arising from changes in the company's business. Companies now have to form their own opinion in order to conduct the dialogue with their auditors on an equal footing, and the auditors, in order to minimize their legal liabilities, tend more than before to always favor the most cautious option even when it is not necessarily the best one. Accounting, as we have seen, is no exact science, and a systematically conservative orientation of accounting policies is not necessarily in the best interests of companies, investors, or the economy as a whole. But as an indirect consequence of Andersen's fall, companies find themselves increasingly on their own in determining their accounting policies and the arguments to defend them. Auditors are simultaneously subject to pressure to stick ever more closely to their role of verifying the books while scaling down other aspects of their relationship with their clients.

In a number of cases, this trend may have the side effect of less transparency in the auditors' access to information. Companies that had grown used to giving their auditors, literally and figuratively, the keys to the offices and filing cabinets of their finance departments will no longer be ready to maintain such a close relationship. Furthermore, the growing quest for legal guarantees on the part of auditors will require companies to increase the volume of written or electronic backup documentation on their operations, probably resulting in more rigorous management but also possibly increasing rigidity and administrative costs. Finally, defending their accounting policies vis-à-vis the auditors will increase the companies' recourse to other outside financial experts such as investment banks or financial appraisers, for example to justify the value attributed to certain assets and liabilities—especially in Europe, where the adoption of IFRS greatly increases the number of accounting items that require being recorded at fair value. This also means increased costs for companies and greater complexity in managing the preparation of financial statements.

The combination of these changes is likely to lead to a more distant, less personal, and in the end less trustful relationship between companies and their auditors, for better or worse. Though the increased awareness of responsibilities has obvious advantages, it can also lead to unintended consequences. Auditors may ask chief financial officers to sign ever lengthier "representation letters" in which they confirm the validity of certain pieces of information and certain assumptions. This tendency may, in addition, create the risk of a certain loss of substance of audits: the representation letters partially relieve the auditors of their liability to verify the mentioned items, but they hardly contribute to the protection of shareholders. The Parmalat example illustrates an extreme case of the potentially perverse effect of such representation letters. The auditors, Deloitte at the parent-company level and Grant Thornton for the Caribbean subsidiaries, accepted the written assurances of Parmalat and its subsidiaries on foreign bank accounts, which they subsequently neglected to verify. Specifically, the auditors should have directly asked Bank of America about a particular offshore account said to have been credited with no less than €3.95 billion, but instead they relied on Parmalat, which forged an imaginary bank statement for this account that turned out never to have existed. If auditors are to avoid a hollowing-out of their work, caused by too much reliance on the audit client's representations, they would need to investigate more rigorously than in the past and to verify more systematically the information provided, through direct contact with the client's financial and commercial partners. This trend, in turn, may further increase the scope for tension in the auditor/audited relationship.

Finally, parallel trends are appearing in corporate boardrooms and audit committees. In the United States as in Europe, boards have tended to be excessively complacent vis-à-vis managers, but developments such as the settlements eventually entered into by Enron's and WorldCom's directors in 2004, where directors had to pay from their own pockets without being covered by the respective companies' insurance policies, are slowly changing corporate directors' behavior.[11] On average, more distance and even confrontation can be expected there, too, in the years to come.

The Unresolved Competition Quandary

As has been noted at the beginning of this chapter, competition is one of the essential factors in the regulation of professions, where it probably plays an even greater role than peer review or (where it exists) government oversight. In this competition, the more critical the task is seen to be, the greater role the reputation effects are bound to play. This is just as true for auditors as it is for architects or surgeons. An auditor's job requires an ever higher degree of expertise to cope with the increasing complexity of financial practices, the globalization of business, and the advent of accounting standards that place greater weight on individual judgment. Logically, given this increasing complexity, competition and selection by reputation should have more prominence than ever in the audit industry.

But this is not what seems to happen currently. The market for auditing large, international companies is concentrated in the hands of only four global firms, between which, even in the absence of anticompetitive behavior, competition is necessarily more limited than if there were more players. Through mergers, the "Big Nine" of the early 1980s became the "Big Six" at the end of the decade, then the "Big Five" with the merger of Price Waterhouse with Coopers & Lybrand in 1998, and finally the "Big Four," sometimes sarcastically dubbed the "Last Four," following the collapse of Andersen in early 2002. In the United States, these four firms audit 78 percent of listed companies and 97 percent of those with revenues above $250 million. In other words, only relatively small listed companies use the services of other firms than the Big Four. The situation is essentially the same in Europe. Even in France, where the institution of dual statutory auditors enabled a few independent firms, such as Mazars, to survive, all of the largest companies by market value (CAC 40 index) had their 2004 accounts audited by at least one of the Big Four, and for twenty-four of them, both statutory auditors belonged to the Big Four.[12]

The problem is not the existence of this oligopoly, but rather that it is, in economic jargon, unchallengeable. In other words, the obstacles that prevent new firms from entering the market of international companies' audits seem practically insurmountable. No one has yet figured out how to simultaneously build a brand that would inspire confidence in clients and their shareholders, a set of skills capable of dealing with the great technical complexity of the accounting practices of large companies, and a local presence in dozens of countries around the world. Indeed, no new firm in the last decades has been able to challenge the incumbents. The number of firms has decreased as an effect of mergers and of Andersen's fall, but there have been no replacements for those that have gone.

To be very clear, there seem to be no grounds whatsoever for accusing the Big Four of anti-competitive conduct. The persistence of the oligopoly is not attributable to improper practices by the incumbents; quite the contrary, a thorough investigation by the Government Accountability Office (GAO) in 2002–2003 concluded there was no evidence of collusion among the key actors in the market. But the same enquiry precisely identified the barriers to entry into the market, and its conclusion is worth quoting:

> GAO found that smaller accounting firms [than the Big Four] faced significant barriers to entry—including lack of staff, industry and technical expertise, capital formation, global reach, and reputation—into the large public company audit market. As a result, market forces are not likely to result in the expansion of the current Big Four. Furthermore, certain factors and conditions could cause a further reduction in the number of major accounting firms.[13]

Barriers to entry have been unwittingly made even stronger by the provisions of the Sarbanes-Oxley Act, which imposes strict rules governing the independence and rotation of auditors. Moreover, the GAO's investigation revealed that the market is even more concentrated than it first appears to be. This is because each of the Big Four has strong industry specializations, and in some sectors the oligopoly is in fact reduced to a duopoly. For example, Deloitte and Ernst & Young alone account for 80 percent of the audit market for general building contractors (measured in terms of clients' assets), 86 percent of air transportation, and 94 percent of security and commodity brokers. PwC and Ernst & Young together have nearly 95 percent of the audit market for petroleum and coal products and 91 percent for metal mining. Deloitte and PwC together have 89 percent of the audit market for transportation equipment; KPMG and Deloitte, 79 percent of the market for trucking and warehousing, and so on. In Europe, the barriers to entry are just as high. The European Commission recognized them somewhat clumsily in September 2002, when it authorized the integration of Andersen's former French operations into Ernst & Young: as it expressed it at the time, "the hypothetical acquisition of Andersen France by second-tier, French auditing firms, such as Mazars & Guérard or Salustro Reydel, would not be able to replicate the global network and the reputation required to enter the market for quoted and large companies."[14] This statement predictably upset Mazars, but it does have some truth to it.

All this amounts to a serious problem. It is not primarily a classic issue of competition (or lack thereof): after all, the world has become used to the dominance of two or three companies in sectors as various as soft drinks (Coca-Cola and Pepsi), athletic footwear (Nike and Adidas), or soap and detergent (Procter & Gamble, Unilever, and Colgate). But an oligopoly in professional services such as auditing is more worrying, because it weakens one of the strongest guarantees of quality, namely competition on the basis of professional reputation. Now that the arrival of new entrants is for all practical purposes excluded, the "last four" have become "too few to fail": everyone knows that reducing their number to three or two would be in no one's interest, and as a result the mechanisms for inflicting penalties for any lapse in performance probably have been blunted. To be sure, the collapse of Andersen demonstrated that this protection was not absolute, and there is no intent here to suggest that the Big Four might give in to the temptation of becoming complacent. But, for example, when the SEC tried KPMG in January 2003 on the fraud in the accounts of Xerox, it felt obliged to state that "no one here wants to see KPMG disappear," although it denied that this concern could lead it to a more lenient approach.[15] The same concerns were also formulated in connection with the Parmalat case, where nobody wanted Deloitte to collapse in spite of its involvement in a scandal of enormous dimensions. A similar story happened when KPMG became embroiled in unlawful tax-shelter schemes, and senior U.S. Justice Department officials expressed concern, as did the United Kingdom's Financial Services Authority.[16] And in the United Kingdom, Parliament has discussed (but not adopted) a draft bill granting auditors specific protection in the form of an upper limit to their liability in lawsuits, in effect a government guarantee on their failings, which is difficult to justify outside the desire to avoid the destruction of any one of them. It increasingly looks as if big accounting firms were protected from sanctions, not by the fact that they behave well but because no one wants to face the consequences if one of them were severely penalized.

Simply stated, the extreme concentration of the large international accounting firms is not troubling because those firms collude with one another or abuse their dominant position, which few accuse them of doing. What is worrying is that the concentration, because of the "too few to fail" factor, results in less pressure on firms to produce independent and high-quality audits. But auditing is not just any profession. The quality of audits is a matter of public interest and is one of the conditions for the confidence of investors in the capital markets. Therefore, the present situation could become a matter for public concern.

If the effect of the tiny number of remaining large international firms were indeed to overprotect those firms from the consequences of their possible failings, then audits in general could suffer from a general loss of confidence. This risk therefore has a systemic dimension, of which the awareness is slowly rising, particularly in the United States. In January 2003, the Conference Board, a business organization, expressed concern about the possible negative effects of the organization and the size of the firms on the quality of the audits they conducted. It asked in a report on restoring business confidence, "Is the huge financial conglomerate the right business model for firms providing professional audit work? Can huge auditing firms be managed in a way to ensure quality audits? Can a culture of professional values be maintained in organizations that, in some cases, have over 100,000 employees?"[17] The already quoted GAO report intensifies these concerns by very clearly determining that market forces will be insufficient to change the current oligopoly setup, which can only get worse if another firm disappears. "It's a national problem. We're concerned about the long-term implications," SEC then-chairman William Donaldson himself admitted, although he took no position on what remedies should be adopted.[18]

Indeed, there is no simple and painless solution to this problem. The nationalization of audits, suggested by some mavericks, would make no sense: audit suffers from too little competition among professionals, not too much, and the job is too complex and too fast-moving to be optimally carried out by civil servants. Another radical approach, suggested by the chief executive of the United Kingdom's Financial Reporting Council, Paul Boyle, would be to end the requirement that audit firms take the legal form of partnerships and allow them to be developed or taken over by outside investors; but this would also create intractable new conflicts of interest.[19] As the Conference Board report suggests, the ideal would be for credible answers to come from the large accounting firms themselves, which must have the most acute awareness of the imperfections of the current market structure. They can grasp the issue on its necessary global scale better than any national government agency could. The large accounting firms would have to demonstrate a great deal of leadership, and even abnegation, to themselves initiate reforms that might impair the strength of the market positions they have gradually acquired. And yet, such reforms may prove necessary to ensure a sustained or improved quality of audits, the long-term credibility of the profession, and hence, ultimately, its survival. In any case, there is little doubt that the debate about the structure of the audit market will grow in importance in the coming years.

CHAPTER 6

POWER TO THE INVESTORS?

We now proceed downstream, from the preparation and audit of financial statements to their use by various participants in the capital markets. The dominant trend here is the gradual gathering of power by investors, which further focuses the requirements placed on financial statements while giving rise to new tensions and potential conflicts.

We have seen how, in the late Middle Ages, the demands of shareholders were a driving force behind the invention of double-entry bookkeeping. Likewise, accounting standards came into existence to protect investors following the 1929 crash. The current reassertion of shareholder power can thus be seen as a step back to basics. A simultaneous factor is that most of the existing intermediaries between companies and their investors, such as rating agencies, financial analysts, and mutual fund managers, have seen their roles called into question, while the borders between the professions of accounting, risk analysis, and investment research have become increasingly blurred.

The Global Rise of Institutional Investors

"Where stock is held by a great number, what is anybody's business is nobody's business." This was a favorite maxim of Andrew Carnegie (1835–1919), the Pittsburgh steel magnate who was considered the richest man of his time. Today, the difficulty of efficient governance of companies with scattered shareholders arises not only from the number of parties involved but also from the fact that their holdings are rarely direct. A growing proportion of shares are held by "institutional" shareholders, which aggregate individual holdings and thus stand between companies and their ultimate owners. These can be mutual funds or UCITS,[1] investment operations of insurance companies, hedge funds, or pension funds. Many of these institutional investors are not household brands, but they play a key role of aggregating savings invested in various asset categories and, most important for our purposes here, in shares of publicly listed companies. As of March 2005, U.S. institutional investors accounted for 48 percent of the total ownership of U.S. equities, whereby direct holdings by U.S. individuals were only 38 percent (the remaining 14 percent being mostly foreign investors). At that date, the financial assets managed in the United States by life insurance companies amounted to $4,166 billion, by other insurance companies to $1,197 billion, by private pension funds to $4,286 billion, by federal, state, and local government retirement funds to $3,054 billion, and by mutual funds to $7,284 billion.[2]

For a long time, however, institutional investors have not engaged very actively in exercising control over the companies in which they have holdings. Their principal form of expression used to be to "vote with their feet," by selling shares in those companies they considered mismanaged and by buying shares in seemingly well-governed ones. Institutional investors always made intensive use of financial information about companies to make their purchase and sale decisions, but they used to have little influence on the way in which this information was provided to them. There are several reasons why institutional investors long did not get more deeply involved in corporate governance. A single fund generally holds a relatively small proportion of a large listed company's equity, making necessary the formation of alliances in order to be able to influence management. Another factor is that "activist" investors may face legal risks, in some national legal systems, where they can be held individually responsible for company decisions. But a key factor, historically, has been the scope for conflict of interest linked to the business model of institutional investors, which is no smaller than for other players of the financial ecosystem and has been richly documented in recent times.

A High Potential for Conflicts of Interests

The fact is that few institutional investors can be considered entirely independent. Many of them are investment management subsidiaries of banks and insurance companies, or they have a commercial relationship with large corporations for whom they manage pension funds or other assets, or both. In the case of fund management firms that are owned by a bank or an insurance company, which is common in continental Europe, there is a risk that the commercial interests of the parent financial institution may influence investment choices. As an extreme example, the fund manager may be prompted to over-invest in companies to which its parent institution has made loans, or from which it is seeking banking or insurance business. Neither the establishment of "Chinese walls" (tight operational separations between different departments of the same firm), nor the legal autonomy granted to asset-management subsidiaries by financial institutions can provide tight guarantees to avoid this kind of interference, even though it is tending to become less frequent than it was in the 1980s or early 1990s.

In the case of fund-management companies tied by their own direct commercial interests, which is most common in the United States, the potential conflict is of a different nature. If a mutual-fund firm derives a substantial part of its revenue from contracts to manage the pension funds of large listed companies, there can be a suspicion as to the objectivity of their investment decisions regarding shares in those companies that are clients, or of those likely to become so in the future. Indeed, the management of corporate pension funds by mutual-fund-management firms is on the increase: in the United States, from 5 percent of the total assets under management in 1991 to 36 percent in 2004, amounting to a total of $3.1 trillion.[3]

Interference can also come directly from the companies issuing shares, for example, by leaning on the investment behavior of their own employees. In some cases, companies have thus encouraged their employees to invest disproportionately in their own stock through the corporate pension fund. In 2001, no less than 41 percent of Enron's pension fund was invested in Enron shares, and therefore the company's bankruptcy led many employees to lose not only their job but also a significant share of their lifetime's savings. And in this respect at least, Enron was not the most extreme case. For example, at the same time the employees of Procter & Gamble had been encouraged to invest as much as 90 percent of their retirement savings in the company's stock.[4]

In addition to all these possible conflicts, asset-management firms that manage the institutional investors' assets may be subject to the temptation of mismanaging them for their own profit, or for the profit of some privileged customers or partners. This has been highlighted by the crisis that since September 2003 has shaken America's mutual funds. Overall, mutual funds have experienced strong growth in the past decade, and some of the companies that manage them have become large and respected players. Fidelity, the number one, had a total of $1.1 trillion under management by the end of 2004. As has been previously mentioned, the clients of such mutual-fund companies are typically individuals who entrust them with their savings and companies that delegate to them the financial management of their pension funds.

But the crisis of the fall of 2003 revealed that many of these mutual funds had in fact routinely engaged in illegal practices consisting of tilting their operations in favor of certain clients or their own employees, to the detriment of the majority of their investors. The initial accusation was centered on two practices known as "late trading" and "market timing," which proved to be surprisingly widespread. To understand this malpractice, one must remember that every day at the close of stock exchange trading (4 p.m. in New York), each mutual fund records a closing price, but the prices of the underlying assets can continue to change after 4 p.m. "Late trading" consists of the fund manager allowing some investors to continue buying shares of the fund after the closing but at the closing price, which represents a near-certainty of profit if the underlying assets have gained in value in the meantime. This practice favors some investors in the fund to the detriment of all the others, which justifies its prohibition in order to preserve equality of treatment. "Market timing" is another form of arbitrage that is based on the fact that the closing price of the fund is not always exactly equal to its fair value. This, too, is a practice detrimental to long-term investors in the fund.

The outrage provoked by the revelations about widespread late trading and market timing led to proposals for stricter supervision over the operations of mutual funds in the United States, particularly by having independent directors participate in the oversight of the good management of each of the funds. The SEC adopted new governance rules applicable to funds in July 2004, which had to be re-adopted on June 29, 2005, the last day of Chairman Donaldson's mandate, following a fierce procedural battle by the U.S. Chamber of Commerce. However, it is too early to assess the effectiveness of these measures. One may hope that the increased pressure on fund managers will lead to more independence and better performance for all investors, but only time will tell if this actually happens.

In any event, there remain many situations in which the incentives surrounding institutional investors may lead to investment decisions that are not necessarily optimal for the people whose savings they manage. And the conflicts of interest, even when they are only potential, may dissuade institutional investors from adopting an active attitude to influence the conditions under which companies prepare and disseminate financial information.

The Activist Momentum

In spite of the significant conflicts of interest, institutional investors on the whole tend to grow globally more powerful and more independent, leading to an increasing degree of shareholder activism. The pioneers in this respect have certainly been large U.S.-based public employee pension funds, such as CalPERS (California State employees) or TIAA-CREF (teachers). These have experienced significant growth in importance on the financial scene in the course of the last twenty years. The CalPERS investment portfolio, for example, grew from $32.7 billion in 1985 to $180 billion in April 2005. Public pension funds are structurally independent from other business interests and, unlike mutual funds, they generally do not solicit investment management contracts from third-party companies (conversely, they are generally more exposed to political interference because of their public status). They also tend to be the most active in the governance of the companies in which they invest. CalPERS, in particular, has long been known for the constant pressure it exerts on the management of underperforming companies, leading in past years to a measurable "CalPERS effect" of performance improvement following an investment by the fund. A 1997 study concluded that companies in which CalPERS had invested outperformed the stock market by 23 percent on average in the five years following the investment, whereas those same companies had performed 89 percent below the market in the five years preceding it.[5] CalPERS has even dedicated a specific website to issues of corporate governance,[6] where it publishes general recommendations as well as particular demands to certain companies considered of concern, which are placed on a public "focus list." This is not pure rhetoric: CalPERS was instrumental in the dismissal of several CEOs in the past, starting early in the 1990s in cases with companies such as General Motors, IBM, and American Express in 1992 and 1993, or Kmart in 1995.

This combination of independence and activism could gradually extend beyond public pension funds, to the private sector. There could be a backlash in the future against the big corporations' involvement in the management of their own pension funds, which led to Enron's employees being ruined by the double loss of their jobs and of their retirement investments as has been described earlier. If the employers' influence over the handling of their employees' retirement savings was diminished, then corporate pension funds could adopt a higher profile than currently and become gradually more active as regards issues of corporate governance and transparency, because they would not be open to the same potential conflicts of interest as today.[7]

Another clear trend of institutional investment is the impressive pace at which its reach extends beyond national borders and becomes increasingly global. For example, the proportion held by non-resident shareholders, many of which are institutional investors, in the capital of companies in France's CAC 40 stock market index has risen from around 10 percent in the mid-1980s to nearly 44 percent in the early 2000s.[8] In the United States, too, the share of corporate equities owned by foreign residents tripled in the past thirty years, increasing from 4 percent in 1975 to 11.2 percent in 2004.[9] One consequence is a growing fluidity of the market for corporate ownership and control, which was well illustrated in France by the takeover of former national manufacturing icon Pechiney, an aluminum producer, by Canadian rival Alcan in July 2003. Contrary to what could have been expected, Pechiney's then CEO Jean-Pierre Rodier, in spite of being a former civil servant, did not invoke any consideration of national interest or protection but instead focused essentially on the price of the bid. There is little doubt that this attitude was influenced by the fact that the three largest Pechiney shareholders at the time were foreign institutional investors, namely two mutual funds based in the United States, Franklin Templeton and Fidelity, and AGF, an insurance company majority-owned by Germany's Allianz, which at the time held respectively 7 percent, 5 percent and 6 percent of the company's shares. By contrast, Danone, a French food-products company in which no foreign institutional investor has a strong position, called for protectionist stonewalling when it was hit by rumors of a hostile takeover by PepsiCo in July 2005. These two contrasting French examples illustrate how the globalization of shareholding structures can have an impact on corporate behavior.

One key channel for shareholder activism in the governance of companies is the shareholders' annual general meetings (AGM). Admittedly, the starting point here is a rather low one. Theoretically, the AGM is the primary locus of power in corporations, as it alone has the authority to appoint the members of the board of directors, to approve the accounts, and to authorize major equity transactions. However, the realities behind this appearance of authority are, for the most part, utterly disappointing. AGMs generally do not host any substantial discussions, and they rarely do more than merely rubberstamp decisions that have already been made. The board of directors controls the agenda and the conduct of the meeting, in which dispersed shareholders have few resources to make their voices heard, find it difficult to come together, and anyway are allowed little room for initiative by the rules of procedure. Imagine a parliament with a single annual session lasting half a day, with no party caucuses, no committees, and the members practically unable to propose legislation. This is what the so-called shareholder democracy most frequently amounts to, even though the situation varies among companies and countries.

Shareholder activism in AGMs has nevertheless been on the rise. Large independent pension funds increasingly apply pressure on individual companies. They also have initiated a number of lobbying actions to change the rules governing AGMs and to allow more shareholder expression, and such actions are often relayed by nationwide organizations, such as the Council of Institutional Investors (CII), which a number of pension funds established in the mid-1980s, or by global ones, such as the International Corporate Governance Network

(ICGN), created in 1995. Shareholder pressure exerted through the channel of corporate boards has played a key role also in the replacement of the chief executives of several large companies in recent years, such as Disney, Shell, Deutsche Börse, or DaimlerChrysler. And as these examples illustrate, such activism is not limited to the United States but has spread extensively through Europe and, to a lesser degree, Japan. In France, the Association française de la gestion financière (AFG), which represents asset management firms, has played a pioneering role in promoting active participation by its members in AGMs, and now systematically analyzes the resolutions proposed at those meetings for a number of large listed companies and makes voting suggestions to its members. This kind of attitude would have been unthinkable as recently as ten years ago and is likely to contribute to a gradually more active posture on the part of institutional investors.

Shareholder involvement also takes the form of legal challenges to companies. In the United States, there has been a marked increase in the number of shareholder class action lawsuits since the Private Securities Litigation Reform Act was passed in the mid-1990s. The size of awards or settlements continues to grow larger. From $122 million in 1997, total amounts in such lawsuits reached $997 million in 1999 and $5.5 billion in 2004.[10] In 2005, this figure is set to rise above a breathtaking $20 billion, including at least $7 billion of settlements related to Enron and $6 billion linked to WorldCom.[11] Often criticized for the excess litigation they may produce, class actions have in practice become, for better or worse, one of the most powerful means of regulation in the U.S. business world. The passing of the Class Action Fairness Act of February 2005, new legislation meant to curb excesses of class action suits, may change certain practices but is unlikely to reverse that momentum. In fact, in an increasing number of cases (including Vivendi Universal and Parmalat), non-U.S. shareholders in non-U.S. companies have sought protection of their interests through initiating class actions with U.S. courts. As the *Economist* pointed out, "as long as European countries fail to offer effective remedies against fraud in civil actions, lawyers will continue to turn to U.S. jurisdictions to file European complaints."[12] All these elements together result in a level of pressure exerted by investors on listed companies that is now arguably higher than at any time for at least several decades.

The Changing Landscape of Intermediaries

In making their investment decisions, institutional investors are crucially dependent on information intermediaries, such as financial analysts and rating agencies, which analyze the financial information provided by companies and thus influence and facilitate investment decisions. These information intermediaries did not escape the general crisis of confidence that followed Enron and the bursting of the technology bubble.

Investment Research in Jeopardy

Financial analysts were among the most affected by the shock wave of accounting scandals in 2002 and, more broadly, by the end of the technology bubble. Beyond the revelation of conflicts of interest and professional malpractice, the legal actions that ensued have highlighted structural weaknesses in the very business model of financial research, and prospects for overcoming such weaknesses remain unclear to this day.

Financial analysts fulfill an essential function of mediating, sharing, and summarizing corporate information for investors. Individual investors or portfolio managers rarely have the time to dissect the information published by listed corporations and to directly form their own estimates of their value. This evaluation, based primarily on the corporations' financial statements and other financial disclosures, is at the heart of the analysts' job. The "buy" or "sell" recommendations they provide are only one (arguably minor) part of the service they deliver to investors, which also, and more importantly, includes models for valuation, scenarios for future business prospects, and the many other kinds of information included in their research notes and reports.

Many problems stem from the fact that reports by analysts from investment banks and brokerage firms (known as the "sell side," by contrast to "buy-side" analysts who are employed by investors themselves) are not marketed at cost price. This service is rarely billed as such to clients and is generally included as part of a comprehensive brokerage service package, for which the main compensation takes the form of brokerage fees. Theoretically, research reports are reserved for the broker's customers, but in practice they tend to be widely disseminated across the capital markets. Financial analysis and research is thus essentially distributed for free by investment banks and brokerage firms, although it obviously has a cost. This has some perverse effects. Most investment banks have tended until now to believe they needed to provide research, if only for prestige reasons, but they have also sought a return on this expense by other means. This has generally meant using their analysts as auxiliaries to commercial operations, especially when it comes to recommending the purchase of securities that they place in the market on behalf of clients. In other words, the fact that investment research does not autonomously generate a flow of revenue has proved fatal for its independence. Sanford Weill, the often ruthless creator of today's Citigroup, is reputed to have often asserted in the past that investment research "has no value except of course to get banking fees."[13]

Following the bursting of the technology bubble in 2000–01, investment research has been widely discredited by the realization that it had been routinely used for raw commercial purposes. Harry Blodget, a Merrill Lynch "star" analyst for Internet and media companies, was discovered to have recommended stocks in his reports, which at the same time he dismissed in internal e-mails as being valueless. In an internal e-mail published by prosecutors, he described one of the companies whose IPO Merrill Lynch was promoting as "such a piece of crap." In another e-mail, he wrote of another hotly promoted stock, "I can't believe what a piece of sh-t that thing is. Shame on me/us for giving them any benefit of the doubt." The Enron case was less rude but no less shocking. On November 1, 2001, well after the first earnings restatements and only a month before bankruptcy was declared, ten of the fourteen analysts following Enron still recommended it as a "buy," seven of them even as a "strong buy." It is difficult to regain the confidence of the public after such facts have been commented on by all the national media.

The coverage of technology companies by analysts eventually led to prosecution by New York State, which was highly publicized by State Attorney General Eliot Spitzer and was followed on the federal level by the SEC. On April 28, 2003, a settlement was reached for the unprecedented total amount of $1.4 billion, to be paid by the ten banks and brokerage firms involved in the accusations of misbehavior.[14] The agreement provided for changes in the organization and reporting processes of the banks' research departments, as well as for a specific funding of $450 million over five years to be distributed to independent financial research firms.

But already at that time, the slump in financial markets and securities transactions had reduced the overall resources available for financial research. When the market environment deteriorated in 2001 and then turned disastrous in 2002, many investment banks severely cut back on their research budgets, which in the previously euphoric climate had been kept at high levels. Analysts often came to be seen mainly as a cost center rather than as a source of added value.

Almost all attempts to make financial analysis profitable by the direct sale of analysts' reports have failed. Market players do not appear to be inclined to pay for information they think they can find elsewhere for free or nearly free, and the April 2003 settlement, in spite of its record-breaking amount, probably remains too small to provide a sustainable response to that challenge. An increasing number of "small-cap" and "mid-cap" companies (i.e., not those with the largest market capitalization) are no longer covered by sell-side analysts, and many others have seen their coverage shrink compared with what it was until 2002.[15] In Europe, the reduction in research budgets is arguably even more marked than in the United States, and some banks, such as BNP Paribas, have even divested their research departments.

What is most likely to develop in the future is a sort of dispersion of analysis and research beyond the brokerage firms, where it used to be mainly hosted, to the entire chain of financial information users. To start with, companies may tend to publish their information in a more readable and structured way (for example, using the XBRL standard mentioned in chapter 4), which would decrease the need for interpretation and analysis by financial research specialists. Then, investors may partly assume for themselves the tasks for which they used to rely on sell-side research, by entrusting them to their own in-house buy-side analysts. It is doubtful, however, that this transformation means an increase in overall efficiency. Sell-side analysts, for all their shortcomings, have generally played a useful role of sharing the effort to understand and process company data among many market participants. Therefore, the apparently persistent weakening of sell-side investment research is not good news for the use and control of financial information.

Rating Agencies Called into Question

The job of financial rating agencies is to evaluate the risk associated with an issuer of bonds or other securities, or with a particular security, by giving it a rating based on a scale ranging from the safest (lowest probability of default) to the riskiest (very high such probability). The ratings either fall into "investment grade" category (from AAA to BBB downwards on Standard & Poor's scale) or, for the riskiest issuers, are considered to be of "speculative" or "junk" status (beginning with BB+ on the same scale). The agencies rate all kinds of organizations that borrow on the capital markets, particularly large corporations (publicly listed or not, including government-owned ones) as well as governments ("sovereign issuers") and other public entities such as large municipalities. As has been described in chapter 1, all three firms that dominate today's world market for external credit rating, namely, Standard & Poor's, Moody's, and Fitch, were created in the United States in the late nineteenth and early twentieth centuries. Standard & Poor's is now a subsidiary of the McGraw-Hill media and business-information group; Moody's is an independent listed company; and Fitch has become a subsidiary of Paris-based Fimalac.

The questions raised about rating agencies are different from those concerning analysts. To start with, they rely on a slightly different approach. Financial analysts mainly assess a company's value, while rating agencies provide an opinion about its risk of default, expressed by a rating on a scale that is specific to each agency. Beyond the different tasks, the agencies' business model is entirely different from that of investment research, as the rating agencies are mainly paid by the companies that issue the securities they rate and not by investors or other information users. Unlike financial analysts that remain a cost center, this feature has allowed rating agencies to enjoy spectacular operating profit margins, which in recent years typically reached more than 20 percent for Fitch, more than 30 percent for S&P, and more than 50 percent for Moody's. This model is also another potential source of conflicts of interest, a bit like in the case of auditing, as the companies the agencies have to rate are also their clients. In principle, these conflicts are minimized by the "Chinese walls" the agencies claim to have put in place between their sales force, who take charge of client relationships, and the analysts, who prepare the ratings. The agencies' concern for their own reputation is also claimed to be a strong safeguard against any temptation of interference between commercial concerns and rating independence. However, the fact of owing their livelihood to the companies they oversee creates an inevitable tension.

Although (unlike financial analysts) they have not been directly tainted by convictions and scandals, the rating agencies have been severely criticized for their glaring inability to detect in advance many large financial crises in recent times. Enron was downgraded to speculative ("junk") status only a few days before its declared bankruptcy; for Parmalat, there was a hardly better interval of two weeks between the two events. The quality of the agencies' methodology has therefore been called into question, along with alleged flaws in the competitive situation. If the market for financial rating had been more open to competition, perhaps new entrants would have better predicted recent bankruptcies. However, and in spite of some similarities, the competitive situation is not identical to the one in the audit market. In particular, it is difficult to imagine how the market could live with many agencies, each with its own rating scale and methodology, because it would have enormous difficulty in handling the resulting complexity. For this reason, a necessary (but not necessarily sufficient) condition for the appearance of new entrants would probably be the standardization of the rating scales and methodologies, which would in turn raise issues of efficiency and independence of the corresponding standard-setting authority. Not surprisingly, the agencies are fiercely opposed to any such idea.

In addition to the intrinsic barriers to competition, because of the power of incumbency, reputation effects, and the magnitude of the initial investment required, the situation is made arguably worse by the fact that the agencies are subject since 1975 to a formal registration procedure by which the SEC grants them a status of "nationally recognized statistical rating organizations" (or NRSRO), which creates an additional hurdle for potential new entrants to overcome. The SEC has grown aware of the problems created by this setting and in 2003 solicited public comment on possible changes in its regulatory system, going as far as to consider abolishing the NRSRO status, but thus far it has decided not to substantially change the existing framework.[16]

A further contentious issue often goes unmentioned in the debates about financial rating. Like auditors, but unlike financial analysts, the rating agencies have a right to access insider corporate information, such as business plans and details of certain contracts (e.g., loan agreements), on the condition, of course, that they respect confidentiality and make sure that no insider trading occurs as a consequence. The justification of this special informational privilege granted to rating agencies, which may possibly take a part in their huge profit margins, remains somewhat fragile and could well be challenged in the future, which would mean that the rating analysts, like all other financial analysts, would have to rely exclusively on public information. If this were to happen, it would probably also imply a strengthening of the overall requirements for public disclosure of financial and non-financial data.

The rating agencies engage in constant efforts to defend the trust placed in them. Partly as a result of the failings of the agencies in cases such as Enron and Parmalat (or, for that matter, the Asian and Argentine financial crises of the past decade), more and more market participants, including banks and institutional investors, have developed their own credit research departments besides the equity research activity that deals with value, rather than risk, analysis. A similar lack of trust is illustrated by the increasingly frequent discrepancies between risk levels implied by the markets in interest rate premiums (or "credit spreads") required from issuing companies, and those that would result from the ratings assigned to the same companies by the rating agencies.[17] In other words, investors seem to display a diminishing trust in the rating agencies, which puts a question mark on the long-term sustainability of their business model in spite of its current high profitability.

Accounts for Investors

How does all this affect the use and preparation of accounting and financial reporting? The change in the context in which institutional investors and information intermediaries operate justifies a reminder of the origins of financial accounting as they have been described in the first part of this book. Just as investors were the driving force for the very invention of financial accounting, their increased muscle logically brings about a corresponding increase in the importance of financial reporting, along with intensified demand for quality and precision in its content. Increased investor power means that companies may be required to disclose ever more complete and specific information, and that they may be asked for greater attention as to the reliability of their accounts and audits.

A greater density in the information disclosed to markets is a first aspect of this trend. Investors want accounts to contain enough detail to enable them to form their own ideas about the value of listed companies, which may mean some fairly detailed information. Generally speaking, countries where the "investor culture" is quite widespread, such as the United States, also enjoy a higher average level of accounting knowledge in the business community than countries where investor awareness has tended to be weak in the past, such as France in the second half of the twentieth century (even today, the accounting literacy of many French business executives is worryingly low, and CEOs with an initial training in accounting, such as Terry Semel at Yahoo! or Douglas Ivester at Coca-Cola, are virtually unheard-of figures in Paris). For example, it was investor pressure that led to the presentation in disclosure notes of more information on stock option programs, on cash transfers between companies and their subsidiaries or associated companies, or on the use of derivatives. A similar emphasis on disclosure has occurred for information that investors consider necessary to form an opinion about company managers. They are thus the most active proponents, more even than the trade unions, of transparency as regards executive compensation. Disclosure of managers' compensation conditions has been an SEC requirement since 1993, long before and much more thoroughly than in countries considered prone to "class warfare," such as France.

Another related trend is the fact that information has to be provided in a uniform manner by all companies to all investors. Of course, every participant in the securities markets would like personally to benefit from privileged information. But the collective interest of investors is that any significant new information should be available to all on equal terms, hence their insistence on public disclosure made at the same time and in the same terms to all participants. The regulation known as "fair disclosure" (or "Reg FD"), imposed by the SEC in 2000, drastically curtails the hitherto widespread practice of companies providing supplemental information in meetings with selected financial analysts, a practice that sometimes allowed investment banks to then use this privileged information to the detriment of all other investors. Regulation Fair Disclosure and similar measures adopted in and outside the United States aim to level the playing field between market insiders and the ordinary investors: a goal worth pursuing in the interest of the market as a whole, even though, in the real world, well-connected Wall Street firms may retain an inherent advantage as regards access to information thanks to the centrality of their position in the financial community.

The same concern for uniformity of information explains why investors are as a general rule the most forceful advocates for the adoption of transnational accounting standards. This is the natural next step after the codification of national standards, which, as we have seen, took place in the 1930s in the United States with the aim of protecting investors. A 2002 survey of two hundred institutional investors in thirty-one countries thus found that 90 percent of them were in favor of a single system of accounting standards everywhere in the world.[18]

As we saw in chapter 3, the priority for equity investors in matters of accounting standards is the relevance of the information provided to an analysis of value, while bond investors are more concerned with the analysis of risk. "Fair value" accounting, in particular, assumes a key role in standard-setting decisions whenever the principal concern is to satisfy the needs of investors, which is the case, as we have seen, for both US GAAP and IFRS.

Another indirect consequence, which is not without risk, is the gradual blurring of boundaries between the professional realms of accounting, financial valuation, investment research, and risk analysis. In increasingly frequent occurrences, accounting standards now require the construction of complex valuation models typically based on the discounting of future cash flows, for example, to evaluate any impairment of goodwill or to account for retirement benefits or certain derivatives. The standards also require more and more detailed description in the disclosure notes of the risks to which the company is exposed. The analytical skills required for this are different from those traditionally associated with accountants, but very close to those of financial analysts as well as other professions such as actuaries, appraisers, investment consultants, or investment bankers. This is likely to result in an increased overlap of the professions of accounting, financial analysis, and risk analysis, brought about by accounting standards whose scope may grow ever more ambitious and all-encompassing.

Growing recourse to regulation through the courts, which is one of the elements of shareholder activism, is also likely to exert a specific influence on financial disclosure and accounting standards. Despite the emphasis placed on principles over rules (as discussed in chapter 3), legal pressure leads standard-setters to issue detailed instructions and guidelines to reduce the legal risk of economic agents. Furthermore, the multiplication of lawsuits brought by shareholders or their representatives is also a factor in the acceleration of the distancing of companies from their auditors as described in the previous chapter. The increase in litigation tends to encourage auditors to favor their duty to the shareholders over their duty to the corporate managers who are their immediate clients.

The credibility of audits has become a key demand of shareholders and investors. It was especially obvious in the Parmalat case that once the audit was defective, the other links in the chain of control were all unable to provide a means of detecting even massive gaps in the accounts. In this Italian sequel to Enron, the acknowledgment of failure affected simultaneously the rating agencies, the Italian securities regulator Consob, the oversight exercised by the Bank of Italy, and the financial analysts. As investors are especially driven to demand high-quality audits, they have been granted specific representation in the new federal body regulating auditors in the United States, the Public Company Accounting Oversight Board. One of the PCAOB's five Board members, Kayla Gillan, has spent most of her career at CalPERS where she was the architect of the earlier mentioned corporate governance program. Comparable investor representation has been introduced in the various other national audit oversight bodies created across the developed world after Enron, and investor groups are organizing themselves to wield more influence on the IASB as well. Thus, investors are likely to wield even greater influence in the future, not only in securing more thorough and relevant financial disclosure from listed companies but also, directly and indirectly, in obtaining higher quality audits, and on the setting of accounting standards themselves.

CHAPTER 7

REGULATORS AT THE CROSSROADS

The capital markets are not generally known for their fondness for government intervention. Most of their participants profess to value contractual freedom, free enterprise, free trade, and the primacy of the individual over collective constraints, with the free operation of market forces fostering individual and collective enrichment by Adam Smith's "invisible hand" with as little government intervention as possible.

A functioning public authority, however, is indispensable for the proper operation of the markets. In fact, the United States, where the financial markets are most extensively developed, is arguably the country where the public authority over them is strongest. At least since the 1929 crash, America's capital markets have been subject to a strikingly powerful and elaborate system of public regulation and control.

The regulatory system includes a tangled web of public, semi-public, and private institutions entrusted with enforcing, monitoring, and updating the rules that allow the markets to properly operate. Along with the changes set out in the three preceding chapters, changes in the organization and policies of the regulatory system are set to influence heavily the way companies prepare and disclose financial information in the future, with challenging choices ahead in the United States as well as in Europe.

Institutions for the Markets

Collective and public institutions entrusted with the regulation of capital markets have grown gradually out of stock market crises, when spontaneous mechanisms of self-regulation turned out to be insufficient to prevent misconduct and the destabilization of the financial system. Such institutions are located at the junction between the private and public sectors, with the difficulties implied by that hybrid position. Therefore, the question of their own responsibility to the public arises constantly, and the answer given has varied widely depending on the country and the point in time.

Government regulation of capital markets was not entirely unknown before the 1929 crash. Its current shape, however, in the United States and in most other developed economies, has its essential roots in the Securities Act of 1933 and the Securities Exchange Act of 1934, which are among the earliest legislation of Franklin Delano Roosevelt's New Deal.

In 1929, approximately twenty million individual investors held securities, half of which turned out to be worthless after the stock market crash. This fact alone required a political response—even though other severe consequences of the market collapse, such as the drying up of business credit and the advent of mass unemployment, were soon to follow. The ensuing legislation of 1933 and 1934, which created the SEC and built the foundations of modern market regulation, can be summed up in two simple principles. First, "companies publicly offering securities for investment dollars must tell the public the truth about their businesses, the securities they are selling, and the risks involved in investing." Second, "people who sell and trade securities—brokers, dealers, and exchanges—must treat investors fairly and honestly, putting investors' interests first."[1] Securities regulation is thus primarily directed toward protecting investors, both by means of the adequacy of information, above all financial, provided by listed companies and through appropriate conduct on the part of market intermediaries. These conditions, which are necessary for investor confidence and the effectiveness of their investment decisions, are not a natural fact of life. Without government regulation, companies may be tempted to give a false or distorted view of their operations—we saw many such examples in the course of this book—and intermediaries may act against the interests of their clients, as when insider trading occurs, or in the cases of investment research and mutual-fund misbehavior as exposed in the previous chapter.

The powers of the SEC, as well as those of most of its counterparts in other countries, have been strengthened after every market crisis, for example in the United States in 1964, 1975, and 1988–90. The latest crisis was no exception to the rule. Following the defaults of Enron and WorldCom, the Sarbanes-Oxley Act of July 2002 gave the SEC new powers in many areas, including the establishment of the PCAOB under its authority to oversee auditors and a doubling of its budget in the course of two years—to around $900 million in 2004. After some internal turmoil and difficulties during the controversial mandate of Harvey Pitt in 2001–2002, the SEC recovered a high degree of authority under William Donaldson, a respected Wall Street veteran whose stint as chairman from February 2003 to June 2005 has been marked by wide-ranging regulatory initiatives and aggressive enforcement actions.

The centrality of the SEC's regulatory role is recognized by all participants in the U.S. market, including many who may otherwise be wary of government intervention. In its year-end issue, which attempted to summarize the lessons of 2002, *BusinessWeek* listed as item number 2 that "regulation is essential," just after the bleak recognition of the systemic nature of the shortcomings revealed by that year's accounting scandals.[2]

A Brief Typology of Financial Regulation

A degree of government regulation is necessary to ensure trust in markets, particularly in light of market crises. But conversely, too much regulation risks hampering entrepreneurial spirit, discouraging risk taking, and curbing the efficiency of market mechanisms. A delicate balance thus has to be reached.

As a consequence, the nature of public regulation varies considerably in different areas of market activity. Some segments are lightly or not at all regulated. In the case of hedge funds, this is because the wealthy individuals or sophisticated organizations that invest in those funds are expected to have a good understanding of the risks to which their investments are subject. Another very lightly regulated market is the one for sovereign debt issued by national governments. Public regulation would make little sense there because it would have no enforcement capability; a sovereign state, whose assets cannot be seized by creditors, cannot easily be constrained to honor its debt.

The kind of market under consideration is not the only aspect according to which the degree of government regulation may vary. Because the confidence of market participants is often a matter of circumstances, the country and the time period involved are also factors. In addition, means of intervention and imposing penalties also have to be adjusted to match the diversity of contexts. A useful distinction can be made between *ex ante* regulation, in which certain operations are subject to prior explicit approval by the regulatory authority, and *ex post* intervention, which concentrates only on cases where serious problems have been identified. This distinction mirrors the one that has been developed in political science literature between "police patrol" and "fire alarm" approaches to Congressional oversight of public agencies.[3] The first approach, which is prominent in countries with a strong administrative tradition such as France, involves centralized and direct surveillance, as in the case of a police patrol that constantly has to inspect the streets of its district; it often provides a greater sense of security but can also lead to excessive rigidities and inefficiency. The second approach, which is more broadly embedded in British and even more in U.S. tradition, is decentralized and reactive: the parallel is with a team of firemen that only goes to places where a fire has broken out, and therefore acts only where it is most urgently needed without spending its time watching all the places that may one day catch fire. This option is more flexible and responsive but presupposes a high degree of maturity and responsibility on the part of individual market participants. In many respects, the SEC has essentially followed the fire-alarm route, even though it has tended to increase the police-patrol dimension of some of its actions following crises of confidence.

On another level, two different approaches can be considered as regards enforcement and penalties. The emphasis can be either on punishing the individuals guilty of fraud, typically with criminal sanctions, or on fining and condemning faulty companies, whose managers and directors are then encouraged to put in place the right internal incentives and mechanisms to discourage misconduct. The second approach used to be the more prevalent in the United States, but this is changing. The Sarbanes-Oxley Act has sharply increased the individual responsibility of corporate executives over the publicly disclosed financial statements, with individual criminal penalties introduced in cases of fraud.

The centrality of the SEC's role should not overshadow the many other participants that together are involved in the regulation of increasingly interdependent global capital markets. In the United States itself, the SEC is far from alone. It has delegated some of its regulatory authority to separate bodies, such as the PCAOB to oversee auditors, the FASB for drafting the US GAAP accounting standards, and the so-called self-regulatory organizations (SROs). Under the SEC's watch, SROs, such as the New York Stock Exchange and the National Association of Securities Dealers (which supervises Nasdaq) do many day-to-day tasks of market regulation which, under the 1933–34 legislation, could have been taken over by the SEC itself. Moreover, for historic reasons, the futures markets are outside the remit of the SEC and are regulated by another federal agency, the Commodity Futures Trading Commission, established in 1974.

Several states where a lot of financial firms are located, such as New York, Massachusetts, and, since 2004, California, have also set up specific regulatory mechanisms that sometimes overlap with the federal authority of the SEC. In New York, Attorney General Eliot Spitzer played an important role in discovering and publicizing several market scandals and imposing sanctions on those involved, including on the role of analysts during the technology bubble, unlawful practices of large mutual funds, and questionable disclosure practices of insurance behemoth AIG, which led in 2005 to the resignation of its until then all-powerful chairman and CEO Maurice "Hank" Greenberg. The overlapping of federal and state jurisdictions is the subject of vigorous debate in the United States, to which we will return later.[4]

Outside the United States, all developed countries have in turn established market regulatory authorities which, like the SEC, control corporate public disclosures and oversee market intermediaries such as stock exchanges, brokers, and retail-oriented asset managers. Belgium established a national securities regulator as early as 1935; France did so in 1967, Italy in 1974, Spain in 1988, and Luxembourg in 1990. However, the respective tasks of Europe's financial regulators vary widely from country to country. The United Kingdom's Financial Services Authority (FSA) and Germany's BAFin have been given roles in the prudential supervision of banks and insurers, which is not the case for France's AMF or Italy's Consob.

In this picture, the SEC's authority over U.S. accounting standard-setting is a distinctive feature. It was framed in the New Deal securities legislation as a subcategory of the SEC's duty to oversee corporate financial disclosures. Since then, the SEC delegated the day-to-day task to various successive private-sector bodies, most recently the FASB since 1973, but the SEC constantly kept watch over it, including by issuing its own interpretations that are technically part of US GAAP. In other countries, however, accounting standards have generally been entrusted to agencies separate from the securities regulator, either because the government wanted to keep more direct control over them (as in France or, to a lesser degree, in Germany[5]) or, on the contrary, because they have remained under a self-regulatory framework with only loose oversight by the state (as in the United Kingdom). Moreover, with the recent adoption of IFRS by countries representing most of the capital-markets activity outside the United States, accounting standards in these countries have been radically decoupled from the authority of national securities regulators.

In all countries, courts also play a major role in the regulation of markets. Only they have the authority to impose certain penalties, although the SEC and other regulatory authorities in different countries have enforcement powers of their own over several market participants. In the previous chapter, we saw how shareholders, particularly large institutional investors, are ever less reluctant to challenge companies in court. The way in which this mechanism operates also varies widely from one country to another. Some courts are highly specialized and can host an informed discussion with market participants, including on the most arcane aspects of the preparation of financial statements. In others, judges have only general legal training and sometimes experience great difficulties in unraveling the complexities and ambiguities of financial practices.

Finally, ministries and legislatures themselves have various levels of influence on securities regulation, depending on the country considered. How the U.S. Congress put pressure on the FASB in 1993 to prevent the mandatory expensing of stock options has been described in chapter 3. And, especially since the adoption of IFRS, European Union institutions such as the European Commission, the European Parliament, and the Committee of European Securities Regulators (CESR), a group that brings together all national counterparts to the SEC in the twenty-five EU member states, play an increasing role in regulating financial markets. In total, for better or worse, the large number of governmental or quasi-governmental authorities simultaneously involved in the oversight of financial activities has become a structural feature of today's financial life, resulting not only in a sometimes mind-numbing complexity of rules but also, increasingly often, the risk of overlapping jurisdictions and of uncertainties as to the precise remit of each of them.

The Junction between Government and Markets

Beyond the multiplicity of participants, the special character of the regulation of financial markets is that it takes place at a critical junction between the public and private realms. To be effective, regulation must handle this delicate position in a way that is both consistent and flexible, which raises the much-debated issue of the boundary between regulation and self-regulation.

Since Enron, self-regulation has been challenged in several instances. In the case of the audit profession, it was abruptly ended in almost all developed economies and replaced by varying schemes of public oversight, as has been described in chapter 5. But the boundary between private sector self-regulation and public oversight can be a rather subtle one. In the world of finance, the communities of public regulators on the one hand, and private practitioners on the other, are not always tightly separated, which means that in practice some features of public regulation involve dynamics that are not essentially different from self-regulatory mechanisms of peer judgment. The last three chairmen of the SEC, Arthur Levitt (1993–2001), Harvey Pitt (2001–03), and William Donaldson (2003–05), all spent a large part of their career on Wall Street. Even in France, where the statist tradition of an autonomous civil service is very strong, the board of AMF, the national securities regulator, contains a majority of members with a private sector background.

In accounting standards-setting, the preeminence of the private sector and the self-regulatory dimension are even more prevalent, even though, as we have seen in chapter 3, the standards themselves have to be considered a matter of public policy. In almost all developed countries, it is participants in the capital markets—current or former auditors, preparers of accounts (in the finance departments of companies), or investors—who play the main part in setting the accounting standards. In the United States, the FASB's seven full-time members include three former auditors, two former employees of investment banks, one former CFO, and one former university professor. Similar proportions are found in other national accounting standard-setting bodies, for example in Germany and the United Kingdom, as well as at the IASB, a private-sector organization that depends on no particular government.

The strong involvement of individuals with a private-sector background in the regulation of financial activities is justified by the sheer technical complexity of market practices. Only individuals with experience in capital markets can efficiently scrutinize their mechanisms and thwart fraud or irregularity. One could perhaps say that regulatory authorities have something in common with computer-security companies that recruit former hackers to devise antivirus or firewall software. When the menace is complex and fast-moving, practitioners are much better equipped than career civil servants to track it, even if they may not always be the most immune to suspicions of conflict of interest.

This obviously raises the question of the control over the regulator itself, which should not be allowed to be held hostage by special interests to the detriment of the public good. This is the old problem of the accountability of public authorities, unchanged for almost two thousand years since the Roman satirist Juvenal memorably summed it up with his question, *Quis custodiet ipsos custodies?*[6] This question is especially crucial in democratic regimes, where the authority of the regulator in principle stems from a delegation by the people. In this respect, the regulator's line of accountability is probably clearer in the United States than in most other countries, because of the pivotal role between government authority and private market operations assigned to the SEC. The Securities and Exchange Commission concentrates in itself the role of interface between executive and legislative authority on the one hand, and most of the non-judicial components of market regulation on the other, whether dealing with matters under its own authority or through the delegation of specialized tasks to bodies such as the FASB, the PCAOB, or the self-regulatory organizations, such as NYSE and NASD. It is the SEC that gives the FASB its authority, appoints the members of the PCAOB, and grants SROs the status that authorizes them to directly oversee market transactions. The other side of the coin is that the SEC constantly interacts with executive and legislative authorities, which is very concretely illustrated by the location of its head office at a stone's throw from the Capitol in Washington, D.C. (rather than, say, in a skyscraper on Wall Street). This interaction takes the form of constant contact between SEC commissioners and employees and the staff of congressional committees and executive department officials, as well as with representatives of numerous lobbies and interest groups. And in addition to formal contacts, there is an active policy discussion taking place in think tanks and other debating venues characteristic of the policy-planning process in the U.S. capital.[7]

Being thus doubly embedded in market activity and in the policymaking community, and despite its complexity and its many imperfections, the institutional system of the United States manages to some degree to reach the diverging goals of market-savvy regulation and public accountability. This does not always prevent bureaucratic drift or capture by special interests, especially when these interests are simultaneously successful in imposing their agenda on the executive branch or Congress. But at the very least, the checks and balances in place ensure a degree of conformity of the regulatory process to the intentions displayed in its founding legislation. The media also play a valuable monitoring role. The national press closely scrutinizes the activity of regulators in the United States and took significant part in the resignation of Harvey Pitt from the SEC in November 2002, following the ill-judged nomination of William Webster as PCAOB Chair. (Webster is a former director of the CIA who was found to have been indirectly involved in accounting irregularities at US Technologies, an incubator of high-technology companies.)

Compared with the U.S. system, European regulators are in general both less accountable and more fragmented as regards their specific tasks and missions. The United Kingdom is a special case because of the long-standing role of self-regulation in the City of

London. The Financial Services Authority, established in 2000 by merging together several previously existing bodies, is a kind of arbiter in a financial community that is otherwise strongly organized, with a dense network of professional associations and clubs playing an essential self-regulatory role. In Germany, market regulation is dispersed among a federal agency that was established as recently as 1994 and then thoroughly restructured in 2002 under the name BAFin, professional organizations, and the *Länder* (semi-autonomous regions) whose importance in the system is still essential. In France, the Autorité des Marchés Financiers (AMF) enjoys a large degree of practical autonomy and is not subject to particularly intense outside supervision by executive or legislative authorities, but it also has a relatively limited mandate as matters such as auditor supervision or accounting standard-setting are outside its remit.[8] In Italy, the Consob is only starting to assert itself as a credible and independent regulator.

The Territorial Challenge

Seen through the lens of institutional settings, financial regulation looks like an essentially national activity, conducted at federal and state levels in the United States and within the borders of each nation in Europe and the rest of the world. But markets increasingly ignore national borders, and the trend toward globalization, which is arguably more advanced for movements of capital than in any other sector of economic activity, raises a formidable challenge to public regulation. The need for common rules is as pressing for cross-border transactions as it is within a national market, and there is no reason why international markets should be spontaneously more competitive or more efficient, or require less regulation, than national ones. This is the territorial challenge of regulation, or how to organize common rules and standards that cover politically separate countries to satisfy the needs of increasingly global investors and other market participants.

This territorial challenge is not entirely new. The dialectic balance between the state and federal levels of financial regulation has been the matter of continuous debate in the United States over the past century. An integrating European Union now experiences similar dilemmas, which are also raised at the international level, most notably with the rise of the IASB as a quasi-global accounting standard-setter.

The Pitfalls of Regulatory Federalism

The case of capital markets illustrates a recurrent theme in debates on regulation, which is whether it is better organized as a natural monopoly or whether instead a degree of competition should be fostered among regulators. This question has been discussed in the United States for decades, and is now increasingly on the agenda of the European Union as it becomes financially integrated but still retains, unlike most of its constituent member states, a high degree of internal political fragmentation.

The establishment of the SEC itself in the early 1930s was not without controversy. In the course of the previous years, several states had adopted their own legislation on the securities market, such as New York's Martin Act of 1921. Many people thought at that time that a securities regulator with nationwide authority would contradict the federal system of government on which the United States was built. Today still, by contrast to securities law (and, incidentally, to bankruptcy provisions which were expressly designated in the constitution as being under federal jurisdiction), corporate law in the United States is almost exclusively a matter of state authority. There is de facto competition among states to become the place of registration of large companies, which in practice resulted in many listed companies registered in the state of Delaware where legislation and courts are considered efficient and business-friendly. Also, the prudential supervision of insurance, of a large share of banking activity, and of many utilities, remains at the state level with limited federal interference. The August 2003 blackout, which paralyzed the Northeast region for a day, illustrated the almost total lack of effective authority of the Federal Energy Regulatory Commission over electric power providers. When the Securities Exchange Act was debated in 1933–34, many members of Congress warned of the danger of excessive bureaucracy and central government abuse that could result from the development of the federal regulation of capital markets.

On balance, the track record of more than seven decades of SEC activity looks overwhelmingly positive. New York has remained the dominant center of global financial activity, and the U.S. capital markets do not seem to have lost their competitive edge. However, the preeminence of the SEC over the U.S. regulatory system remains challenged, for various reasons. In many business circles, there is an inherent suspicion toward any form of federal regulation, and conservative think tanks regularly criticize the SEC for the burden it imposes on companies, particularly as regards financial disclosure obligations. The American Enterprise Institute, for example, took strong positions against the SEC's and FASB's effort on expensing stock options; it has also published a book calling for the restoration of securities market regulation at state level, implying a suppression or scaling down of the SEC's powers.[9] Conversely, Democrats have supported New York Attorney General Eliot Spitzer's effort to protect the "little guy" against what has been denounced as the inertia of the Bush-nominated SEC. In that story line, the SEC is described as being subject to excessive influence from large financial firms to the detriment of new entrants. Such criticism is likely to develop further following the mid-2005 change at the helm of the SEC, when William Donaldson, a moderate who often sided with the Democratic Commissioners, was replaced by Christopher Cox, a more politically engaged figure who was previously a Republican representative for California. The corresponding risk is that the activism of local regulators, particularly in New York and Massachusetts, may lead to more fragmentation of U.S. securities regulation across state borders, which could prove detrimental to the nationwide efficiency of markets.

Europe could be the matter of a similar discussion. For a long time, European capital markets have remained essentially national. Each country had its own currency, financial capital, market arrangements, accounting standards, and national traditions. Cross-border capital flows and business activity had little impact. This is no longer true. Following the adoption of the euro, investors have radically changed their behavior, and they now tend to think of the entire continent as a single market in which the nationality of companies has less and less meaning. Consolidation of stock exchanges, particularly the creation of Euronext from the merger of the exchanges in Amsterdam, Brussels, Lisbon, and Paris, the restructuring of clearing and settlement operators, and the reorganization of investment banks along pan-

European lines all point in the direction of an ever greater integration of the capital markets in Europe.

As a result, the regulation of these European markets, which until recently had been subjected to purely national frameworks, presents a similar problem to what existed in the United States just before the federal securities legislation of 1933–34, that is, a fragmented regulation for a market that is increasingly integrated throughout the continent. As in the United States at the time, the big question is whether that fragmentation leads to a "race to the bottom," with companies deciding to issue their securities in countries with the laxest regulation and the least investor protection, thereby increasing the general level of risk; or a "race to the top," with a healthy competition among national systems, stimulating innovation and fostering the spread of best practices. The integration is too recent and has been insufficiently analyzed to allow definitive conclusions to be formed, but the first of these two dimensions—the "race to the bottom"—may well exist at least in certain market segments.

The European Union (EU) has identified some of the corresponding risks and has set up a complex process to reach some degree of uniformity of rules, even though their implementation and enforcement remains conducted by different agencies in different EU member states. Several directives (framework legislation) have been adopted at EU level to harmonize national securities laws. A formal EU-wide process has been put in place, known as the "Lamfalussy process" in reference to a 2001 report by Alexandre Lamfalussy, a former president of the predecessor organization to the European Central Bank in the late 1990s. This process has been intended to foster shorter lead times to adopt directives on securities legislation, better consultation of market participants, and perhaps most important, better coordination among national regulators that now form a permanent committee known as CESR (the Committee of European Securities Regulators, generally pronounced "Caesar"). However, CESR is for the moment hardly more than a forum for discussion among national regulators, with a role to advise the European Union's institutions but no autonomous powers of decision or enforcement, and it can in no way be considered a European authority for securities regulation, even in embryonic form. The possibility of creating such an EU-wide agency dealing with financial regulation is therefore still an open question for the future, much as it was in the United States during the roaring twenties.

The same dialectic between unity and competition exists, on an even wider territorial scale, for accounting standards. In this area, the decision by the European Union to adopt IFRS for the consolidated financial statements of all its listed companies has radically changed the picture. Before that decision, each developed economy had its own national standards, a reflection of its particular traditions and of the respective strength of different market participants as has been illustrated in chapter 3. At that time, only the US GAAP could credibly pretend to benchmark status for other developed countries, in line with the dominant position of U.S. capital markets. This has changed dramatically in the course of the past few years. To borrow a term from the foreign-policy vocabulary, the world of accounting standard-setting has become bipolar, with a mixture of cooperation and competition between the two dominant systems, the US GAAP and IFRS. Other systems of accounting standards, principally in Asia, cannot claim the same level of preeminence and are quite likely to gradually follow the IFRS in the years to come. In March 2005, the Accounting Standards Board of Japan and the IASB held the first in a series of planned meetings to discuss convergence of their standards, and in booming China, where thousands of companies already publish nominally IFRS-compliant accounts in order to attract investments from abroad, the authorities have recently spoken in favor of convergence of local GAAP toward IFRS, describing the standards' worldwide adoption as an "inevitable trend."[10]

Whether the worldwide unification of accounting standards is desirable is a complex question. Such a unification is the implicit mandate assumed by the IASB, the committee developing international financial reporting standards, and it is now also advocated by the European Union. But the questions that arise in this discussion are comparable to those mentioned in the debate on regulation. Unification would have the obvious advantage of reducing the costs currently associated with reconciling the financial statements of companies that need to report under both IFRS and US GAAP, which includes all European companies listed in the United States. More to the point, it would make it possible to reach one of the ultimate aims of accounting, that is, the immediate comparability of the financial statements of all companies independently of their country of incorporation. Unification could thus eliminate some of the competitive distortions that different systems of accounting standards now induce between companies located in different places of the world. But conversely, some observers point to the fact that the simultaneous existence of two main systems of reference, the IFRS and US GAAP, could encourage competition and thereby foster the quality, innovativeness, and responsiveness of the standard-setting process. This is the argument in particular of many who try to defend the sovereign right of the United States on accounting standard-setting, whereas European and other countries have delegated their sovereign power to the IASB to set such standards.

The IASB: A Power on a World Scale

Behind its colorless acronym, the International Accounting Standards Board (IASB) has indeed become a powerful organization that has provided an original response to the challenges posed to regulators by increasingly global capital markets. Because of its status as an entirely private body whose organization, governance, and resources owe nothing to national state authorities, the IASB is an emblem of the possibilities and difficulties of global governance, at least as regards economic and financial matters.

The history of international accounting standards began in 1973 with the creation of the International Accounting Standards Committee (IASC), which was comprehensively overhauled in 2000–01 with the creation of the current two-level organization modeled on existing precedents in the United Kingdom and the United States.[11] Since 2001, the IASC Foundation, a private entity registered in Delaware, collects the funds, makes the key appointments, and guarantees the independence of the standard-setting process. The IASB (or IAS Board) itself, which develops the standards in full independence, is a London-based private entity under British law that is wholly owned and funded by the IASC Foundation, which appoints all IAS Board members. These are twelve full-time members who, once appointed, must sever all ties with their former employers, and two part-time members who continue their professional employment. The IASB's budget was on the order of 11 million British pounds (about 20 million U.S.

dollars) in 2004, and, in addition to the board members, has a permanent staff of about forty based on 30 Cannon Street in London.

The IASC Foundation is currently chaired by Tommaso Padoa-Schioppa, an Italian former central banker who succeeded Paul Volcker in 2005. Its nineteen trustees include six North Americans, six Europeans, six members from the rest of the world (Japan, Hong Kong, Brazil, Australia, and South Africa), and one representative from the Bank for International Settlements in Basel. The current chairman of the IAS Board is David Tweedie, a Scot who had previously held the same position in the United Kingdom's Accounting Standards Board.

The IASB is often criticized in non-English-speaking countries for an alleged imbalance in the nationalities of its members. As a matter of fact, ten of its fourteen current members come from English-speaking countries, with the United Kingdom and the United States alone accounting for seven members (i.e., half the board, including the chairman and vice-chairman), plus one Canadian, one Australian, and one South African. The four remaining current members are from France, Germany, Japan, and Switzerland. The IASB's line of defense against the often-heard charge of not being geographically balanced points out that the most highly qualified international accounting professionals generally come from English-speaking countries, which also are host to a large part of the world's capital-markets activity.

The organizational structure of the IASB is further supplemented by a Standards Advisory Council and an International Financial Reporting Interpretations Committee (IFRIC), whose function is to determine the interpretation of standards in situations considered ambiguous. As in national standards organizations, the accounting profession is well represented in these bodies, but the IAS Board also includes other financial professionals with backgrounds in corporate finance, banking, investment management, and academia.

The rationale for the European decision to adopt IFRS, which was essentially made in 2000, was quite straightforward. The first step was a recognition that the integration of Europe's capital markets led to the necessity of unifying the accounting standards used by listed companies across the continent. Second, it was clear that the attempt to gradually harmonize the systems of national standards through European directives, which had been attempted in the late 1970s and early 1980s, had been a failure. Third, the European Commission had neither the technical capacity nor the credibility to create, on its own and from scratch, a system of European accounting standards of sufficient quality. Hence, if no action were taken, the US GAAP would impose themselves as the default standard for large European companies, which at the time were all looking for a listing on the New York Stock Exchange or the Nasdaq. In other words, the choice of IFRS was in essence a defensive one, as they were the only credible alternative that could be quickly implemented to thwart what was identified by then as the risk of a massive migration of European blue-chip companies from national accounting standards toward US GAAP.

The European Union nonetheless attempted to keep some degree of control by defining a so-called endorsement mechanism for the adoption of IFRS, which was enshrined in the 2002 regulation that set the general framework and deadlines for IFRS adoption. Under this framework, each individual standard and interpretation is applicable to listed European companies only after its formal endorsement by the European Commission, following a vote by an Accounting Regulatory Committee (ARC) made up of representatives of member states voting under qualified-majority rule in accordance with usual EU decision-making processes.[12] The crucial point here is that the European Commission may adopt or reject any individual rule (which include the IAS and IFRS standards and their revisions and also the interpretations issued by the above-mentioned IFRIC and its predecessor called SIC), but that in principle it cannot amend their content—precisely as a measure to maintain the unity of the body of international standards. In practice, the European Commission adopted all existing IAS and IFRS standards in 2003 and 2004, except for the IAS 39 standard on financial instruments from which, as has been already described in chapter 3, provisions were "carved out" about the "fair value option" and "macro-hedging," a politically expedient choice whose legal status under the 2002 regulation is doubtful at best and has been stated by the European Commission as being an exceptional and temporary fix.

The existence of the endorsement mechanism undoubtedly encourages preliminary discussion between the European Commission and the IASB on drafts of new standards, so that the final texts can be adopted smoothly by the European Union. However, this should by no means lead to the conclusion that the IASB is working primarily for Europe. The relationship between the IASB and the European Union is entirely different from the one between a national standard-setter (say, the FASB) and its political counterpart (say, Congress), because the IASB's territorial remit has no boundaries and potentially extends to any country in the world, without giving Europe any privileged role. And as a matter of fact, the European Union is far from being alone in having made IFRS mandatory for its listed companies by 2005. This is also the case for dozens of countries as varied as Egypt, Norway, Peru, and Russia and China for listed financial firms and companies whose shares can be purchased by foreign investors (so-called B-shares). In addition, places such as Australia, New Zealand, Hong Kong, and Singapore use national accounting standards that are replicates of IFRS for most practical purposes. Moreover, the IASB sees this as a dynamic expansion, and perhaps its single most important strategic objective now is of one day having its standards recognized in the United States. In the fall of 2002, the IASB and the FASB signed a common document known as the Norwalk Agreement (named after the town in Connecticut where the FASB has its offices), to signal their intention to move toward "convergence" of their respective standards. This means an effort to eliminate, to the extent possible, the existing differences between IFRS and US GAAP, and a joint *ex ante* work on drafts of new rules. With this stated convergence aim, which will necessarily result in the IASB sometimes aligning itself on existing or planned US GAAP rules (the reverse may also occur), the United States now probably has more direct and decisive influence on the evolution of IFRS than Europe does—however paradoxical this may sound to European ears, as the EU has adopted IFRS and the United States has not. In any event, and even though the adoption of IFRS in the EU has been without question a crucial step in the growth of the IASB's global influence, Europeans are mistaken whenever they are tempted to see the IFRS as mainly European standards.

The same discrepancy in perceptions may explain some of the difficulties in the current dialogue among Europeans, public authorities and private operators alike, and the IASB. The IAS Board sees itself as completely independent, accountable in principle to only the trustees of the IASC Foundation. The Europeans, who are aware of the significant real-world implications of the standards (which, as has been seen in chapter 3, are far from economically neutral), consider it indispensable that the IASB fit in one way or another into a system of collective responsibility toward the European public. But at the same time, most European policy makers also wish that the United States authorities adopt IFRS instead of US GAAP, or at least give them some degree of official recognition, which would eliminate the possible distortions in transatlantic competition based on accounting standards. The paradox here is that such U.S. recognition of IFRS, which the SEC declared in April 2005 that it would consider (but with no binding timetable), would mean an even more limited European influence on the IASB, which would then arguably become even more sensitive to U.S. constituencies than is currently the case. Moreover, any current efforts by the EU to assert control over the IASB can only hamper the prospect of IFRS recognition in the United States and would therefore be at least partly counterproductive.

In other words, the choice made by the European Union in 2000–02 has proved to be a radical abandonment of policy sovereignty for the sake of more efficient and transparent capital markets. Seen retrospectively, the decision to transfer responsibility for accounting standards to a private body independent of any political authority and with global ambitions was an unprecedented and strikingly bold move. The way in which the consequences of this choice will unfold in the coming years will be decisive for the future of the IASB as well as for the future of corporate financial reporting in Europe. The key question is how, under these circumstances, the IASB will be able to gradually assume its responsibility toward the public it serves, without losing the independence that is a crucial driver of its credibility: the fact that they now have a direct responsibility vis-à-vis the public is a major new challenge for the IASB, described by Alexander Schaub, the top EU bureaucrat on these issues, as "a deep change, a real shock to their self-understanding."[13] It seems improbable that over the long run, the setting of accounting standards, with its manifold impacts on the behavior of economic agents and therefore on public well-being, can escape from any form of accountability, however indirect, vis-à-vis the democratic institutions that represent citizens. The endorsement mechanism already set up by the European Union may not be sufficient for that purpose. But the form under which the IASB could make itself accountable to the European Union and the other countries that use its standards has yet to be invented.

Adapting Financial Regulation to Global Interdependence

European misgivings on accounting standards are part of a wider picture, which can be described as a tension between, on the one hand, the leadership and strength of the U.S. national regulatory system and, on the other hand, the increasingly global character of capital markets. This may be seen as a particular case of what *New York Times* columnist Thomas Friedman once termed his "theory of everything": because of its unique power, the United States "touches people's lives—directly or indirectly—more than their own governments. [. . .] Finding a stable way to manage this situation will be critical to managing America's relations with the rest of the globe."[14] Friedman had in mind the discontent of many countries' public opinions about the war in Iraq, but a similar tale could be told about the decisions that shape all countries' capital markets being made predominantly in New York and Washington, D.C. Financial markets have distinctive features of their own, however, and it is quite possible that original governance solutions may emerge for them which cannot be transposed to other matters of international relations and policy.

Examples have abounded in the past few years to strengthen the feeling that the rules of the game for capital markets are disproportionately made in the United States, without other countries having much possibility to influence the policy outcomes. Through the granting of the NRSRO status (see chapter 6), the SEC is in all practical matters the only regulator in the world that has any authority over the major financial rating agencies. This was plainly acknowledged by a 2005 report of the Committee of European Securities Regulators (CESR), which candidly concluded that in considering possible European actions to regulate rating agencies, "there is an argument for the wait and see approach."[15] The Sarbanes-Oxley Act's extraterritorial provisions imply that the U.S. PCAOB has, in principle at least, the power to inspect and to impose its standards on any audit firm that has clients listed on the U.S. markets, even if that listing is only a secondary one. Section 404 of the same act has become the main driving force behind the reshaping of internal controls in corporations all around the world. As mentioned in chapter 6, the U.S. jurisdictions have also taken a lead in what law experts call "global forum-shopping," so that European minority shareholders in Vivendi Universal, Parmalat, or other companies find it attractive to sue these companies in the United States rather than in their home countries to take advantage of the possibilities offered by U.S. class actions. Regulatory initiatives are also more responsive, powerful, and authoritative in the United States. As discussed earlier in the Parmalat case, the SEC was quicker in launching an investigation than its Italian counterparts. In total, more than one hundred non-American companies listed in the United States have been prosecuted by the SEC or the Justice Department between 1995 and 2004, which makes it more likely that they will be exposed to legal proceedings than U.S. companies themselves.[16] And as we have seen, as a consequence of the IFRS-US GAAP convergence process and of greater technical expertise, the SEC and FASB probably now have more influence on the IASB than any player in the European Union, even though only the latter has adopted the international standards to this date. As one European observer put it, "the IASB listens carefully to the SEC but not so closely, it seems, to the European Union,"[17] perhaps at least partly because the SEC has been able to assemble more skilled teams than the Europeans in monitoring standard-setting. The SEC has announced it would be active in monitoring the implementation of IFRS in the European Union, with the implication that it is likely to have more influence than any other player in the crucial debates ahead on the implementation and interpretation of IFRS rules in the European context.[18] The SEC's comment letters to companies on IFRS implementation will probably de facto become an important part of the body of rules European companies will feel they must apply in order to be compliant with IFRS.[19]

As these examples show, the United States' predominance in global financial regulation does not result solely from the sheer size of its markets. Although that size is impressive, the financial world is far from being "unipolar"—it is rather bipolar in fact, with the aggregated European market capitalization at 68 percent of the U.S. one, and the two together totaling as much as 73 percent of global equity capitalization in the world.[20] In some aspects, Europe actually supersedes the United States, such as in the issuance of new bonds for which, since the creation of the euro, the amount issued in euros has been higher than the amount of new bonds issued in dollars.[21] But in regulatory matters, the SEC and other components of the U.S. system reign virtually all-powerful over their international counterparts, as *Financial Times* columnist Brian Groom bluntly but accurately expressed in February 2004 when he described the SEC as "the world's de facto [securities] regulator."[22]

The specifically transatlantic dimension of this global imbalance is arguably much less due to American "imperialism" than to Europe's internal weakness, as it results from the fragmentation of its financial regulation that remains organized along purely national lines, and moreover is often divided among several different institutions within each country.[23] Each of these jealously autonomous national regulators is of negligible weight in comparison with the SEC. For example, France's AMF had in 2004 a budget of €46 million, roughly twenty times less than the SEC's $893 million—not counting all the bodies that are placed under SEC authority, such as the FASB ($30 million in 2004), the PCAOB ($70 million in 2004, $136 million in 2005), and the SROs whose costs incurred for regulatory functions under the SEC's watch also range in the hundreds of million dollars. But any talk of further regulatory integration is considered politically incorrect in Europe, because it would be seen as yet another "abandonment of sovereignty" in a low-trust context, which has been highlighted in May and June 2005 by the rejection of the proposed European constitutional treaty in the referendums held in France and the Netherlands—even though the integration of Europe's capital markets is arguably already too advanced for any national authority to continue making much sense and impact.

In the United States, the stakes are even higher as regards future policy choices. In addition to the transatlantic relationship, the U.S. regulators will increasingly have to manage relations with Asian countries that are bound to gain in importance and weight on global capital markets in the years to come, in line with the emergence of China and India as global economic powerhouses.

In this respect, what happens in the area of accounting standards may perhaps be an indication of the shape of things to come. The U.S. authorities are in an ambiguous position as regards the prospect for official recognition of IFRS (i.e., authorizing companies listed in the United States to publish their financial statements using IFRS instead of using US GAAP as is now obligatory). On the one hand, maintaining this prospect is a huge lever of influence over the IASB, through the IFRS–US GAAP convergence process and other ongoing discussions such as the so-called constitution review, a limited overhaul of the IASB's governance framework. On the other hand, eventually granting equivalent status to the IFRS would mean a significant loss of influence of US GAAP and, through this, of the U.S. national regulatory system over its international counterparts. Even with a disproportionate degree of influence, the SEC can only be one among many stakeholders of the IASB and IFRS, whereas it has undisputed and exclusive authority over the FASB and US GAAP. In the end, the choice on accounting standards—and this framework of options could well extend to other regulatory issues in the years to come—is between taking advantage of the current U.S. leadership to gain a large stake in a globally accepted multilateral system, or trying to maintain the dominance of U.S. national rules.

As mentioned earlier, it would be misleading to look at this dilemma through only the transatlantic lens. If the United States and Europe were alone, the best option for the United States would probably be to prolong the current situation that combines high leverage over the IASB (and over the implementation and interpretation of IFRS in Europe itself, through the oversight of U.S.-listed European corporations) with complete autonomy in setting, updating, and implementing US GAAP at home. But the rise of Asian economies and especially China, which for obvious political reasons will never adopt US GAAP as such, introduces a strong incentive for the United States to promote and strengthen the IASB, in which the SEC and FASB are influential, rather than see the Asians develop autonomous sets of standards if the IFRS' prospects in the United States are dimmed. The future of accounting practices in tomorrow's global capital markets will thus crucially depend on the leadership and vision that the SEC and other U.S. authorities may, or may not, display in the next few years.

CONCLUSION

May 2016: Smoke & Mirrors, Inc., has reinvented itself as a vendor of computer-simulation software for the design of complex fireworks, mostly exported to China. Its financial statements are now published every two weeks, in compliance with a new regulation jointly adopted by the SEC and Eurofin, the European securities regulator that was created in 2010 following an unprecedented series of interrelated accounting scandals in the United Kingdom, Poland, Malta, and Luxembourg. The statements are audited every month by Grazzi, Skjellsgård, Suryanarajayavarman & Zhuo (GSSZ), one of the fifteen international audit firms that resulted in 2012 from a comprehensive reform of the accounting profession. The overhaul was undertaken at the initiative of the three major firms remaining after one of the erstwhile "Big Four" had disappeared following a nasty shareholder lawsuit in New Zealand. Although listed in New York, Smoke & Mirrors, Inc., uses IFRS for its financial statements, thanks to an endorsement of these standards by the SEC in 2014. The talk now is of transforming the IASB into a public international organization modeled after the International Monetary Fund. This proposed reform was set by the United States and China as a condition for abandoning their national accounting standards altogether and for mandating the use of IFRS for all corporations listed in their respective territories.

Joseph Smith has retired from his CEO position. He, James Littleman, and John Wills have come together as partners to found a new firm, which advises large institutional investors on improving their monitoring of the performance of corporations in which they own shares. But Smoke & Mirrors, Inc., of course, is not included in the companies monitored, as a consequence of the very strict internal policies adopted by Smith, Littleman & Wills to avoid any possibility of conflict of interest.

Global markets are moving fast. The accounting scandals of the early 2000s, Enron first among them, highlighted the profound changes affecting financial reporting in an environment where corporate operations are less stable and more affected by disruptive innovations, and where investors are requiring ever more precise and elaborate data. At stake in these developments is nothing less than the way in which the various economic agents in the financial ecosystem interact and enable companies to find the capital they need to grow.

The awareness of accounting's shortcomings, as revealed by the recent accounting scandals, combines with the pressure resulting from the increase in investor influence, with the likely effect of leading to a rise in the quality required from corporate financial statements. Simultaneously, a continuous flow of financial innovation will inevitably lead to more complex and demanding accounting standards and policies, as practitioners adapt to the possibilities offered by new financing techniques and by emerging uses of information technology, among which XBRL may feature high in the years to come. At the same time, the combination of European integration, Asian growth, and globalizing capital means that the traditional centering of financial markets on the United States (and, to a lesser degree, the United Kingdom) is likely to evolve toward a more distributed structure with multiple centers of influence. This is bound to result in an even more complex financial reporting environment in the future, which in turn calls for even more attention from the general public over accounting issues.

Our journey in the realm of accounting and financial reporting highlights some important lessons. Financial accounting is a key enabler of capitalist activity, along with which it was born in the late Middle Ages. Financial transparency, in this view, is not an end in itself, but is increasingly a necessary means to satisfy the growing requirements of investors. Accounting also relies almost as much on human judgment about the future as it does on fact-collection about the past. As a consequence, high-quality accounting standards are crucial in order to diminish as far as possible the scope for manipulation and misrepresentation while providing users with relevant information—even though perfectly reliable and accurate accounts will always remain an unattainable ideal. Standards are modeled on the requirements of particular users; they cannot be neutral and are bound to influence corporate behavior in a number of areas. Therefore, their preparation is a matter of public interest, the oversight of which is an important regulatory task that needs to be adapted to the changing features of today's markets.

Accounting is not the arcane and peripheral field it seems to be at first sight. On the contrary, it is one of the most important foundations of any market-based economy. A better public understanding of its underpinnings, and of what is at stake with accounting standard-setting and enforcement, is necessary to adequately meet the challenges of the globalization of capital flows. Our hope is that the policy makers, regulators, business leaders, and practitioners who all have a stake in the financial reporting framework will develop enough knowledge, understanding, and vision on these issues to make the right choices in the years ahead.

APPENDIX 1: FINANCIAL STATEMENTS

OF SMOKE & MIRRORS, INC.

The initial balance sheet and income statement of Smoke & Mirrors, Inc., before the conversation described in the prologue, were as follows:

Table 3. Balance Sheet

($ millions, as of December 31)			
Assets		Liabilities and Equity	
Cash and cash equivalents	100	Accounts payable	140
Accounts receivable	100	Long-term financial debt	700
Inventories	200	Share Capital	500
Property, plant & equipment	900	Profit / loss of the current year	(40)
Total assets	1,300	Total liabilities and equity	1,300

Income Statement	
Revenue	550
Cost of goods sold	(400)
Gross margin	150
Sales & Marketing expenses	(40)
Research & Development expenses	(15)
General and Administrative expenses	(35)
Earnings before Interest & Tax (EBIT)	60
Interest expense	(52)
Profit/(loss) from discontinued operations	(48)
Profit/(loss) before tax	(40)
Corporate income tax	0
Net profit/(loss)	(40)

The financial ratios used are defined as follows:

$$\text{Net profitability} = \frac{\text{net profit/loss}}{\text{revenue}}$$

$$\text{Return on equity} = \frac{\text{net profit/loss}}{\text{shareholders' equity}}$$

$$\text{Debt ratio} = \frac{\text{net debt}}{\text{shareholders' equity}}$$
$$= \frac{\text{financial debt} - \text{cash and cash equivalents}}{\text{shareholders' equity}}$$

The corporate income tax rate is 30 percent.

Step 1: Transfer of corporate headquarters

The building is sold to a special-purpose entity (SPE) for a price of $190 million, whereas its net value on the balance sheet was $150 million. Thus, the transaction leads to recognition of a capital gain of $40 million. In return, Smoke & Mirrors commits to pay the SPE a yearly rent of $20 million. Because the sale takes place at year-end, this rent has no impact on the current year and will appear only in the next one.

The current year's pretax profit is increased by the amount of the capital gain, that is, $40 million. Because Smoke & Mirrors previously had a loss of that amount, the increase does not result in a requirement to pay corporate income tax (to simplify, we assume here that the fiscal device of loss carry forward does not apply). As a result of the SPE's payment, Smoke & Mirrors' cash on hand increases by $190 million.

US GAAP status: The kind of operation described was allowed under US GAAP until 1988. Sale-lease back transactions had been increasingly popular in the United States, from the 1950s to the late 1980s. In 1988, FASB statement No. 98 (FAS 98) strengthened the criteria required for such so-called synthetic leases, with the following four conditions to allow for an off-balance sheet treatment:

- the non-cancelable lease term has to be less than 75 percent of the useful life of the asset;

- the present value of payments for rent has to be less than 90 percent of the market value of the transferred asset;

- there must be no "bargain option" at the end of contract;

- there must be no automatic transmission of the asset at the end of the contract.

In practice, FAS 98 has considerably restricted the possibilities for off-balance sheet treatment of sale-lease back transactions. A similar rule exists under IFRS (IAS 17).

Step 2: Transfer of accounts receivable

$100 million of accounts receivable are sold to the SPE, and the proceeds from the sale result in an increase in cash. As in the previous step, the transaction occurs on December 31 and thus has no impact on the current year's interest income. Because the receivables are sold at face value, the transaction does not generate a capital gain or loss.

US GAAP status: Operations not very different from the one described were allowed under US GAAP until 2003. Rules concerning the deconsolidation of special-purpose entities were overhauled in 2003 following the Enron collapse. FASB interpretation No. 46, which was adopted in January 2003, foresees that companies must consolidate SPEs for which an outside equity investor does not bear the economic risk of the transferred assets. Before this interpretation was issued, the criteria considered for off-balance sheet treatment were looser, focusing exclusively on the company's voting rights and equity stake in the SPE. Similar rules exist under IFRS (IAS 27 and SIC 12).

Step 3: Change in inventory accounting method

The inventory at the beginning of the year consisted of 20,000 tons of explosive powder valued at $15,000 per ton, that is, a total of

$300 million. In the course of the year, 20,000 additional tons were bought at $10,000 per ton, and 20,000 tons were also used in production.

With the "first-in, first-out" (FIFO) method formerly used, the powder used during the year was valued at $15,000 per ton. At the end of the year, the use of powder thus represented an operating expense of $300 million, and the remaining inventory was valued at $10,000 per ton, that is, $200 million for 20,000 tons.

With John Wills's "weighted average cost" method, the powder is valued at $12,500 per ton for both material used during the year and inventory left at the end of the year:

$$\frac{20{,}000\times15{,}000+20{,}000\times10{,}000}{20{,}000+20{,}000}=12{,}500$$

The corresponding operating expense is thus $250 million, and the inventory at the end of the year is also recorded at a value of $250 million.

With the reduction in operating expense, the pretax profit increases by $50 million. The company must now pay 30 percent tax on $50 million—$15 million—which is paid immediately and thus deducted from cash on the asset side of the balance sheet.

US GAAP status: The kind of operation described is allowed under US GAAP. To change the valuation method from FIFO to weighted average, Smoke & Mirrors would only need to provide an economic justification for its decision. The one-time profit derived from the change in accounting policy would be recorded as nonoperating income and included in the net profit. A similar rule exists under IFRS (IAS 2).

Step 4: Use of interest-rate derivatives (interest rate swap)

The transaction described involves the entire financial debt of $700 million. Its impact on the profit account is thus $(8\% - 4\%) \times 700 = \$28$ million on pretax profit, and $19.6 million on net profit after tax. Because the transaction takes place on December 31 as well, this impact appears only in the following year.

US GAAP status: The kind of operation described was allowed under US GAAP until 1999. Rule FAS 133, adopted in 1998 and effective since 1999, requires that derivatives be recognized at market value, so that expected losses resulting from future negative cashflows would have to be recognized by Smoke & Mirrors, Inc. Prior to the adoption of FAS 133, derivatives were usually valued at historic cost, that is, cash flows were recorded only at the time they occurred. A similar rule exists under IFRS (IAS 39).

Step 5: Reduction of salary for employees and granting of stock options and pension benefits

The operation results in a reduction of $40 million in salary costs. As a result, operating expenses decrease by the same amount, pretax profit increases by $40 million, net profit increases by $28 million, and corporate income tax by $12 million. Here too, the impact occurs only in the year following the current one. As in the preceding case, commitments created by the transaction will not materialize until several years later.

US GAAP status: The kind of operation described was allowed under US GAAP until 1993 (as regards pensions) and 2005 (as regards stock options). In 1993, Rule FAS 106 mandated the recognition of pension liabilities on an accrual basis. As for stock options, it was only in 2004 that the FASB required in its declaration 123(R) that they would have to be recognized as an expense, starting in 2005 or 2006 depending on fiscal-year closing dates. Before, the decision was left to the discretion of companies, which generally chose not to expense stock options and to only report them in the disclosure notes. Similar rules exist under IFRS (IAS 19 for pensions, IFRS 2 for stock options and other share-based payments).

Summary

The sequence of accounting changes is summarized in the following table:

Table 4. Summary of Steps 1 to 5

	Year N				Year N+1		
	Initial	Step 1	Step 2	Step 3	Budget	Step 4	Step 5
			($ millions)				
Balance sheet items as of December 31							
Cash and equivalents	100	290	390	375	425	445	473
Accounts receivable	100	100	0	0	0	0	0
Inventories	200	200	200	250	260	260	260
Property, Plant & Equipt	900	750	750	750	714	714	714
Total Assets	1,300	1,340	1,340	1,375	1,399	1,419	1,447
Accounts payable	140	140	140	140	150	150	150
Long-term debt	700	700	700	700	700	700	700
Total Liabilities	840	840	840	840	850	850	850
Share Capital and reserves	500	500	500	500	535	535	535
Profit/loss of current year	(40)	0	0	35	14	34	62
Total Shareholders' Equity	460	500	500	535	549	569	597
Income statement items							
Revenue	550	550	550	550	620	620	620
Cost of goods sold	(400)	(400)	(400)	(350)	(450)	(450)	(425)
Gross Margin	150	150	150	200	170	170	195
SG&A expenses	(90)	(90)	(90)	(90)	(100)	(100)	(85)
Interest income/(expense)	(52)	(52)	(52)	(52)	(50)	(22)	(22)
Other than current operations	(48)	(8)	(8)	(8)	0	0	0
Net profit/(loss)	(40)	0	0	50	20	48	88
Corporate Income Tax	0	0	0	(15)	(6)	(14)	(26)
Net profit/(loss) after tax	(40)	0	0	35	14	34	62
Key financial ratios				(%)			
Net profitability	–7	0	0	6	2	5	10
Return on equity	–8	0	0	7	3	6	12
Debt ratio	130	82	62	61	50	45	38

Steps 4 and 5 do not have an impact the first year but only the following year after the transactions are completed. Therefore, the column describing the impact of steps 4 and 5 above refer to expectations for that following year.

It may be noted that most operations suggested by John Wills have an overall negative tax impact. By artificially increasing profits, they proportionately increase tax due in the short term. Although the accounting manipulations give the impression that Smoke & Mirrors' situation has improved, their aggregate effect on the company's effective wealth and value is negative.

APPENDIX 2: SELECTED CONTROVERSIAL CASES OF CORPORATE ACCOUNTING

Ahold

Ahold is a Dutch company, established in 1887, which had become the third largest mass merchandise company in the world (after Wal-Mart and the French company Carrefour), with sales of $59.2 billion in 2002. Despite its European origins, 74 percent of those sales were made in the United States. The principal executives at the beginning of February 2003 were Cees van der Hoeven, chairman of the board, and Michael Meurs, CFO. The accounts were audited by Deloitte.

On February 24, 2003, Ahold disclosed irregularities in the accounts of its American subsidiary US Food Service and indefinitely postponed the publication of its financial statements for the year 2002. The CFO and the chairman of the board instantly resigned. Immediately thereafter, Deloitte retrospectively withdrew its unqualified audit opinion of the accounts for 2000 and 2001. Within a few days, Ahold stock lost two-thirds of its value. After those dramatic episodes, a new management team was set up and the company launched a radical program of selling assets to secure cash, cleaning up its balance sheet, and reorganizing its business.

The principal element in question in Ahold's accounting irregularities concerned payments made to US Food Service by its suppliers for "promotional allowances" (or "vendor rebates"), a common practice in the retail sector, which were systematically entered in the accounts on dates prior to receipt. In 2003, Ahold stated that the accounting irregularities resulted in an overstatement of net income by $1.2 billion. Accounting irregularities in other subsidiaries were also disclosed.

In July 2003, the Amsterdam prosecutor opened a criminal investigation into "possible falsifications and the possible publication of inaccurate annual profit figures" for joint ventures in Latin America and Scandinavia.

In early January 2004, VEB, a Dutch shareholders' association, began proceedings against Ahold, calling for revision of the company's accounts for the period from 1998 to 2002.

The SEC opened an investigation into possible violation of American law, as Ahold had been listed on the NYSE since 1993. It accused Ahold of having overstated its net income by more than $800 million and its net sales by about $30 billion during the period 2000 through 2002. Thanks to its cooperation in the investigation, Ahold eventually avoided being fined by the SEC. A group of former employees of Ahold's subsidiary US Food Service, however, are still being sued by the SEC, and an investigation is being carried out by the Department of Justice.

In parallel, a class action suit was launched, which has not yet been settled. By July 2005, Ahold's stock value had nearly recovered its pre-scandal level of $12 billion.

AIG

Founded in 1919 in Shanghai, American International Group (AIG) is the biggest insurance company in the United States by most measures, and one of the largest insurers worldwide, with approximately $800 billion of assets at the end of 2004.

In February 2005, a transaction for $500 million appears to have been improperly accounted for by AIG as an insurance premium in order to inflate its revenue and its reserves. The ensuing resignation in March (at the board's request) of its charismatic CEO, Maurice "Hank" Greenberg, after a reign of nearly forty years at the helm of the company, was a shock. On March 30, the company publicly acknowledged improper accounting for several transactions in the previous years, which were all aimed at making the financial situation of the company appear stronger than it actually was. AIG stated that its

net worth may have been overstated by $1.7 billion. Filing of the an-
nual accounts for 2004 was delayed, and Standard and Poor's immediately downgraded the rating of the company.

When the improper accounting of those transactions was disclosed,
AIG was already under investigations by the SEC and by the attorney
general of New York, Eliot Spitzer. A fine of $126 million had been paid
by AIG in 2004 for deals structured for clients that allegedly violated
insurance accounting rules, although AIG admitted no wrongdoing.
The company had also been accused of helping the insurance broker
Marsh & McLennan in fraudulent schemes in which Marsh illegally
pushed its clients to subscribe to insurance contracts with the insurance companies that proposed the highest commissions to the broker
(those commissions are known as "placement services agreements").
Jeffrey Greenberg, the son of Hank Greenberg, had to resign from his
position of CEO of Marsh & McLennan in October 2004.

In late May 2005, the SEC and the New York attorney general sued
AIG, Hank Greenberg, and Howard Smith, AIG's former CFO. The
company also announced that it had to restate its earnings for four
years by an amount of $4 billion. Greenberg disputed the grounds for
the restatement, calling many of the items "exaggerated and unneces-
sary,"[1] and pointed out that the responsibility of overseeing AIG's
accounting was equally shared by many people, including the company's audit committee as well as its auditor, PricewaterhouseCoopers.

In June 2005, an executive of General Reinsurance, the insurance
company that helped AIG set up the $500 million transaction that was
initially disclosed, decided to plead guilty. He admitted the transaction had no economic substance and "was designed solely for the purpose of achieving a specific, and false, accounting effect on [AIG's] financial statements."[2]

In July 2005, AIG announced it had named Arthur Levitt, the former chairman of the SEC from 1993 to 2001, as special advisor to the
board of directors on corporate governance issues. Indeed, Hank
Greenberg had put in place a system that has often been described as
the quintessential "Imperial CEO Rule," with weak governance and
the concentration of considerable power in the hands of the CEO, including a unique degree of personal control over AIG's scheme of ex-

ecutive compensation. This may have contributed to the deficiency of controls on the accounting issues at the root of the scandal.

AIG's accounts have been audited by PricewaterhouseCoopers (and its predecessor firm Coopers & Lybrand) for more than 20 years.

After a high on February 11, 2005, just before the first disclosures, AIG's share dropped 32 percent by the end of April. In about two months, its market capitalization thus decreased by $60 billion. Part of the losses were nevertheless regained afterward, and in August 2005 the stock quoted about 17 percent below its pre-scandal value.

AOL Time Warner

The Internet service provider AOL and the media giant Time Warner announced their merger in early 2000, in the midst of the "technology bubble," thereby creating the world's largest media company. Warner Bros. movie studio began production in 1922, the same year as *Time* magazine, with which it merged in 1990, whereas AOL was established in the 1980s. In 2002, AOL Time Warner had revenues of $41 billion and 91,000 employees worldwide. Its market capitalization immediately after the merger rose above $240 billion. At the time, the principal executives were Steve Case, former CEO of AOL, and Gerald Levin, who had held the same post at Time Warner. The accounts were audited by Ernst & Young.

In July 2002, AOL Time Warner disclosed the opening of an SEC investigation into questionable accounting methods for its advertising revenues. In August, management stated that it was unable to certify the company's accounts as required by the recently passed Sarbanes-Oxley Act. In early 2003, the company depreciated $99.8 billion dollars of goodwill for the year 2002, and as a result declared a $98.7 billion loss, the largest ever recorded by a company in the United States.

The SEC investigation related to advertising transactions, particularly those involving payment in kind (see chapter 4), which were thought to have been recorded on the AOL accounts for amounts significantly higher than their real value. This represented several hundred million dollars for the period 1999–2001, for example, a $100 million contract signed in 1999 between AOL and Monster.com, an online employment service. Other transactions, notably with World-Com, Qwest, and Vivendi Universal, are reportedly under investigation.

Numerous executives from AOL, including CEO Steve Case, have since left the company, which resumed the name Time Warner, Inc., in September 2003. In May 2005, Time Warner even indicated that it could spin off its AOL division, thus effectively reversing the merger.

In October 2003, the SEC investigated a $400 million contract signed with the German media conglomerate Bertelsmann after the merger between AOL and Time Warner in 2001. The services provided under this contract did not appear to justify its recording as advertising revenue. Time Warner agreed in December 2004 to pay $210 million to settle with U.S. Department of Justice charges, and in March 2005, $300 million to settle SEC charges that it had inflated its advertising revenues and the number of its Internet subscribers.

Several civil actions are under way. In February 2003, the Minnesota Board of Investment, a government fund management agency, was named lead plaintiff in a federal class action suit against AOL Time Warner, Steve Case, and several other company executives, who are accused of having overestimated revenues by $1.7 billion and of insider trading for selling stock at prices inflated by accounting irregularities. A similar suit, one of whose plaintiffs is the University of California, was filed in California State court in April 2003. In August 2005, the company announced that it would settle lawsuits from shareholders and employees for $3 billion.

The market capitalization of Time Warner in July 2005 was on the order of $76 billion, after a low point of $42.5 billion in August 2002.

Crédit Lyonnais

This large French bank, founded in 1863, nationalized in 1945, and privatized in 1999, had revenues of €6.7 billion in 2002, with 41,000 employees. In 1991–92, Crédit Lyonnais was headed by Jean-Yves Haberer, and its two chief operating officers (*directeurs généraux*) were François Gille and Bernard Thiolon. Its auditors were Ernst & Young and Coopers & Lybrand, now PricewaterhouseCoopers.

Beginning in the mid-1980s, Crédit Lyonnais entered on a policy of financing major acquisitions and investments in a wide array of industries, such as entertainment (acquisition of Metro Goldwyn Mayer) and real estate. A large number of these assets were hit by the recession and real estate crisis of the early 1990s. Unpleasant surprises were encountered in some acquisitions (including MGM), which together with the difficulties of investment subsidiary Altus Finance made the financial situation of Crédit Lyonnais delicate by 1991. However, the bank largely omitted to account for these difficulties in its financial statements for 1991 and 1992. Two years later, in 1994, the French State had to bail it out with a capital injection of 4.9 billion French francs (about $900 million). Soon thereafter, a book amount of 130 billion French francs ($23.5 billion) in bad loans and other questionable assets was transferred to a state-owned ad hoc entity, the Consortium de réalisation (CDR). After securing approval for these operations from the European Commission in 1998, the bank was privatized the next year, and eventually acquired by Crédit Agricole in 2003, thus putting an end to one hundred and forty years of independent existence.

Several former executives of Crédit Lyonnais, former statutory auditors, and officials in charge of government regulation were defendants in a criminal proceeding instituted in April 2000 and appeared in Paris criminal court in early 2003. They were accused of having prepared or of having accepted the preparation of misleading accounts for the years 1991 and 1992, and in particular of having knowingly underestimated the financial risks incurred by subsidiaries. Indictments had been issued for "presentation of inaccurate accounts and complicity," "dissemination of false or deceptive information and complicity," "failure to disclose criminal acts," and "certification of deceptive information."[3] The prosecution evaluated the additional provisions that should have been recorded in the accounts at 440 million euros for 1991 and 570 million for 1992.

Defense lawyers took advantage of the vagueness surrounding the notion of accuracy of accounts, relying on the very diverse evaluations of the extent of accounting manipulation presented by different expert witnesses. Under the judgment issued in June 2003, the former managers were convicted, with an eighteen-month suspended prison sentence and a €50,000 fine for former CEO Haberer, and lesser penalties for Mssrs. Gille and Thiolon (all three appealed the judgment). However, the other defendants, regulatory officials and statutory auditors, were all acquitted. The court merely noted in its grounds for decision that the auditors "demonstrated negligence" in "not insisting on receiving information." An appeals court confirmed in February 2005 the sanction for Haberer and Gille.[4]

Enron

See also chapter 2.

Enron was created in 1985 by the merger of InterNorth and Houston Natural Gas, two natural gas distribution companies. In the 1990s, it became an important player in the energy market, with revenues of $100 billion in 2000 and with a workforce of 20,600. Its market capitalization reached a high of $66 billion in September 2001 and was of the order of 25 billion in mid-October of the same year. Its principal executives were Kenneth Lay (chairman and CEO until the end of 2000), Jeffrey Skilling (chief operating officer, and then CEO for a few months until his sudden resignation in August 2001), and Andrew Fastow (CFO). Its accounts had been audited from the mid-1980s by Arthur Andersen.

The principal accusations made against Enron are the illegal arrangements used to deconsolidate special-purpose entities, misstatement of the value of certain assets, and improper accounting of the revenues of trading business. Enron is also accused of having played a key role in the crisis in the California energy market during the summer of 2000 by manipulating energy prices. This crisis deprived millions of residents of electricity, threw (among others) the utility Pacific Gas & Electric into bankruptcy, and cost the state of California several billions of dollars.

About twenty former executives of Enron faced criminal charges. Fifteen of them decided to plead guilty. At the time of writing, two of them have been sentenced and imprisoned: Ben Glisan Jr., the former treasurer of Enron (five years), and Lea Fastow, the wife of Enron's former CFO (one year). Her husband, Andrew Fastow, accepted in January 2004 a plea bargain involving a prison term of ten years and nearly $24 million in forfeiture, but his sentence is still to come.

The first criminal trial began in September 2004 and concerned the sale of a Nigerian barge by Enron. One former Enron employee as well as four former employees of Merrill Lynch were convicted of conspiracy to commit wire fraud and conspiracy to falsify books, records, and accounts and were sentenced to prison. A second trial, involving five former executives of Enron Broadband Services, began in April 2005. The court case involving Enron's highest executives, Kenneth Lay and Jeffrey Skilling, began in January 2006. In February 2004 Jeffrey Skilling faced an indictment for conspiracy, securities fraud, and insider trading, risking more than 325 years in prison and a fine of several hundred million dollars. As for Kenneth Lay, he was charged with eleven criminal counts in July 2004, including securities and bank fraud, risking a sentence of up to 175 years of imprisonment. Both men, along with former Enron chief accounting officer Richard Causey, are defendants in the trial.

Besides those criminal cases, fines of up to several millions dollars were paid in settlements between several former Enron executives and the SEC.

In addition, a large number of civil actions have been filed by former shareholders who believe they were misled by the information made public by the company on its financial health. The main class action suit, with the University of California (which itself manages a large investment fund whose returns are financing some of its legal expenses) as lead plaintiff, and with the participation of many pension funds, claims damages of more than $30 billion from the company, about thirty former executives of the company, its lawyers, Arthur Andersen, and several banks. It was in the context of this proceeding, which charges large-scale insider trading, that Arthur Andersen (or rather, what little is left of it) agreed to pay $40 million in November 2003. Settlements with banks reached unprecedented amounts: JP Morgan paid $2.2 billion; Citigroup, $2 billion; Lehman Brothers, $222.5 million; Bank of America, $69 million; and Canadian Imperial Bank of Commerce, $2.4 billion. Former Enron directors also paid significant amounts. Settlements thus far total up to nearly $7.1 billion. A trial is scheduled in October 2006 for defendants that would not settle, which may include Merrill Lynch, Deutsche Bank, Credit Suisse First Boston, and Barclays.

Creditors have sued the company's lawyers, Arthur Andersen, and more than thirty former company executives, including Mssrs Lay and Skilling, after being authorized to do so by a Bankruptcy Court judge in Manhattan in December 2003.

In connection with the Enron affair, and separately from the above-mentioned class actions, the SEC in July 2003 also imposed fines on the banks JP Morgan Chase ($135 million), Merrill Lynch ($80 million), Citigroup ($120 million), and, in December 2003, the Canadian Imperial Bank of Commerce ($80 million). All these banks were accused of having helped Enron conceal its real financial condition by means of structured financing operations.

As for the claims that Enron played a role in the California energy crisis in 2000, a settlement was reached in August 2005, and Enron agreed to pay $1.5 billion to the state of California and other parties involved.

In November 2004, Enron's shares were cancelled in the framework of the bankruptcy proceeding. The remaining assets of the company will serve to repay creditors, who should recover an estimated 20 percent of the face value of their credits.

Fannie Mae and Freddie Mac

The Federal National Mortgage Association, better known by its nickname Fannie Mae, was created by the U.S. Congress in 1938 to help the housing industry during the Depression. It turned private in 1968 and has operated since then as a Government Sponsored Enterprise (GSE),[5] with a mission to provide stability and liquidity on the secondary mortgage market. Fannie Mae hence does not directly lend money to home buyers but plays a key role in the mortgage market, acting as a secondary-level lender that either repurchases or insures loans granted by mortgage brokers to households. Fannie Mae's charter specifies that it should promote access to mortgage credit to low- and moderate-income families, as well as to people living in underserved areas. To carry out these public purposes, Fannie Mae receives support by the federal government in the form of a line of credit from the U.S. Treasury, exemption from state and local income taxes, and exemption from SEC oversight.

Its special status makes it possible for Fannie Mae to borrow money on financial markets at rates close to those of U.S. Treasury securities. Although no explicit guarantee exists from the U.S. authorities for the company's debt, it is widely believed among investors that the federal government would intervene if a GSE were to become insolvent. In 1970, a second GSE was created in the mortgage sector, the Federal Home Mortgage Corporation (nicknamed Freddie Mac).

At the end of 2003 Fannie Mae's total assets amounted to $1,009 billion, making it the biggest GSE and the third-largest global financial group,[6] whereas Freddie Mac's assets amounted to $797 billion. Together, the two GSEs either hold or provide a warranty for 46 percent of the $7,700 billion U.S. mortgage loan market.

In 2002, both Fannie Mae and Freddie Mac agreed to voluntarily register their common stock with the SEC and follow federal corporate disclosure requirements, despite the exemption in their charter, in order to address the criticisms that had been raised against their privileged status as GSEs and the proposals made to repeal part of their charters' provisions.

In January 2003, under the advice of its new auditor, PricewaterhouseCoopers, Freddie Mac announced that some applications of its accounting policies, including those involving derivatives and mortgage assets, were out of line with generally accepted accounting principles (GAAP). As a consequence, the mortgage company, which acknowledged having understated its earnings to "smooth out volatility in profits," restated its accounts for 2000, 2001, and 2002 by $4.4 billion upwards. Through misapplication of the accounting rules for derivatives and hedges (FAS 133), it had understated earnings by $1.12 billion in 2000 and by $4.35 billion in 2002 while overstating earnings by $989 million in 2001, in order to maintain a regular increase of its income (in the profession, this kind of artificial reserve is known as "cookie jar" or "rainy day"). President and chief operating officer David Glenn was dismissed, while Leland Brendsel, Freddie's chairman and CEO, and Vaughn Clarke, its CFO, had to resign. Freddie Mac subsequently paid a $125 million fine to its regulator, the Office of Federal Housing Enterprise Oversight (OFHEO).

One year later, in September 2004, the OFHEO made public the conclusions of the report of an investigation into Fannie Mae's accounting practices and accused the company of having manipulated its accounts in order to meet the earnings per share targets that permitted bonuses be paid to the company's executives. The improperly accounted items identified by the OFHEO were, as in Freddie Mac's case, derivatives misclassified as hedges, whereas they should have been marked to market, and amortizations of profit and losses related to mortgage-backed securities, for which the FAS 91 rule had been misapplied. Unlike Freddie Mac, which had mainly understated its performance, Fannie Mae turned out to have overstated its income by an estimated $8.4 billion, according to declarations made by the company in December 2004 after the SEC had confirmed the misapplication of GAAP and asked the company to restate its financial statements. The company's CEO Franklin Raines and its CFO Timothy Howard had to resign, and KPMG, the auditor of the company since 1969, was dismissed. Raines and Howard, who signed Fannie Mae's financial statements in 2002 and 2003, may face charges pursuant to the Sarbanes-Oxley Act, and KPMG could go under an investigation by the newly created Public Company Accounting Oversight Board (PCAOB).

As of August 2005, Fannie Mae had still not been in a position to make public the restatement of its accounts. In addition, it declared that further accounting problems were identified, so that it may also have to restate transactions for which US GAAP rules FAS 149 (Amendment of FAS 133 on Derivative Instruments and Hedging Activities) and FAS 115 (Accounting for Certain Investments in Debt and Equity Securities) were not properly applied. The total restatement could reach $11 billion, according to the company.

A federal class action suit was initiated by the Ohio attorney general against Fannie Mae and its former executives Timothy Howard and Franklin Raines, on behalf of the Ohio Public Employees Retirement System, the State Teachers Retirement System of Ohio, the Ohio Bureau of Workers' Compensation, and all other defrauded shareholders.

Parmalat

Parmalat, a dairy products and food processing company, was until late 2003 the seventh largest private company in Italy. Its sales were €7.6 billion in 2002, of which 35 percent were in Europe, 35 percent in North America, and 20 percent in Latin America. Its market capitalization was on the order of 1.8 billion euros at the beginning of November 2003, down from a peak of 3.5 billion in April 1998. The principal executives at the end of 2003 were Calisto Tanzi, CEO and founding shareholder, and the CFO Fausto Tonna. The accounts were audited until 1999 by Grant Thornton Spa, an Italian accounting firm associated with the North American Grant Thornton, the largest U.S. accounting firm outside the "Big Four." In 1999, Grant Thornton gave up its place to Deloitte, in accordance with an Italian law dating to the late 1970s requiring a regular rotation of auditing firms. Grant Thornton nevertheless remained as auditor of many non-Italian subsidiaries, notably several offshore companies that Parmalat had set up in the West Indies.

On November 11, 2003, the market learned that Deloitte had decided to raise reservations about the accounts for the first six months of 2003. On December 15, Calisto Tanzi resigned. On the 24th, Parmalat asked to be placed under bankruptcy protection. Its debts amounted to €14.5 billion, two-thirds of which were owed to foreign institutions. A bankruptcy administrator was appointed to carry out the restructuring of the company.

In December 2003, the principal executives of Parmalat were arrested by the Italian authorities and placed in preliminary detention for criminal conspiracy. In early January 2004, the auditors of the Grant Thornton Spa accounting firm were arrested as well, along with the lawyer Gian Paolo Gini who had helped devise the contested arrangements. In February 2004, Calisto Tanzi's children, Stefano and Francesca, were placed in detention and accused of "criminal conspiracy," "fraudulent bankruptcy," and "false financial statements." Along with their father, they are suspected of having participated in the diversion of around one billion euros for themselves or for companies under their control.

The SEC, for its part, initiated a civil proceeding against Parmalat, which it accused of having sold more than $1 billion in debt securities to American investors on the basis of falsified accounts. According to the complaint of the SEC, Parmalat overstated its assets by nearly $5 billion as of year-end 2003 and understated its debts by $10 billion. As a consequence, the net worth of the company amounted to a negative $13 billion on December 31, 2003, instead of $2.4 billion as reported in Parmalat's financial statements.

Several tactics seem to have been used by the company to hide its true financial situation, and it may have begun to set up arrangements designed to falsify its financial statements more than a decade before the scandal burst out. Parmalat had established a number of offshore nominee companies, to which it transferred debt guaranteed by assets that existed only on paper. In particular, an account allegedly opened in the New York branch of the Bank of America, listed in the assets for 3.95 billion euros, appears never to have existed and to have been justified to the auditors by falsifying the books. The nominee entities also entered into transactions (loans, interest rate swap, fictitious sales) with Parmalat's operating subsidiaries aimed at hiding losses made by those subsidiaries and artificially diminishing the debt appearing on the consolidated financial statements of the group.

In addition, in January 2004, a civil suit including a request for class action status was filed by a group of investors in state court in New York against leading executives of Parmalat and several firms accused of having provided them with advice: the audit firms Deloitte and Grant Thornton, the New York law firm Zini & Associates, and several banks (Citigroup, CSFB, Banca Nazionale del Lavoro). The plaintiffs accuse them of having set up a system for falsifying company accounts over a period of more than ten years, in particular by recording fictitious bank accounts, by falsifying financial documents, and by declaring fictitious transactions. The executives and their accomplices are also accused of having secretly diverted or aided in the diversion of approximately $1 billion. According to the complaint, 40 percent of the total assets declared by Parmalat did not in fact exist.

The SEC proceeding against Parmalat was settled in July 2004 and the company agreed to change its internal corporate governance rules, including on the election of the board of directors by the shareholders, its composition of independent individuals who will serve finite terms, and the obligation that the positions of chairman of the board and chief executive be held by two separate individuals.

In June 2005, a first trial was held in Italy and eleven former executives, including three former CFOs of Parmalat, were sentenced to prison terms of up to two and a half years. The investigation led by the Italian prosecutors will continue, and future trials should concern other former executives, the company's founder Calisto Tanzi, the auditors of the company, and also possibly financial institutions for their role in aiding the firm to raise cash in bond issues.

A number of civil actions were launched in the aftermath of the scandal. As already mentioned above, class action suits were initiated by investors. Parmalat also launched cases against a group of forty-five financial institutions that had lent it money in order to obtain the cancellation of part of its debts, claiming that they had been aware of its situation and had nevertheless continued to lend. As of July 2005, only Morgan Stanley had agreed on a settlement with Parmalat, whereas the other claims, including a claim for damages of $10 billion against Citigroup, were still pending.

Vivendi Universal

The old Compagnie Générale des Eaux, renamed Vivendi in 1998, merged with Seagram in 2000, giving birth to Vivendi Universal, and subsequently gradually withdrew from its traditional business of providing water and other services to municipalities (which were grouped together and spun off under the name Veolia Environnement). In 2001, the entire firm had revenues of €28.1 billion. Its market value reached a peak of almost €88 billion in January 2001, falling to 67 billion at the end of 2001, and around 50 billion in March 2002. Jean-Marie Messier was the company's CEO from 1996 until the summer of 2002 and was assisted by Éric Licoys, COO, and Guillaume Hannezo, CFO. The company was audited by Arthur Andersen and Salustro Reydel.

In March 2002, Vivendi Universal disclosed a write-down of €15.7 billion in its 2001 accounts in relation to several acquisitions made during the "technology bubble." Jean-Marie Messier claimed at the time that "Vivendi Universal is doing better than well," but its stock price accelerated the decline that had begun in late 2001. On July 2, the board forced Jean-Marie Messier to resign, leaving to his successor Jean-René Fourtou a heavily indebted company described by the new management team as on the verge of a cash crisis. The next day, the press revealed that there had been a sharp dispute between Vivendi Universal and the COB, France's securities regulator, at the end of 2001 over the accounting treatment of its investment in the British television network BSkyB.

A criminal investigation was begun in France in October 2002 into the "dissemination of false or deceptive information on the prospects for Vivendi Universal in 2001 and 2002" and the "publication of false balance sheets for the years 2000 and 2001."[7] There were additional allegations of misuse of company property in a complaint filed by the Association of active small shareholders (Appac) with respect to the salaries and severance benefits of Jean-Marie Messier and Edgar Bronfman Jr., former vice-chairman of the board of directors, as well as of possible insider trading.

Similar accusations were made by the SEC in its sanctions proceeding initiated against Jean-Marie Messier and Guillaume Hannezo in September 2003. The SEC accused them of having violated United States law applicable to listed companies by making deceptive statements in 2001 and 2002 about Vivendi Universal's liquidity and cash flow, by inappropriately changing the company's accounting methods in 2001 so as to give the impression that the EBITDA targets had been met, and by having concealed financial commitments and certain risks connected with subsidiaries that should have been included in disclosure notes. In late December 2003, the SEC reached a settlement with Jean-Marie Messier, by the terms of which he agreed to pay a penalty of $1 million to investors harmed by the fall in the share price, and to give up the severance package of €21 million that he claimed from Vivendi Universal. He is also barred for ten years from being a director of a company listed in the United States. Guillaume Hannezo is subject to the same prohibition for five years, along with a $120,000 fine.

The SEC accusations were repeated in a class action suit filed in California State court in 2002 against Vivendi Universal, Jean-Marie Messier, and Guillaume Hannezo. This suit, which concerns the period from February 11 to July 2, 2002, also accuses the company and its executives of having failed to depreciate the goodwill and other intangible assets connected with the mergers with Seagram and Canal Plus, and of having published deceptive information about the 2001 acquisition of MP3.com, an online music site. The Association for the defense of minority shareholders (Adam), headed by Colette Neuville, is handling this case in the United States in the name of three French shareholders.

In July 2005, the market capitalization of Vivendi Universal had gone back up to about €29 billion, after a low point of €10.1 billion in August 2002.

WorldCom

WorldCom was founded in Mississippi in 1983 by Bernard Ebbers, a media-savvy businessman, and then grew relentlessly through a series of acquisitions in the sectors of computer networks and Internet data transmission. In 1996, with the purchase of the telephone company MCI, WorldCom became the second largest long-distance carrier in the United States, just behind AT&T. Total revenues in 2001 reached $35.2 billion, and the company had 85,000 employees worldwide. Its market capitalization had reached a peak of $180 billion in June 1999 and was still above $40 billion in January 2002. The principal executives were Bernard Ebbers, until his replacement by John Sidgmore in April 2002, and the CFO, Scott Sullivan (until June 2002). The company was audited by Arthur Andersen until May 2002 and thereafter by KPMG.

On June 25, 2002, WorldCom declared large-scale accounting irregularities in the financial statements for 2001 and the first quarter of 2002. The share price collapsed. On July 21, 2002, the company requested bankruptcy protection. This was the largest bankruptcy in U.S. history, larger even than Enron. In November 2003, the company came out of Chapter 11 proceedings and was renamed MCI for the occasion, indicating a break with its more recent past.

The principal irregularity identified was booking current expenses (such as rental costs for the use of certain communications lines) in the accounts as investments that were depreciated over several years, a flagrant accounting fraud committed in this case on a very large scale. The SEC estimated at $9 billion the costs incorrectly accounted for between 1999 and 2002.

Scott Sullivan pleaded guilty to charges including conspiracy, securities fraud, and submitting false documents to the SEC. Bernard Ebbers, also indicted in early March 2004, was found guilty for all nine counts brought against him, after a trial that lasted until March 2005. Ebbers and Sullivan were sentenced to twenty-five years and five years in prison, respectively, in July and August 2005.

On July 7, 2003, the SEC, which had begun proceedings against WorldCom for fraud, reached a settlement with the company for the unprecedented amount of $750 million.

On the civil side, a New York judge in October 2003 authorized WorldCom shareholders and creditors to sue former executives, directors, and investment banks that had sold company shares for fraud, opening the way to a large number of class action suits. To settle the proceedings, seventeen banks that were involved agreed to pay more than $6 billion ($2.6 billion for Citigroup and $2 billion for JP Morgan alone), thus making WorldCom's class action the largest one in history as measured by the amount recovered (the previous settlement record, in a case against Cendant Corp., was little more than half as large). Former directors of WorldCom also came to an agreement with the plaintiffs and agreed to pay more than $20 million in March 2005.

Market Intermediaries

See also chapter 6.

Equity Research

In June 2002, Attorney General Eliot Spitzer of New York made public an investigation of alleged conflicts of interest in several large Wall Street banks. They were accused of orienting the recommendations that came from their investment research departments to favor the interests of third parties—parties connected with their investment banking business and their relations with certain client companies.

The investigation led to the signature on April 28, 2003, of a settlement agreement between the SEC, Eliot Spitzer, other regulatory authorities, and ten banks, involving a total amount of $1.4 billion (including $400 million from Citigroup, $200 million from Credit Suisse First Boston, and $200 million from Merrill Lynch). In addition to the payment of fines, the agreement provides for new rules of operation for the financial analysis departments of these banks in order to strengthen their independence, along with specific funding for independent investment research firms.

Mutual Funds

Mutual funds, which account for a substantial portion of total investments in the United States, were also subject to a proceeding instituted by Eliot Spitzer that was made public in September 2003. The practices involved, principally late trading and market timing, are described in chapter 6.

The case launched by Eliot Spitzer was joined by the SEC. In the course of three months, Putnam, Strong Mutual Fund, Securities Trust (dissolved in November), Charles Schwab, Alliance Capital (a subsidiary of Axa), and Invesco were all prosecuted. The New York attorney general reached settlements with several of them, and they have agreed to lower their commissions by 20 percent for at least five years. For its part, the SEC, initially accused of inertia, imposed several large fines. For example, Alliance Capital agreed in December 2003 to pay $250 million. At the same time, the SEC started to work on stricter regulation of the sector: in January 2004, Chairman William Donaldson proposed to require that chairmen of the boards of mutual funds be independent of the management company, along with three-quarters of the directors, and to require increased transparency on the part of fund managers. This led to the adoption by the SEC, in July 2004, of new governance rules applicable to funds. The U.S. Chamber of Commerce immediately engaged a fierce procedural battle against SEC's decision, and, in order to validate them, the SEC re-adopted the rules on June 29, 2005, the last day of Chairman Donaldson's mandate. The rules are applicable starting in 2006.

NYSE Specialists

Unlike most stock exchanges in the developed world, the NYSE still relies on physical operations: orders pass through the hands of human traders who make the connection between offer and demand and determine the best price for each stock. These traders, known as "specialists," must belong to one of the seven authorized firms that exclusively conduct this activity. When there is no simultaneous offer and demand for a stock, and only in that case, specialists can intervene in the market using their own funds. By doing so, they ensure market liquidity and are in these circumstances known as "market makers." But when offer and demand occur simultaneously, they do not have the right to intervene.

A substantial number of specialists seem nevertheless to have suc-cumbed to the temptation of the practice, known as "interposition-ing." In April 2003, the NYSE disclosed that an investigation was under way, conducted concurrently by the exchange's oversight au-thorities and the SEC. In December 2003, the California public pen-sion fund, CalPERS, filed suit in state court in New York, accusing NYSE specialists of having engaged in conspiracy and of having "pursued a fraudulent scheme to bilk investors" and "engaged in a wide range of manipulative self-dealing, and deceptive and mislead-ing conduct."[8] In 2004, two separate agreements were announced be-tween the SEC and the seven specialist firms, according to which they had to pay total civil penalties and disgorgements of $247 million. This amount was placed in a fund to be distributed to investors who were victims of the firms' conduct. Further to the action against the firms, the SEC initiated in April 2005 a new proceeding against twenty former individual NYSE specialists accused of interposition-ing. The SEC also charged the NYSE with failing to adequately police the specialists, and the NYSE agreed, in settling the charges, to reme-dial measures designed to strengthen its oversight. Moreover, the NYSE agreed to an undertaking of $20 million to fund regulatory au-dits of its own regulatory program every two years through 2011. The NYSE also committed itself to implement a pilot program for video and audio surveillance on its trading floor. As to individual special-ists, they not only face civil charges but for fifteen of them also crimi-nal charges: if they are convicted, they could be sentenced to up to twenty years in prison and fines of between $1 million and $5 million.

ABBREVIATIONS

AFG	Association française de la gestion financière, the French association of asset managers
AGM	annual general meeting
AICPA	American Institute of Certified Public Accountants (United States)
AIG	American International Group, a leading global insurance company
AMF	Autorité de Marchés Financiers, France's securities regulator
ARC	Accounting Regulatory Committee (European Union)
BAFin	Bundesanstalt für Finanzdienstleistungsaufsicht, Germany's financial regulator
Big Four	international auditing firms Deloitte, Ernst & Young, KPMG, and PricewaterhouseCoopers
CAC 40	France, index of top 40 companies by market capitalization (originally published by the Compagnie des Agents de Change, the former organization of French broker-dealers)
CDR	Consortium de réalisation, an entity that took over Crédit Lyonnais's dubious assets in the 1990s (France)
CESR	Committee of European Securities Regulators (aka "Caesar")
CII	Council of Institutional Investors (United States)

CNC	Conseil National de la Comptabilité, France's main advisory body on accounting standard-setting
CNCC	Compagnie nationale des commissaires aux comptes, France's organization of auditors
COB	Commission des Opérations de Bourse, France's securities regulator until the creation of AMF in 2003
Consob	Commissione Nazionale per le Società e la Borsa, Italy's securities regulator
CRC	Comité de la Réglementation Comptable, a committee that advises the French government on accounting standards
EBITDA	earnings before interest, tax, depreciation, and amortization
EDF	Electricité De France, France's state electricity company
EFRAG	European Financial Reporting Advisory Group, a private-sector body that advises the European Commission
EITF	Emerging Issues Task Force (within FASB)
ERP	Enterprise Resource Planning
EU	European Union
Fannie Mae	Federal National Mortgage Association (United States)
FAS	Financial Accounting Standards (one element of the US GAAP body of accounting standards)
FASB	Financial Accounting Standards Board (United States)
FIFO	"first-in, first-out" method of expensing materials
Freddie Mac	Federal Home Mortgage Corporation (United States)
FSA	Financial Services Authority, the United Kingdom's financial regulator
GAAP and US GAAP	Generally Accepted Accounting Principles
GAO	Government Accountability Office (United States)
GOSPLAN	Gosudarstvennyi Komitet Planirovaniya, the State Planning Committee of the former Soviet Union
GSE	Government Sponsored Enterprise, e.g., Fannie Mae and Freddie Mac (United States)

IAS	International Accounting Standards, developed by the IASC until 2001 and updated since by the IASB
IASB	International Accounting Standards Board
IASC	International Accounting Standards Committee, the predecessor body to the IASB (until 2001)
IASCF	IASC Foundation, the body that funds and supervises the IASB
ICGN	International Corporate Governance Network, a global investor group
IFRIC	International Financial Reporting Interpretations Committee, a committee related to the IASB
IFRS	International Financial Reporting Standards, developed by the IASB since 2001 (by extension, include IAS)
IPO	initial public offering
IT	Information technology
M&A	mergers and acquisitions
NASDAQ	National Association of Securities Dealers, Automatic Quoting system
NRSRO	nationally recognized statistical rating organizations (United States)
NYSE	New York Stock Exchange
OFHEO	Office of Federal Housing Enterprise Oversight (United States)
PCAOB	Public Company Accounting Oversight Board (United States)
PCG	Plan Comptable Général or general chart of accounts (France)
PwC	PricewaterhouseCoopers (one of the Big Four)
SAB	Staff Accounting Bulletin (issued by the SEC, part of US GAAP)
SAS	Statement of Auditing Standard (United States)
SEC	Securities and Exchange Commission, federal securities regulator (United States)
SME	Small- and Medium-sized Enterprises
SPE	special-purpose entity
SPV	special-purpose vehicle
SRO	self-regulatory organization (United States)

S&P	Standard & Poor's, a rating agency and financial-information company
UCITS	Undertakings for Collective Investment in Transferable Securities (Europe)
US GAAP	U.S. Generally Accepted Accounting Principles
XBRL	eXtensible Business Reporting Language

NOTES

Prologue

1. The impact of John Wills's proposals on the balance sheet and income statement of Smoke & Mirrors, Inc., and a description of the treatment of such transactions under past and present U.S. generally accepted accounting principles (US GAAP), are set out in appendix 1.

Introduction

1. In this book we do not thoroughly explore recent trends in Asia, although many developments in Japan and South Korea broadly mirror the ones we analyze for continental Europe. Accounting in China and other emerging economies remains to this day underdeveloped as compared with the countries mentioned in this book, even though this situation is changing rapidly as China initiates efforts to integrate itself with the world's capital markets.

Chapter 1. The Common Language of Capitalism

1. This is obviously the case in English, but also, for example, in German (*Buchhaltung*) and in Spanish (*teneduria de libros*).
2. Thomas Hobbes, *Leviathan* (1651; Oxford: Clarendon Press, 1952), 178–79.
3. Luca Pacioli, chapter entitled *"Particularis de Computis et Scripturis"* in *Summa de Arithmetica, Geometria, Proportioni et Propornionalita*, published in Venice in 1494. Incidentally, this book, considered the first comprehensive manual of accounting, was also one of the first to be printed in Italy using the Gutenberg process.

4. Max Weber, *The Protestant Ethic and the Spirit of Capitalism,* trans. Talcott Parsons (1930; London and New York: Routledge, 1993), 21–22.

5. For a penetrating analysis of these effects of the limitation on shareholder liability, see David Moss, *When All Else Fails: Government as the Ultimate Risk Manager* (Cambridge: Harvard University Press, 2002).

6. From 1973 to 2000, the international accounting standard-setting body was known as the IAS Committee or IASC and issued in total 41 International Accounting Standards (some of which were later suppressed), numbered IAS 1 to IAS 41. In 2001, it adopted a new governance structure and changed its name to IASB; from that date on, newly issued standards are known as International Financial Reporting Standards (IFRS 1 to IFRS 7 by late 2005), but the old IAS, including their ongoing revisions, still apply and form an integral part of the body of standards known collectively as IFRS. This confusing alphabet soup does not seem to bother the standard-setters, although it has often led to some head scratching among practitioners.

7. Individual investors who speculate daily on market volatility, usually through online brokerage sites.

8. The view of employees or their representatives may, in some cases, also be helpful to other users of accounting information. In the case of Parmalat, an employee union was among the first to question the company's financial strategy several months before the financial scandal hit the headlines.

9. IASB, *Framework for the preparation and presentation of financial statements* (1989), § 10.

10. This last category has tended to shrink in recent years, as most systems of accounting standards have tightened rules on what can be considered extraordinary.

11. In 2003, Suez crossed the threshold of ownership of more than 50 percent of Electrabel's shares, which allowed it to consolidate under US GAAP as well.

Chapter 2. "Creative Accounting"

1. Also known as special-purpose vehicles (SPV), another term designating the same kind of financial engineering.

2. Staff Accounting Bulletin (SAB) of the SEC no. 101, December 1999; interpretation of the Emerging Issues Task Force (EITF) no. 99–19, July 2000. Rules of this kind are an integral part of US GAAP.

3. A reduction from €7.2 billion to €214 million. Of course, this change in revenue recognition had no impact on net income, and the apparent net profit margin of the trading business was thus considerably increased, rising (again for fiscal year 2002) from 0.6 percent according to French

standards to 21 percent according to IFRS. Presentation of accounts by EDF for the first half of 2003 with partial adoption of IFRS, October 2, 2003. No fraud was involved in this case, which is purely an illustration of the change of standards.

4. In May 2005, the U.S. Supreme Court overturned Andersen's condemnation for the destruction of documents. However, even if the trial had been decided differently in 2002, it is unlikely that Andersen could have survived the crisis undamaged.

5. Mr. White was reported to have personally collected more than $12 million from the sale of Enron stock between May and December 2001, which later prompted some controversy.

6. *BusinessWeek*, December 30, 2002.

7. The quote is from Neal Batson, an Atlanta lawyer who was appointed as examiner in the bankruptcy proceedings following the Enron collapse, in the *Houston Chronicle*, November 25, 2003.

8. Howard Schilit, *Financial Shenanigans: How to Detect Accounting Gimmicks and Fraud in Financial Reports* (New York: McGraw Hill, 1993; rev. ed. 2002). Prof. Schilit now heads the Center for Financial Research and Analysis, an independent consultancy.

9. Ibid., 24–25.

10. Earnings Before Interest, Tax, Depreciation, and Amortization: a non-accounting financial balance used by many companies in their financial publicity; see below.

11. United States District Court for the Southern District of New York: Securities and Exchange Commission, Plaintiff, vs. Xerox Corporation, Defendant; Civil Action No. 02-272789 (DLC). On the SEC's website: http://www.sec.gov/litigation/complaints/complr17465.htm.

12. It is estimated that around 30 percent of companies listed on the New York Stock Exchange in 1929 did not publish any accounts. Still today, a number of states do not specifically require any financial reporting statements.

13. Sean M. O'Connor, "Be Careful What You Wish For: How Accountants and Congress Created the Problem of Auditor Independence," *Boston College Law Review* 45 (2004).

14. Securities Exchange Act of 1934, Section 13, b, 2. See for example website http://www.law.uc.edu/CCL/index.html.

15. Statement of Auditing Standards (SAS) No. 69, included on April 16, 2003, in the US Public Company Accounting Oversight Board's body of Interim Auditing Standards, AU Section 411.05a. Available on PCAOB's website http://www.pcaobus.org.

16. The expression "true and fair view" was introduced in the United Kingdom's legislation in 1947, replacing a previous requirement (dating from 1929) that the accounts must give a "true and correct view." At that

time, the accounting profession successfully argued that it would prove unrealistic to define a reference against which the "correctness" of accounts could be assessed. Similar legislative debates have occurred in most European countries. In 1966, French deputies suggested a legal requirement for "exactness (*exactitude*) of accounts," but this proposal was eventually rejected in the *Sénat*, France's upper house.

17. European Community's Fourth Directive on company law, issued on July 25, 1978.

18. See for example Tim Bush, "Divided by Common Language—Where Economics Meets the Law: US versus non-US Financial Reporting Models," pamphlet published by the Institute of Chartered Accountants in England and Wales and available on http://www.icaew.co.uk, June 2005; and John Plender, "Fight for truth and fairness in Europe's accounts," *Financial Times*, July 11, 2005.

19. See Oriol Amat, John Blake, and Ester Oliveras, "Spanish Auditors and the 'True and Fair View'," Universitat Pompeu Fabra, Department of Economics and Business Working Paper No. 409, October 1999, published on SSRN website http://ssrn.com/abstract=199062.

20. IASB, *Framework for the Preparation and Presentation of Financial Statements*, 1989, § 22.

21. *Le Figaro Économie* and *Les Échos*, March 6, 2002. Translation by the authors.

22. Communiqué of the Commission des Opérations de Bourse, France's stock market regulatory agency, March 12, 2003.

23. *Financial Times*, April 25, 2003.

Chapter 3. Standard-setting and Its Challenges

1. Available on the Financial Accounting Standards Board's website at http://www.fasb.org.

2. *IASC Foundation Constitution* (2000) article 2 (a).

3. We refer here to the neutrality of the standards themselves, not to that of the accounts in the way in which the IASB uses the word ("financial statements are not neutral if, by means of the selection or presentation of information, they influence decision making or judgment in order to reach a predetermined result or conclusion," IASB, *Framework for the Preparation and Presentation of Financial Statements* [1989] § 36). The authors are grateful to Olivier Davanne for his contribution to this development.

4. See, for example, Peter Wallison, "Give us disclosure, not audits," *Wall Street Journal*, June 2, 2003.

5. Gordon M. Bodnar and Gunther Gebhardt, "Derivatives Usage in Risk Management by U.S. and German Non-financial Firms: A Comparative Study," *NBER Working Paper*, no. 6705 (1998).

6. Study by PricewaterhouseCoopers quoted in "IFRS Put Damper on Share Option Schemes," *Financial Times*, August 11, 2005.

7. See, for example, Robert Litan, *The Enron Failure and the State of Corporate Disclosure* (Washington, D.C.: Brookings Institution, 2002).

8. Securities and Exchange Commission, *Study Pursuant to Section 108(d) of the Sarbanes-Oxley Act of 2002 on the Adoption by the United States Financial Reporting System of a Principles-based Accounting System*, July 25, 2003.

9. Excerpt from the July 2003 report. The SEC is not entirely fair in this description, as it does not mention the constant efforts by the IASB in recent years to eliminate as many as possible of the numerous options which indeed exist in the IFRS standards.

10. In a clarifying press release published a few days after his testimony to the Senate quoted above, David Tweedie stated, a little awkwardly, that he had indeed *not* said that the use of IFRS would have averted the Enron fraud. He went on: "History is full of examples of those who said 'it couldn't happen here' and came to regret it. I do not plan to repeat that mistake."

11. IASB, *Framework for the Preparation and Presentation of Financial Statements* (1989) § 35.

12. Umberto Eco, *Dire quasi la stessa cosa. Esperienze di traduzione* (Milan: Bompiani, 2003).

13. Walter Benjamin echoed this orientation in his essay "The Task of the Translator," published in *Illuminations* (Schocken Publishing, 1969).

14. Bernard Colasse and Peter Standish, "De la réforme 1996–1998 du dispositif français de normalisation comptable," *Comptabilité-Contrôle-Audit* vol. 4, part 2 (September 1998). "Colbertism" refers to Jean-Baptiste Colbert, a minister under Louis XIV in the seventeenth century and a champion of state intervention in the economy.

15. Seven government officials out of fifteen CRC members, the others being three representatives of the accounting profession, three representatives of companies, and two members of nationally recognized trade unions.

16. Eugen Schmalenbach, "Der Kontenrahmen," *Zeitschrift für handelswissenschaftliche Forschung* no. 9 (1927).

17. In Germany, the Goering Plan was disposed of after 1945. There is now an "Industrial Chart of Accounts" (*Industrie Kontenrahmen* or IKR), but it has been developed by the private sector and its application is entirely voluntary.

18. Or "property, plant & equipment," as tangible fixed assets are usually referred to in the English-speaking world.

19. Pierre Rosanvallon, *Le Modèle politique français* (Paris: Seuil, 2004).

20. Alan Roberts, "The development of the French Plan Comptable Général: a New Zealand perspective," working paper presented at the Business History and Europe Conference, University of Canterbury, September 5, 2003.

21. Warren Buffett, annual letter to the shareholders of Berkshire Hathaway, 1999.
22. Ibid.
23. "S&P Data to Include Option Costs," *Wall Street Journal*, November 21, 2005.
24. Thomas Friedman, "Homeland Insecurity," *New York Times*, March 17, 2005.
25. We quote an article by Michael Rothschild in *Upside* Magazine, ominously titled "Gain without Pain," in April 1993: "The double-entry and zero-sum mentality that governs the thinking of the FASB and politicians from the 'industrial age' is quite simply incompatible with the economic dynamics of the 'information age,' which is a positive-sum game that creates wealth. They are completely unable to understand that the new wealth comes out of no one's pocket, that there really can be profit without cost, revenue without expense. Stock options are extraordinary because they make the perfect win-win situation attainable, a true partnership between employees and shareholders." And this was years before what is considered the beginning of the "technology bubble."
26. To be precise, another compulsory disclosure, of the fully diluted earnings per share (calculated by assuming that all stock options are vested and exercised), is affected by stock options. This indicator reflects the number of options but not their value or cost, however, and is usually the focus of relatively little attention in comparison to net earnings or net earnings per share.
27. Quoted in John Cassidy, "The Greed Cycle: How the Financial System Encouraged Corporations to Go Crazy," *New Yorker*, September 23, 2002, from an interview with the author.
28. "I'm not sure that the presented fix doesn't create more problems than it actually solves. (. . .) Putting a fair value on something as complicated as long-term stock options is almost an impossible task." Transcribed by the online journal CFO.com, January 12, 2004.
29. The Basel Committee is hosted by the Bank for International Settlements, the oldest international financial institution (established in 1930), which makes possible cooperation between central banks and other participants with a view to protecting the stability of global financial exchanges. The system for calculating the solvency ratio now in force is known as the "Cooke ratio," defined in the late 1980s; several countries are now considering a shift to new rules known as "Basel II" or the "McDonough ratio," taking more account of the complexity of current financial techniques and establishing a link to changes in accounting standards.
30. IASB, *Framework for the Preparation and Presentation of Financial Statements*, 1989, § 37.
31. According to statistics of the U.S. Department of Labor.
32. Joint Working Group of Standard Setters, "Financial Instruments and

Similar Items, Draft Standard and Basis for Conclusions," 2000, summary, page iii.

33. Securities & Exchange Commission, *Report and Recommendations Pursuant to Section 401(c) of the Sarbanes-Oxley Act of 2002 on Arrangements with Off-Balance Sheet Implications, Special Purpose Entities, and Transparency of Filings by Issuers*, June 2005.

34. The letter is quoted on the French Banking Federation's website at http://www.fbf.fr.

Chapter 4. Capitalism in Flux

1. Peter Hall and David Soskice, *Varieties of Capitalism: The Institutional Foundations of Comparative Advantage* (Oxford University Press, 2001). Two earlier, seminal books on the comparative political economy of capitalism are John Zysman, *Governments, Markets, and Growth: Financial Systems and the Politics of Industrial Change* (Cornell University Press, 1984); and Suzanne Berger and Ronald Dore, eds., *National Diversity and Global Capitalism* (Cornell University Press, 1996).

2. Another example of the close business-politics connection is the chairman of the Republican National Committee from 2003 to 2005, Ed Gillespie, who had long been one of the most influential corporate lobbyists in town through the firm Quinn Gillespie & Associates, which incidentally counted Enron (before the collapse) among its most well-known clients.

3. Raghuram Rajan is chief economist of the International Monetary Fund in Washington, D.C., and Luigi Zingales is a professor of entrepreneurship and finance at the University of Chicago. We refer in particular to "Which Capitalism? Lessons from the East Asian Crisis" (working paper, University of Chicago, 1998) and "Banks and Markets: the Changing Character of European Finance" (working paper, University of Chicago, 2003), as well as *Saving Capitalism from the Capitalists* (New York: Crown Business Press, 2003).

4. This had not always been the case: in the period immediately preceding the First World War, the French economy was very open and the capital markets played an important role. See Suzanne Berger, *Notre première mondialisation. Leçons d'un échec oublié* (Paris: Seuil, 2003).

5. Philip Gordon and Sophie Meunier, *Le Nouveau Défi français* (Paris: Odile Jacob, 2002).

6. Antoine Bozio, "La capitalisation boursière en France au XXe siècle," DEA thesis, laboratoire DELTA (Paris), 2002, and authors' calculations.

7. Thomson Financial website at http://www.thomson.com (accessed July 2005).

8. Based on the "FT Global 500" survey, June 11, 2005.

9. Bruno Husson and Nicolas Véron, "Attention aux goodwills," *Option Finance*, March 29, 2004.

10. Civil complaint filed by the SEC in January 2005 in the U.S. District Court for the District of Columbia. Since the early 2000s, new standards have restricted the scope for such malpractice.
11. SEC news release, February 25, 2003.
12. *L'Expansion*, April 24, 2002; authors' translation.
13. See the website http://www.xbrl.org for more detail.
14. Securitization is a technique somewhat comparable to sale-leaseback, whereby the special-purpose entity acquires a financial rather than a tangible asset: for example, in the securitization of loans, the company transfers the rights attached to them to the special-purpose entity, which then receives subsequent payments from the debtors in place of the initial lending company.
15. Calculated respectively by the World Bank and by MSCI (Global Capital Markets Index), see website http://www.msci.com.
16. "Application of Option-pricing Theory: Twenty-five Years Later," Nobel Prize acceptance speech, December 9, 1997, in *American Economic Review* 88, no. 3 (June 1998).
17. Adam Smith, *An Inquiry into the Nature and Causes of the Wealth of Nations*, vol. 2 (1776; Oxford: Clarendon Press, 1976), 741.
18. Michael C. Jensen and Kevin J. Murphy, "CEO Incentives—It's Not How Much You Pay, But How," *Harvard Business Review*, May–June 1990.
19. See Daniel Bergstresser and Thomas Philippon, "CEO Incentives and Earnings Management," Harvard Business School working paper, 2003, available at website http://pages.stern.nyu.edu/~tphillip/.
20. Joseph Blasi, Douglas Kruse, and Aaron Bernstein, *In the Company of Owners* (New York: Basic Books, 2003).
21. Study by William M. Mercer, quoted in the *Wall Street Journal*, April 12, 2001.
22. "Barons of Bankruptcy," *Financial Times*, July 31, 2002.
23. Shane Johnson, Harley Ryan, and Yisong Tian, "Executive compensation and corporate fraud," April 2003, available at website http://ssrn.com/abstract=395960.
24. Lucian Bebchuk and Yaniv Grinstein, "The Growth of Executive Pay," Harvard Law and Economics Discussion Paper No. 510, April 2005.
25. Nicholas D. Kristof, "Captains of Piracy," *New York Times*, March 19, 2005.
26. "My Big Fat C.E.O. Paycheck," *New York Times*, April 3, 2005.

Chapter 5. Auditors under Scrutiny

1. Arthur Levitt, "Accountants Must Put Investor First," *Financial Times*, November 24, 2003. The "sublimely unique" quote is from a speech by then-chairman Levitt at the Fall Council of the American Institute of Certified Public Accountants in Las Vegas, October 24, 2000.

2. Statement of The Honorable Charles A. Bowsher, Chairman, Public Oversight Board, before the Senate Banking Committee; March 19, 2002.

3. The logic of this extraterritorial jurisdiction stems from the following reasoning. If any individual U.S. household can buy Sinopec shares on the NYSE in the same way it would buy shares in General Motors, then Sinopec's financial statements must provide the same guarantees of transparency and quality as General Motors'. Therefore, Sinopec's auditors must be as open to inspections by the PCAOB as the auditors of General Motors in Detroit.

4. In spite of the apparent similarity of purposes, the European audit regulators can in reality be extremely different, and generally weaker, than the PCAOB. For example, France's *Haut Conseil* has a yearly budget of approximately €650,000 and has no legal autonomy from the Justice Ministry that hosts it. By contrast, the PCAOB had a budget of more than $136 million in 2005.

5. See Stephen Taub, "Audit Firms Focusing on Audit Fees," in the online journal *CFO.com*, July 7, 2004. The firms covered by the study were the "Big Four" (i.e., Deloitte, Ernst & Young, KPMG, and PricewaterhouseCoopers), plus BDO Seidman and Grant Thornton.

6. *BusinessWeek*, January 12, 2004.

7. "Ex-KPMG Execs Could Face Crime Charges," *CFO.com*, August 3, 2005.

8. The gradual corruption of the high ethics that had been imposed on the firm by its founder Arthur Andersen, a Norwegian immigrant in Chicago, down to its eventual collapse have been described by Barbara Ley Toffler, *Final Accounting—Ambition, Greed, and the Fall of Arthur Andersen* (Broadway Books, 2003).

9. Quoted in "The Auditors' Progressive Voice," *Financial Times*, October 6, 2005.

10. "Sorry, the Auditor Said, But We Want a Divorce," *New York Times*, February 6, 2005.

11. Eleven WorldCom ex-directors agreed to pay a total of $20 million in March 2005 as part of a settlement with New York State's Comptroller Alan Hevesi. The sum was said to represent roughly 20 percent of the directors' aggregate net worth, not counting their primary residences and retirement accounts. At Enron, ten former directors agreed in October 2004 to pay a total of $13 million to settle a class action suit. *New York Times*, January 8 and March 19, 2005.

12. These figures take into account the merger of RSM Salustro Reydel with KPMG, which was approved by both firms' governing bodies in early 2005.

13. General Accounting Office, *Public Accounting Firms: Mandated Study on Consolidation and Competition*, July 2003, available at the website http://www.gao.gov.

14. European Commission, news release of September 5, 2002.

15. *Economist*, February 1, 2003.

16. "Ex-KPMG Execs Could Face Crime Charges," in the online journal *CFO.com*, August 3, 2005, and "European Regulators Express Concern on Possible US Prosecution of KPMG," *Financial Times*, July 11, 2005.

17. The Conference Board, *Commission on Public Trust and Private Enterprise*, part 3, "Audit and Accounting," available at website http://www.con ference-board.org.

18. *BusinessWeek*, September 1, 2003.

19. "Bring Down Barriers to Outside Capital in Audit—External Investors Could Help Challenge the Big Four," *Financial Times*, October 31, 2005.

Chapter 6. Power to the Investors?

1. "Undertakings for Collective Investment in Transferable Securities" (UCITS), a term of euro-jargon that covers many funds managed in the European Union.

2. *Flow of Funds Accounts of the United States, First Quarter 2005*, Federal Reserve Board, June 2005.

3. Investment Company Institute, "*2005 Investment Company Fact Book*," May 2005.

4. *BusinessWeek*, January 11, 2002.

5. *Financial Times*, July 21, 2003.

6. See website http://www.calpers-governance.org.

7. Following Enron, the House of Representatives adopted a draft Pension Security Act, which would have been a step in that direction, but it was later rejected in the Senate. However, this issue is likely to resurface in future legislative debates.

8. Survey by Georgeson Shareholder, *Le Monde*, July 29, 2003. Conversely, French investors are investing more and more abroad as protectionist tax regulations, which in the past encouraged investment in French shares, are being dismantled under pressure from the European Union.

9. Federal Reserve Board.

10. Laura Simmons and Ellen Ryan, "Post-Reform Act Securities Settlements—updated through December 2004" and "Securities Class Action Case Filings, 2004: A Year in Review," publication of the Stanford Law School Class Action Clearinghouse in cooperation with the Cornerstone law firm, 2005.

11. "A Blazing Summer," *Economist*, August 13, 2005.

12. "Litigation Risk: All American Now?" *Economist*, January 10, 2004.

13. Quoted in "The Crux of Reform: Autonomous Stock Rating," *New York Times*, October 7, 2002.

14. These were Bear Stearns, CSFB, Goldman Sachs, Lehman Brothers, J.P.

Morgan, Merrill Lynch, Morgan Stanley, Citigroup, UBS, and U.S. Bancorp Piper Jaffray.

15. Marie Leone, "The Flight of the Sell-Side Analyst," in online journal *CFO.com*, July 8, 2004.

16. Partly to deflect criticism, the SEC also granted NRSRO status to two new firms in addition to S&P, Moody's, and Fitch, namely Toronto-based Dominion Bond Rating Services in 2003, and AM Best, which specializes in rating insurance companies, in March 2005. However, the recognition of these smaller players is unlikely to significantly alter the overall competitive landscape.

17. See, for example, Long Chen, Pierre Collin-Dufresne, and Robert S. Goldstein, "On the Relation Between Credit Spread Puzzles and the Equity Premium Puzzle," May 2005 at website http://ssrn.com/abstract= 687473; and Jeffrey D. Amato and Eli M. Remolona, "Is There a Credit Premium Puzzle?" Bank for International Settlements, 2003.

18. Survey conducted by McKinsey in April and May 2002, cited in "Investors Want Single Accounting Standard," *Financial Times*, July 8, 2002. Unsurprisingly, however, opinions diverged on what body of standards should be chosen, with 78 percent of Europeans favoring IFRS, while 76 percent of North Americans preferred US GAAP.

Chapter 7. Regulators at the Crossroads

1. From website http://www.sec.gov.

2. *BusinessWeek*, December 30, 2002.

3. Mathew D. McCubbins and Thomas Schwartz, "Congressional Oversight Overlooked: Police Patrols versus Fire Alarms," *American Journal of Political Science* 28 (1984).

4. To complete this quick summary of the U.S. regulatory landscape, one has to mention the supervision of banks and insurance companies by a complex network of state regulators and, for banking, federal agencies that include the Federal Reserve System and the Office of the Comptroller of the Currency.

5. In Germany, the task of setting accounting standards was delegated in the 1990s to a private association, the Deutscher Standardierungsrat. However, each standard still has to be individually approved by the Minister of Justice, which is, as in France, particularly responsible for corporation law and the protection of creditors. This institutional setting reflects to some degree the traditional importance of banks and credit in the German financial system.

6. "Who shall oversee the overseers?" Quote from Juvenal (55–140), *Satires*, VI.347.

7. A contrast between these interactions and the relative rigidity of the

French regulatory framework can be found in Pierre-Henri Conac, *La Régulation des marchés boursiers par la Commission des opérations de bourse et la Securities and Exchange Commission* (Paris: LGDJ, 2002; English translation forthcoming at Jurispublishing).

8. See Solveig Godeluck, *Entre Gens de Bonne Compagnie* (Albin Michel, 2005).

9. Roberta Romano, *The Advantage of Competitive Federalism for Securities Regulation* (Washington, D.C.: AEI Press, 2002).

10. Speech by the People's Republic of China's Assistant Finance Minister Wang Jun at the ICAEW Annual Conference, reported in Kevin Reed, "China vows to endorse IFRS," in online journal *AccountancyAge.com*, June 29, 2005.

11. While owing nothing to governments, the IASC was from its creation tied to the international expansion of the major accounting firms. Henry Benson, generally considered the father of the IASC, was a partner in Coopers & Lybrand, and was also, on his mother's side, a descendant of the Cooper family who founded that firm in London in the nineteenth century. His autobiography, *Accounting for Life*, was published in 1989 (London: Kogan Page).

12. This committee is itself advised on technical matters by a private-sector body called EFRAG (European Financial Reporting Advisory Group).

13. Interview of Alexander Schaub, Director-General for the Internal Market at the European Commission, "Is a Clear Picture of Corporate Health Being Obscured by New Accounting Rules?" *Financial Times*, October 17, 2005.

14. Thomas Friedman, "A Theory of Everything," *New York Times*, June 1, 2003.

15. "CESR's technical advice to the European Commission on possible measures concerning credit rating agencies," March 2005, item 265; available on the website http://www.cesr-eu.org.

16. Study by PricewaterhouseCoopers cited in the *Economist*, January 10, 2004.

17. Quote from Stig Enevoldsen, chairman of the European Financial Reporting Advisory Group (EFRAG, see note 12), "Is a Clear Picture of Corporate Health Being Obscured by New Accounting Rules?" *Financial Times*, October 17, 2005.

18. Donald Nicolaisen, "A Securities Regulator Looks at Convergence," *Northwestern University Journal of International Law and Business*, April 2005. Donald Nicolaisen was the SEC's chief accountant at that time and specified in this article (as the SEC has done in other statements) that "securities regulators, including the SEC, need to ensure that compliance [of European companies' financial statements with IFRS] is enforced. The SEC [. . .] may find it necessary from time to time to weigh in on particular accounting interpretations."

19. See "EU regulators unite over IFRS," *Financial Times*, August 8, 2005.
20. From the World Federation of Exchanges, *Annual Report and Statistics*, 2004.
21. See Jacques de Larosière, "Good News and Bad on Europe's Financial Markets Integration," *Europe's World*, Autumn 2005.
22. Brian Groom, "European Comment. No Need to Fear the Reach of the SEC," *Financial Times*, February 13, 2004.
23. Some tentative ideas for a more balanced securities regulation on both sides of the Atlantic have been explored in Benn Steil, *Building a Transatlantic Securities Market* (Zurich: International Securities Market Association in association with the Council on Foreign Relations, 2002).

Appendix 2

1. Quoted in Jenny Anderson, "Greenberg Fires Back at Directors," *New York Times*, August 5, 2005.
2. Website of the Securities and Exchange Commission, http://www.sec.gov/news/press/2005-85.htm.
3. *Le Nouvel Observateur*, January 7, 2003.
4. This case is entirely distinct from the one on Executive Life, in which Crédit Lyonnais was also involved alongside French businessman François Pinault and which resulted in hundreds of millions of dollars of fines following a Californian prosecution in 2004.
5. GSEs are private companies that are backed by the U.S. government in order to reduce the capital cost for certain borrowing sectors of the economy.
6. Behind Citigroup and AIG (from Forbes Global 2000 for the year 2003).
7. *La Tribune*, June 22, 2004.
8. Press release of California State Treasurer Phil Angelides, December 16, 2003; available on website http://www.treasurer.ca.gov.

BIBLIOGRAPHY

Accounting and Financial Reporting

Benson, Henry. *Accounting for Life*. London: Kogan Page, 1989.

Benston, George, Michael Bromwich, Robert Litan, and Alfred Wagenhofer. *Following the Money: The Enron Failure and the State of Corporate Disclosure*. Washington, D.C.: AEI-Brookings Joint Center for Regulatory Studies, 2003.

Boyle, Phelim, and Feidhlim Boyle. *Derivatives: The Tools that Changed Finance*. London: Risk Books, 2001.

Briloff, Abraham. *The Truth about Corporate Accounting*. New York: Harper & Row, 1981.

Casta, Jean-François, and Bernard Colasse, eds. *Juste Valeur: Enjeux Techniques et Politiques*. Paris: Economica, 2001.

Colasse, Bernard. *Les grands auteurs en comptabilité*. Paris: EMS, 2005.

Crouzet, Philippe, and Nicolas Véron. *Accounting For Globalisation: The Accounting Standards Battle*. Paris: En Temps Réel, 2004.

DiPiazza, Samuel, and Robert Eccles. *Building Public Trust—The Future of Corporate Reporting*. New York: John Wiley & Sons, 2002.

Finnerty, John D. *Project Financing: Asset Based Financial Engineering*. New York: John Wiley & Sons, 1996.

Leuz, Christian, Dieter Pfaff, and Anthony Hopwood, eds. *The Economics and Politics of Accounting, International Perspectives on Trends, Policy, and Practice*. Oxford: Oxford University Press, 2004

Pratt, Jamie. *Financial Accounting in an Economic Context*. New York: John Wiley & Sons, 2005 (6th edition).

Schilit, Howard. *Financial Shenanigans: How to Detect Accounting Gimmicks and Fraud in Financial Reports*. London: McGraw & Hill, 1993; revised edition 2002.

Smith, Clifford W., Jr., ed. *The Modern Theory of Corporate Finance*. New York: McGraw-Hill, 1989 (2nd edition).

Swartz, Mimi, with Sherron Watkins. *Power Failure: The Inside Story of the Collapse of Enron*. New York: Doubleday, 2003.

Toffler, Barbara Ley, with Jennifer Reingold. *Final Accounting: Ambition, Greed, and the Fall of Arthur Andersen*. New York: Currency Books, 2004.

Financial Systems and Regulation

Albert, Michel. *Capitalism vs. Capitalism*. New York: Four Walls Eight Windows, 1993 (original French publication: *Capitalisme contre capitalisme*, Seuil, 1991).

Allen, Franklin, and Douglas Gale. *Comparing Financial Systems*. Cambridge: MIT Press, 2001.

Berger, Suzanne, and Ronald Dore, eds. *National Diversity and Global Capitalism*. Ithaca: Cornell University Press, 1996.

Berger, Suzanne, and the MIT Industrial Performance Center. *How We Compete*. New York: Doubleday, 2005.

Blasi, Joseph, Douglas Kruse, and Aaron Bernstein. *In the Company of Owners*. New York: Basic Books, 2003.

Braudel, Fernand. *Civilisation matérielle. Économie et capitalisme*. Paris: Armand Colin, 1979; English translation *Civilization and Capitalism*. Berkeley: University of California Press, 1992.

Conac, Pierre-Henri. *La Régulation des marchés boursiers par la Commission des opérations de Bourse et la Securities and Exchange Commission*. Paris: LGDJ, 2002.

Godeluck, Solveig. *Entre Gens de Bonne Compagnie: Comment les Maîtres de la Bourse Trompent les Actionnaires*. Paris: Albin Michel, 2005.

Goodhart, Charles, Philipp Hartmann, David Llewellyn, Liliana Rojas-Suárez, and Steven Weisbrod. *Financial Regulation: Why, How and Where Now?* London: Routledge, 1998.

Gordon, Philip, and Sophie Meunier. *The French Challenge: Adapting to Globalization*. Washington, D.C.: Brookings Institution Press, 2001.

Gourevitch, Peter, and James Shinn. *Political Power and Corporate Control: The New Global Politics of Corporate Governance*. Princeton: Princeton University Press, 2005.

Hall, Peter, and David Soskice. *Varieties of Capitalism. The Institutional Foundations of Comparative Advantage*. Oxford: Oxford University Press, 2001.

Herring, Richard J., and Robert E. Litan. *Financial Regulation in a Global Economy*. Washington, D.C.: Brookings Institution Press, 1995.

Kraakman, Reinier, Paul Davies, Henry Hansmann, Gerard Hertig, Klaus Hopt, Hideki Kanda, and Edward Rock. *The Anatomy of Corporate Law, A Comparative and Functional Approach*. Oxford: Oxford University Press, 2004.

Krugman, Paul. *The Great Unraveling: Losing Our Way in the New Century.* New York: W. W. Norton, 2003.

Levitt, Arthur. *Take on the Street. What Wall Street and Corporate America Don't Want You to Know, and What You Can Do to Fight Back.* New York: Pantheon Books, 2002.

Levy, Jonah. *Tocqueville's Revenge: State, Society and Economy in Contemporary France.* Cambridge, MA: Harvard University Press, 1999.

Mandel, Michael. *The Coming Internet Depression: Why the High-Tech Boom Will Go Bust, Why the Crash Will Be Worse Than You Think, and How to Prosper Afterwards.* New York: Basic Books, 2000.

Miklethwait, John, and Adrian Wooldridge. *The Company—A Short History of a Revolutionary Idea.* New York: Modern Library Chronicles, 2003.

Rajan, Raghuram, and Luigi Zingales. *Saving Capitalism from the Capitalists.* New York: Crown Business Press, 2003.

Stigler, George J. *The Citizen and the State: Essays on Regulation.* Chicago: University of Chicago Press, 1975.

Stiglitz, Joseph. *The Roaring Nineties.* New York: W. W. Norton, 2003.

Zysman, John. *Governments, Markets and Growth: Financial Systems and Politics of Industrial Change.* Ithaca: Cornell University Press, 1984.

Internet Sources

BRUEGEL (Brussels), http://www.bruegel.org

European Commission, a section of their website dedicated to Financial Reporting issues, http://www.europa.eu.int/comm/internal_market/accounting/index_en.htm

Financial Accounting Standards Board, http://www.fasb.org

International Accounting Standards Board, http://www.iasb.org.uk

Public Company Accounting Oversight Board, http://www.pcaobus.org

Securities & Exchange Commission, http://www.sec.gov

Two comparison presentations of US GAAP and IFRS, managed by PricewaterhouseCoopers and Deloitte, respectively. http://www.pwcglobal.com/gx/eng/about/svcs/corporatereporting/SandD_04.pdf and http://www.iasplus.com/usa/ifrsus.htm

INDEX

Page numbers with an *f* indicate figures; those with a *t* indicate tables; those with an *n* indicate endnotes.